DISRUPTING LEADERSHIP IN ENTREPRENEURIAL UNIVERSITIES

Perspectives on Leadership in Higher Education

Series Editors: Tanya Fitzgerald, Helen M. Gunter and Jon Nixon

Perspectives on Leadership in Higher Education provides a forum for distinctive, and sometimes divergent, ideas on what intellectual leadership means within the context of higher education as it develops within the 21st century. Authors from across a number of nation states critically explore these issues with reference to academic and research-informed practice and development, institutional management and governance, the remapping of knowledge as well as sector-wide policy development.

Advisory Board:

Sarah Aiston (University of Teesside, UK), Michael Apple (University of Wisconsin-Madison, USA), Ronald Barnett (University of London, UK), Hamish Coates (Tsingshua University, China), Ann Corbett (London School of Economics, UK), Rosemary Deem (Royal Holloway, University of London, UK), Kevin Dougherty (Teachers College, Columbia University, USA), Claus Emmeche (University of Copenhagen, Denmark), Ase Gornitzka (University of Oslo, Norway), Chris Husbands (Sheffield Hallam University, UK), Will Hutton (Academy of Social Sciences, UK), Fred Inglis (University of Warwick, UK), Niilo Kaaupi (University of Strasbourg, France), Eric Lybeck, (University of Manchester, UK), Bruce Macfarlane (University of Bristol, UK), Jani Ursin, (University of Jyväskylä, Finland), Yuki Takahashi (Tsuda University, Japan), Ly Tran (Deakin University, Australia) and Leesa Wheelahan (University of Toronto, Canada)

Also available in the series:

Cosmopolitan Perspectives on Academic Leadership in Higher Education, *edited by Feng Su and Margaret Wood*
Mass Intellectuality and Democratic Leadership in Higher Education, *edited by Richard Hall and Joss Winn*
Leadership in Higher Education from a Transrelational Perspective, *Christopher M. Branson, Maureen Marra, Margaret Franken and Dawn Penney*
Leadership for Sustainability in Higher Education, *Janet Haddock-Fraser, Peter Rands and Stephen Scoffham*
Scholarly Leadership in Higher Education, *Wayne J. Urban*
Exploring Consensual Leadership in Higher Education, *edited by Lynne Gornall, Brychan Thomas and Lucy Sweetman*

Forthcoming in the series:

Intellectual Leadership, Higher Education and Precarious Times, *edited by Tanya Fitzgerald, Helen M. Gunter and Jon Nixon*

DISRUPTING LEADERSHIP IN ENTREPRENEURIAL UNIVERSITIES

Disengagement and Diversity in Higher Education

Jill Blackmore

BLOOMSBURY ACADEMIC
LONDON • NEW YORK • OXFORD • NEW DELHI • SYDNEY

BLOOMSBURY ACADEMIC
Bloomsbury Publishing Plc
50 Bedford Square, London, WC1B 3DP, UK
1385 Broadway, New York, NY 10018, USA
29 Earlsfort Terrace, Dublin 2, Ireland

BLOOMSBURY, BLOOMSBURY ACADEMIC and the Diana logo are trademarks of
Bloomsbury Publishing Plc

First published in Great Britain 2023
This paperback edition published 2024

A catalogue record for this book is available from the British Library.

A catalog record for this book is available from the Library of Congress.

ISBN: HB: 978-1-3501-3782-0
PB: 978-1-3502-1690-7
ePDF: 978-1-3501-3783-7
eBook: 978-1-3501-3784-4

Series: Perspectives on Leadership in Higher Education

Typeset by Deanta Global Publishing Services, Chennai, India

To find out more about our authors and books visit www.bloomsbury.com and
sign up for our newsletters.

For Julie Rowlands (1963–2021) and Andrea Gallant (1961–2021)
Wonderful friends, selfless colleagues and academic citizens

CONTENTS

Part III
LEADERSHIP DISRUPTORS

Chapter 8
DIVERSIFYING TO DISRUPT LEADERSHIP

Chapter 9
CARELESS MANAGEMENT, THE VULNERABLE UNIVERSITY
AND CRITICAL LEADERSHIP

SERIES EDITORS' FOREWORD

What are universities for in the twenty-first century? This is a question that is now debated not only within universities themselves but within wider society and across the political spectrum: we can no longer assume a consensus regarding the ends and purposes of higher education or the role of universities in fulfilling those ends and purposes. Consequently, leadership within higher education cannot simply be a matter of managing the status quo: leadership necessarily involves an understanding as well as analysis of the twenty-first-century world and of how the university might contribute to the economic, social, cultural and political challenges that we face. In short, it requires leadership that is both visionary and programmatic: visionary in its understanding of the past as well as present and future impacts of globalization and programmatic in its grasp of how universities might respond to that impact.

What might such leadership look like? This series aims to address that question with reference to academic practice and development, institutional management and governance, the remapping of knowledge and sector-wide policy development. Central to each of these areas of concern is the importance of interconnectivity in a context of increasing institutional and global complexity: interconnectivity within and across institutions, regions and cognate fields. The gathering of agreement is one of the prerequisites of leadership at every level – and that requires an understanding of different viewpoints and opinions some of which may be in direct conflict with others. The capacity to balance, respect and contain these differences is what constitutes leadership. This inevitably raises important ethical questions regarding leadership in a more complex and subtle setting, where leadership goes beyond a hierarchical model of telling others what to do and expecting them to do it. The twin themes of interconnectivity and ethics cut across the series as a whole.

Crucially, this series invites authors and readers to rethink the value and purposes of higher education and leadership within higher education. We hope to provoke sustained debates about the unevenness, ambivalences and disruptions that now mark everyday life and interactions. The global pandemic, climate change and the rise of authoritarianism have destabilized individuals, our autonomy and our social realities. How then might we as scholars speak back to our precarious present, the disruptions that continue to emerge, and reclaim what is both important and purposeful? We do not seek in this series to answer these questions but to stimulate debates about the critical importance of higher education in disrupting the status quo.

Disrupting Leadership in Entrepreneurial Universities critically examines the radical restructure of higher education globally, the increasing assertion of executive power and the impacts on academic work and academic practices. Jill Blackmore draws on the theme of disruption to rework understandings of leadership within universities and the sector more globally. She further considers how particular forms of leadership are disruptive of or conducive to productive forms of academic practice and questions more closely the impacts of dominant managerial forms of leadership that work against the core values and purposes of higher education. Blackmore calls for leadership to be disrupting: to fulfil the claims of the academy as being inclusive and diverse in its values, people, ideas, practices and imaginaries and to be more critical and ethical in its leadership in a post-truth and precarious world.

ACKNOWLEDGEMENTS

This study of Australian universities has international relevance because Australia has historically been 'the canary' in the global field of higher education and also illustrative of the impact of neoliberal policies. In the text, I draw on data from an Australian Research Council Discovery Project *Leadership in Entrepreneurial Universities: Cross-National Investigations of Engagement and Diversity*,[1] with initial findings already published in the co-edited text (with Marita Sanchez-Moreno and Narah Sawers), *Globalized Re/Gendering of the Academy and Leadership* (2017, Routledge). There are numerous reasons for the delay of this text – lack of time because of directing a strategic research centre, too many big projects involving large teams, trying to earn funds to build colleagues' research and keep research fellows and academics employed on 'soft money', personal circumstances, and then Covid-19. Only then was the dedicated time and headspace required possible with lockdown. There is therefore an element of retrospectivity which has been of value. The gap of three years since data collection provided the opportunity in the final chapter to indicate how rapidly things have changed in higher education as a result of political volatility, pandemic management, conspiracy theories, social media and fast-moving if not divisive debates over gender, race and climate change in Australia and globally. In the final chapter I analyse the immediate impact of Covid-19 on Australian higher education as well as the responses of leaders in government and universities into 2021.

There are many to thank. Foremost are the 150 academics, administrators, policymakers and consultants who were interviewed. I hope I have provided an accurate, representative and fair, while critical analysis. I also wish to thank Dr Naarah Sawers, who was the Senior Research Fellow, colleague, constant support and friend, going beyond her job description in every way. Likewise, thanks to Kristy McIllvray, a wonderful doctoral student and former community organizer whose research focused on her puzzlement about the lack of collectivism in the academy. Kristy gave up her scholarship to return to the United States to do multiple 'gig' jobs to support her family impacted by severe illness. Their intellectual input and energy are embedded throughout the text.

As always, my colleagues at Deakin have been there for me and I feel their support in our daily interactions, particularly through Deakin being restructured yet again in 2020 and 2021. The sense of collegiality ingrained in Deakin's School of Education affective economy is one based on trust and care, most evident in their collective response to the executive proposal of forced redundancies. I have listened and learned from them about what it is to be an academic, an educator, a researcher and a leader in the contemporary Australian university, and I hope this text makes sense to them. In particular, I dedicate this book to my late colleagues

Julie Rowlands and Andrea Gallant, both selfless colleagues, friends and academic citizens who succumbed to cancer in 2021 – aged fifty-eight and sixty, respectively.

Finally, thanks to my friends and extended family – many of them academics and scientists experiencing the disruption of higher education and the pandemic and with whom I energetically discuss the future of the university. In particular, my late cousin Rod Crewther, a strong union member, fought for an academic voice on the Council of University of Adelaide. I have been supported by my Gen Xer's – Romaine, Justine, Ziggy, Tristan, Ben, Jess, Marc, Shane and Jessica, many of them living with insecure employment in the gig economy. Particular thanks to Ro, my stepdaughter, who has lived and worked with me during the writing of this book while completing her PhD on trans-disciplinarity. Ro has been good intellectual and social company through the groundhog days of lockdown in Melbourne as we worked at opposite ends of the house only to finish our manuscripts within days of each other.

Jill Blackmore, AM, January 2022

ABBREVIATIONS

A/Dean	Associate Dean
AARE	Australian Association of Research in Education
AAUP	Australian Association of University Professors
ARC	Australian Research Council
CPA	Chartered Professional Accountants Australia
CSP	Commonwealth Supported Places
EBA	Enterprise Bargaining Award
DVC	Deputy Vice Chancellors
ECR	Early Career Researchers
EEO	Equal Employment Opportunity
ERA	Excellence of Research in Australia
EOWA	Equal Opportunity Workplace Agency
GDP	Gross Domestic Product
HASS	Humanities and the Social Sciences
HoS	Head of School
HDR	Higher Degree by Research
HR	Human Resources
IDP	International Development
NGOs	Nongovernmental Organizations
PDF	Post-Doctoral Fellow
PVC	Pro Vice Chancellors
PR	Permanent Residency
QILT	Quality Indicators for Learning and Teaching: Graduate Outcomes Survey
NTEU	National Tertiary Education Union
RQF	Research Quality Framework
RTO	Registered Training Organization
STEMM	Science, Technology, Engineering, Mathematics and Medicine
TEQSA	Tertiary Education Quality Standards Agency
UA	Universities Australia
VC	Vice Chancellor
WIL	Work-Integrated Learning

Chapter 1

INTRODUCTION

DISRUPTING LEADERSHIP IN HIGHER EDUCATION

This text sets the scene for understanding the impact of the disruption wrought on Australian higher education and globally by the Covid-19 pandemic in 2020-22. It explains how Australian as other Anglophone universities came to be so vulnerable, and how government, university management and the professoriate responded to multiple external and internal challenges. In particular, the text focuses on leadership, which as a concept and discourse is under-researched in higher education, over-researched in management literature, misused in policy and often abused in practice (Bryman 2007). Leadership, as a situated and relational practice of being, doing, saying and relating, is undertaken formally and informally by many. Leadership is the lens through which approaches to organizational restructuring and change and its effects on academic practice in the context of the disruption of higher education globally are considered (Blackmore et al. 2016).

How leadership is understood and practised, and with what effect, is examined from the perspectives of those in positional roles of academic management (Vice Chancellors, Deputy Vice Chancellors, Pro-Vice Chancellors, Deans and Heads of School) and the professoriate (in Australia and the UK including associate and full professors only) not in formal positions. In so doing, the crisis in leadership, usually depicted as the disengagement of many academics from university management, the lack of gender and cultural diversity in senior positions (Grove 2017) and failure of ethical leadership, unfolds (MacFarlane 2012a). This analysis questions whether Australian universities under current modes of managing have the capacity to serve 'the public good' for a democratic society, to educate professionals and not just train 'job ready' workers while providing sustainable, inclusive and equitable work conditions for academic and professional staff.

To do this, I take a particular feminist position by working on and with Bourdieu's tools to analyse the changing sociopolitical contexts, discourses, regulations, values, categories and hierarchies of universities, the culturally specific nature of university governance, and how these articulate at transnational, national, institutional and individual levels:

> It is increasingly important to map circuits of power between the state, its
> devolved (higher education) agencies and actors . . . to account for relays of power
> that encompass public, professional, private, personal, and affective realms. It
> would require an appreciation of the material and discursive as well as intimate
> dimensions of the regulation of social experience. (Hey and Broadfoot 2004: 694)

The twentieth-century Enlightenment idea, and indeed legitimacy of a
comprehensive university offering a liberal education and serving the public good
(Marginson 2011), has over decades been challenged by interconnected external
pressures, particularly in Anglophone nations, due to the rapidly changing
global context characterized by financial, political and health insecurity and the
reduction of trust in democratic institutions in a 'world risk society' (Beck 2013).
Together with serial organizational restructuring and reform driven by neoliberal
managerial and market logics, the nature of the field of higher education, its
discourses and rules of the game as well as the scope, scale and practice of academic
and leadership work, has been transformed (Marginson 2008).

The conjuncture of pressures reconfiguring higher education include
massification to feed workforce demand (Mok 2016); internationalization
abroad and at home (Jones et al. 2018, Knight 2012, Tran 2016); intensified
competitiveness for research funds and students (Chubb and Watermeyer 2017);
reduced government funding (Watt 2015, Howard 2020); increased accountability
(Stensaker and Harvey 2011); metrics ranking universities and academics
unequally (Analogue University 2019, Amsler and Bolsmann 2012, Currie 2008,
Pusser and Marginson 2013, Symonds et al. 2006, Wildson et al. 2015); research
assessment regimes differentiating between universities and individuals (Besley
2010, Oancea 2019, Rowlands and Wright 2020, Watermeyer 2014); privatization
and new competitors (Slaughter and Taylor 2015); rising student and employer
expectations regarding graduate employability (Blackmore et al. 2016, Brown et
al. 2011); escalating demands for individualized multimodal flexible teaching with
the shift from content to student-centred teaching in innovative learning spaces
(Boys 2015, Colet 2017); a push towards 'impactful' research (Cheng 2011); and
the digitalization and datafication of university governance, teaching, research and
academic life (Sellar 2015, Selwyn 2014, Williamson 2016 b), all aspects shaped by
a new digital architecture of time and space accelerating academic work (Wajcman
and Dodd 2016). These external pressures produce ongoing challenges, require
new directions in strategic thinking by university executives and academics to
reinvigorate the central role of universities and academics in democratic societies,
as universities are being repositioned in relation to the state to merely serve
national economies (Degn 2015, Jameson 2019).

Disrupting Relations between State, Society and Higher Education

The role of the university in state–society–knowledge relations is being disrupted.
The social field of higher education, understood as 'a set of possibilities, or a series

of moves; as a site of particular forms of capital and particular narratives; and especially as a site of regulative and coercive discourses' (Webb et al. 2002: 68), has been reconfigured over thirty years, with a shift in focus from massification in the 1990s to quality in the 2000s, excellence in the 2010s and quantification in the 2020s.

The emergence of new, sometimes interlocking, social fields of transnational governance of supra-national policymaking bodies and policy communities (OECD, IMF, World Bank, UNESCO) (Rizvi and Lingard 2010) discursively developed and legitimated neoliberal theories and ideas such as the knowledge economy, and informed new regional formations such as the EU reconfiguring higher education under Bologna (Delanty 2001, OECD 2008, Peters 2011). The policy imaginary of the knowledge economy, a key discursive strategy of neoliberalism and the 'sliding signifier of our time' in the 1990s (Peters 2011: 12), repositioned universities as critical to government and national economies as a source of innovation, economic growth and in the production of a skilled workforce of lifelong learner-earners. The knowledge economy discourse justified a particularly economic view of the role of higher education relative to the evaluative state and self-interested individual, making a qualitative shift in the discourse by shifting discourses away from education as a human right to how education could be measured and compared between nation states (Robertson 2007). Knowledge economy discourses justified government's tighter coupling of universities as key sites of production, dissemination and legitimation of knowledge to national economies using policy technologies of funding and accountability (Forsyth 2014, Lauder et al. 2012, Sidhu 2006). In so doing, government sought to capture the transnational and relational nature of the higher education field with all its rankings, status hierarchies and 'bundles of relations' such as teaching and research collaborations, cross-national institutional and industry and NGO partnerships.

Rapid growth due to massification after unification of university sectors in the UK, Australia and the EU in the 1990s was increasingly framed by a more instrumentalist than educationalist ideology, particularly with regard to international education. While universities, particularly in the West, were already highly internationalized in terms of their global orientation and research collaborations and with multiple exchange programmes, Stier (2010) argues that the Bologna process unifying EU higher education was specifically focused on competency building for the labour force as part of an 'ideological convergence in much of the world's higher education . . . where the new public management ideology has come to exert much influence on academia, adding terms such as "global competitive-ness", "benchmarking" and "sustainable development" to the vocabulary of policy-makers, university administrators, researchers, educators and students' (Stier 2010: 340).

In the Anglophone nations since the 1980s, universities experienced interconnected processes of unfettered marketization and managerialism, simultaneously experiencing reduced public funding while expected to address massification and equity pressures (Marginson and Considine 2000, Molesworth et al. 2011). Furthermore, knowledge, information and data have become new sources of profit for roving global capital and technopreneurs in emerging digital economies (Williamson 2016a and 2016b) while multinational and national agreements determined knowledge transfer and commercialization (Olssen and Peters 2005). Multiple new private actors and forms of economic capital (edu-businesses, big tech and edu-philanthropists) seek profit out of providing educational services, infrastructure and technologies, taking precedence over the field (Ball 2012, Verger et al. 2016). Universities have forged troubling links with these 'new actors, new markets and new contexts' (Stensaker and Harvey 2011: 8), sometimes joining, other times competing, in 'the practical interplay between roll-back (critique of public education sector) and roll-out (new business opportunities) of neo-liberalism' (Ball 2012: 119), increasing risk for universities regarding corrupt practices and so on. The penetration of these generic businesses into the academy has subtle effects as they treat education as just one arm of a profit-making enterprise next to transport, housing and energy, while offering soft and hard service provision, professional and managerial services, both relying on and exploiting academic credibility and expertise. External actors such as publishers (e.g. Pearson) exploit academic work through data mining of metrics and rankings while positioning universities and shaping academic practice, in a 'purposeful destatalisation and commodification of education' (Ball 2012: 124). Management firms such as EY, KPMG, Deloitte and McKinsey give advice on education policy and change management (Drori 2016). Public universities partner with private for-profit businesses to establish campuses overseas, in Malaysia, Vietnam and Singapore, instances of complex contractual hybrid arrangements of globalizing, neo-liberalizing, and indeed Westernizing edu-capitalism blurring public and private interests. Universities are key actors as their global reach extends through interaction with the private sector, state agencies, international consortia and other nation states (Ball 2012).

Universities therefore work within quasi-markets of higher education, which are globally constituted through national policies and politics, institutional processes, reputation, regulative mechanisms of governance, unregulated flows of products and students at macro (multinational trade agreements, international education), meso (domestic students, for-profit universities, social media such as LinkedIn with 24,000 universities on the platform in 2013) and micro (marketing agencies, price setting) levels. These quasi-markets involve multiple actors (policymakers, international student brokers, university managers, techno-businesses and professional organizations) and require individual, institutional and government investment (Robertson and Komljenovic 2016). Education markets also exploit and are driven by personal preferences and affective cultural economies, playing on the desires as well as fears of students as transnational mobility has become a familial middle-class strategy to enhance their children's cultural and economic capital, particularly for Asia and East Asian families (Tran 2016).

As a transnational social field, higher education also has its own rules of the game (merit, quality, credentials, etc.), hierarchies (research/non-research-intensive universities) and epistemic binaries (science/humanities), forms of distinction (international/domestic, world class) informed by capital formation in terms of economic (money), cultural (forms of knowledge, preferences and taste) and social (familial networks, culture and language) capitals, both processes and products of the field (Kim 2017, Kloot 2009, Marginson 2008, Maton 2005, Naidoo 2004). International education as a market (as distinguished from the processes of internationalization of curriculum, etc.) is both central and marginal to the field, has its own 'rules of the game' (visas, citizenship), hierarchies (student preferences for particular countries and universities, rankings), networks (recruitment, regional, online), unequal social relations (between domestic and international students) and discourses (cultural stereotypes about Asian students, etc.) (Mok 2016, Tran 2016).

Over thirty years, the field of HE has become porous as academics are no longer able to control the rules of the game with an ebbing away at its borders due to cross-field effects of politics, business and economics (Rawolle 2005). These cross-field effects are translated through higher education policy, which in turn re-constitutes the field in the form of texts (strategic plans) and discourses (of leadership) seeking to change the behaviour of institutions and individuals. In so doing, policy has a normative dimension due to its authoritative allocation of values and resources and how it positions different agents and social groups within a field in particular ways, by creating categories (e.g. equity groups). Policy also provides a language and legitimacy for action for some actors and not others, simultaneously drawing on and changing the rules of the game and practices as 'policies link the concerns of government and institutional practices with the individual behaviour of the worker-subject' (Sidhu 2006: 178). The infiltration of neoliberal policies has impacted on the values, vocabularies, rules and practices of higher education field and the formation of academic subjectivities.

The Neoliberal Project in Higher Education

Higher education restructuring over thirty years in Western developed nation states is illustrative of a changing relationship between the state and the individual within a wider shift from state-welfarism to state-managed capitalism (Fraser 2013, Olssen et al. 2004). Neoliberal 'policy technologies' of HE reform have been part of a global trend indicating a shift from the government of a unitary state to governance in and by contractual relations and market principles. The shift from social liberalism to neoliberalism has occurred as economic capital has been more powerful than cultural capital, most evident with the rise of academic capitalism (Fraser 2013, Nussbaum 2010, Slaughter and Rhoades 2004), and the penetration of new players into the field of higher education – edu-philanthropists, multinationals and technopreneurs (Gunter et al. 2016). Bourdieu (1998: 94–5) – reflected that neoliberalism is a 'strong discourse which is so strong and so hard to fight because it has behind it a world of power relations which helps to make it as it is', with its political operation realizing a 'program of methodical destruction of the collectivities' due to its focus on the individual. Academic capitalism also relies on institutionalized structures that are gendered and racialized, with capacity to extract different forms of affective labour.

Neoliberalism does not explain everything as it is only one element of economic globalization and is driven by the dynamics of technology and science, the collapsing of time/space creating greater interdependency. But neoliberalism in higher education, if 'conceptualized not as a fixed set of attributes with predetermined outcomes, but as a logic of governing that migrates and is selectively taken up in diverse political contexts' (Ong 2007: 3), cannot be ignored. Neoliberalism has informed the policy doxa of the knowledge economy and the logics governing the university, where doxa is 'the process through which ideas and concepts come into being in explaining experience of the social world and where those concepts and ideas are accepted as indisputable and "natural"' (Bourdieu 1977: 84). Understanding neoliberalism is critical to understanding higher education reform and its effects (Tight 2014, Connell 2013).

The neoliberal project of higher education reform was premised on three key tenets, particularly in the Anglophone nations, with the shift from welfarism to state-managed capitalism (Fraser and Jaeggi 2018). First, that the market, based on competition and choice, is the most efficient and effective mechanism of delivering goods and services rather than the state. Marketization of higher education was central because universities are key players as knowledge producers, legitimators and disseminators. The market logic when dispersed through policies and practices converted academic education into a commodity (Palfreyman and Tapper 2014) and 'the transformation of what are abstract, intangible, non-material and relational experiences into a visible, quantifiable and instrumentally driven process' (Furedi 2017: 2), as contractual not pedagogic or collegial relationships. The logics and language of the market permeate – explicitly through language. For example, students as consumers or customers need to be 'satisfied'; academics are 'delivering' curriculum as a product and not as a pedagogical relationship; industry and government are 'clients'. The commodification of research and the monetization of all aspects of academic practice are based on individualized transactional relationships of workload formulae (Kenny 2018).

Contrary to classic liberal theories of free markets which freed the individual and the institution for state intervention, neoliberal reforms allowed the state to actively intervene to micro-manage university life, to remedy market inadequacies and impose social norms (Molesworth et al. 2011). State intervention created 'the appropriate market by providing the conditions, laws and institutions necessary for its operation' (Olssen and Peters 2005: 315) by encouraging competition between individual universities, privatization and economic autonomy to enhance responsiveness. Each new external pressure (internationalization, industry partnerships) led to a proliferation of new management positions and development programmes focusing on strategic leadership, as well as the integration of professionally qualified marketing divisions across all aspects of the university (Engwall 2008).

Second, human capital theory is a key ingredient of the policy doxa of the twenty-first-century notion of lifelong learning based on the promise that more education leads to greater economic benefits. Human capital theory assumes an abstract notion of a disembodied race-, class- and gender-free autonomous individual who seeks to maximize their individual gain through choice. Investment in education means the individual accumulates a valued stock of economic, cultural and social capital that is rewarded in the market. Founded on this belief, a new informal social contract was struck between citizens and the state: 'the state would provide the educational opportunities for citizens to ascend the credential ladder and in return they had to study and achieve to the best of their abilities. Through this contract it was thought the state could achieve both economic competitiveness and social justice . . . a social imaginary that has education at its centre' (Lauder et al. 2012: 1). A related skill-bias theory was that technological advances increased (not replaced) demand for higher skills, now revisited with AI (Lauder et al. 2012: 52–3).

Such assumptions justified massification and the introduction of university fees in the 1990s in Australia. Contrary to this, Brown (2015: 103) argues: 'human capital is merely the liberal subject portrayed from a masculinist, bourgeois viewpoint' that assumes a normative white male and ignores how different historical, cultural, economic and social conditions constrain or enable individual choice due to the gender, ethno-racial and class stratification of labour markets. Evidence shows that women and people of colour experience discrimination and lower pay for the same credentials possessed by their white male counterparts (Livingstone et al. 2008).

Third, and conducive to the reception of neoliberalism, was the influence of New Public Management (NPM) in the UK, New Zealand and Australia since the 1980s (Deem and Brehony 2005, Pusey 1991). NPM focused on converting public administration into a service-oriented delivery by imitating private corporate sector governance and promoting structural devolution to facilitate consumer choice, appropriating democratic discourses of citizen rights and counter 'producer capture' by the professions of their fields (public education, health, welfare) (Deem et al. 2007, Olssen and Peters 2005, Slater et al. 2008). In Australia, corporate managerialism, Australia's version of NPM, altered the relationship between government and the bureaucracy federally, with the Ministerialization of policy. Senior bureaucrats were put on contract, reorienting their commitment away from 'the public' to being loyal to the government in power, and Treasury was given power over the education, health and welfare portfolios (Pusey 1991). As stated by a political science professor at one university in this study: 'The Australian government is just a Westminster neoliberal government run by Treasury . . . it bares down on expenditure at all levels and minimizes its obligations . . . pretty similar to the UK.'

Higher education was pressured by federal governments to develop a performance culture through management and the 'techniques of auditing, accounting and management' (Olssen and Peters 2005: 315; Bansel and Davies 2010). Corporate managerialism was manifested post-1990 variously: by a drive for efficiency modelled on business practices, restructuring labour markets to gain flexibility, accountability, performance indicators, target setting, benchmarking, league tables and performance management as well as the outsourcing of services (Deem and Brehony 2005: 220). While few now advocate NPM, its logics and practices are embedded in the next phase of digital governance (Dunleavy 2005) and 'the colonization of analogue life (technologies, institutions and people) by a digital logic expressed through networked computerization' (Hassan 2017: 72).

In Australia, critical to the responsiveness of the higher education workforce, relations between unions, government and business were reconfigured under the National Accord negotiated in 1987 by the federal Labor government (O'Brien 2015). Enterprise bargaining devolved all wage bargaining down to individual enterprises such as universities (economic autonomy) and disallowed cross-sector bargaining, which had historically allowed strong unions (male-dominated and industrial) to support weaker unions (feminized and service-based) (Currie 1992). Enterprise bargaining over three decades has ratcheted up productivity to gain minimal wage increments at the cost of worsening work conditions and reducing academic salaries relative to other professions (Welch 2012). Such structural reforms of industrial relations lacked a moral economy as it reduced the safety net and impacted particularly on women as the higher education workforce became feminized (Bailey et al. 2011).

Putting education at the centre of national competitiveness globally, and in the context of the mobility of talent, led to a focus on accountability, fuelled after 2005 by comparative measures of success such as the global rankings of universities (Times Higher Education, Jinq Qua Tong, QS Quacquarelli-Symonds, University World Rankings) (Deem et al. 2008, Epseland and Sauder 2016, Pusser and Marginson 2013, Robertson and Komljenovic 2016, Stack 2016). Under conditions of heightened competition due to internationalization, being distinctive in the field became critical, foregrounding reputation and excellence. Governments and students used metrics and rankings as proxies for quality because they enabled comparison between academics, within and between universities and systems. In the search for being distinctive in the market, evaluative mechanisms such as research assessment in turn re/produced hierarchies between and within universities and disciplines (Besley 2010, Blackmore 2009a,b, 2020c, Currie 2008, Wright 2009) and increased differentiation between research-intensive and other universities.

As new providers and partners as well as evaluative mechanisms proliferate in the field of higher education, educational policy has been removed from the hands of the education professional and is increasingly informed through circuits of global policy communities, big business, education consultants and philanthro-capitalists with private capital moving into the social space left by the state. This is part of a wider trend of the

> hollowing out of democracy by market forces at two levels: on the one hand, the corporate capture of political parties and public institutions at the level of the territorial state, on the other hand, the usurpation of political decision-making power at the transnational level by global finance, a force that is unaccountable to the demos. (Fraser and Jaeggi 2018: 3)

The disassociation of the economic from the social and political, and the instrumental from the ethical, is embedded in neoliberalism (Brown 2015). Neoliberalism has been depicted as governing through freedom and governing by calculation (Ong 2007: 4). On the one hand, academic knowledge has become critical to national economies, commodified and measured for its economic benefits, and governed by calculation when being held accountable for measurable outcomes, metrics and money or what Fraser (2013) refers to as *economism*. On the other hand, the neoliberal mantra is that the 'leaner' state 'steers from a distance' through policy and funding mechanisms allowing universities to freely choose from the options or 'governing by freedom' in a state-mediated global market (Deem et al. 2007; Olssen and Peters 2005). This leaves space for ethical leadership. University executive management is 'free to choose' how they use their resources within constraints of policy, funding and accountabilities. Despite this, much of the risk and responsibility has been devolved to the individual academic (Saltmarsh and Randall-Moon 2015).

The feminist political scientist Yeatman (2002) offers an alternative conceptualization. She distinguishes between patrimonial contractualism of classic liberalism, premised around established rules and authorities, and market contractualism, which assumes neoliberalism's self-maximizing atomistic individual who is 'self-reliant through market participation' (Yeatman 2002: 71). Neoliberalism promotes a reductionist view of the individual exercising choice without the need for social protections or recognition of the relationships which individuals form. Market contractualism is transactional, limited to what is in the contract, reducing relationships to cost and benefit, and is unable to recognize the relationship individuals form whether through parenting, teaching or collaboration. Yeatman (2002) proposes a social/relational contractualism that assumes a process of individualization which is dynamic and relational, occurring as more choices are available due to the growing interdependency of our social, economic and political worlds, with individuals gaining a sense of self, agency, meaning and belonging. As a mode of governance within a liberal democratic society, relational or social contractualism 'centres on the conduct of ongoing relationships between individuals' and questions what type of institution or conditions are required to develop these, an important question regarding the future of universities (Yeatman 2002: 71).

Arguably, in higher education, market and relational contractualism coexist together with patrimonial (paternal) contractualism, antagonistic modes often in conflict (Rawolle et al. 2016). Liberal notions of contractualism are embedded in institutional design and a master discourse of choice, producing a particular form of contractual personhood (Yeatman 2002). Corporatization of universities saw the growth of contractual relations which were once accompanied by professional judgement and trust but are increasingly replaced by measures of accountability, surveillance and veiled mistrust (Rawolle et al. 2016). Academic and leadership practices are also constituted through implicit informal contracts and a sense of reciprocity which are the 'social glue that informs institutional life and the sense of collegiality is one of its main constituents' (Nixon 2015: 12). Academic identities are formed in a professional world that serves – and is accountable to – the public (Nixon 2015: 12). Contractual personhood is a narrower and more instrumental version of the social contract in which academics are expected to perform in particular ways and be loyal to the university (paternal contract). Hence the tension between practice premised upon collegiality (relational contractualism) and its professional ethical and moral imperatives of responsibility to others, and those premised on individual competitiveness and market contractualism where individuals are limited to undertaking specific work defined in a contract (Bacon 2014, Macfarlane 2017). With relational contractualism, people gift to each other without requiring anything in return, gifting of labour being a common practice underpinning academic relations (Bourdieu 1990, Bullen and Flavell 2017, Cheal 1988, Eriksen 2006).

Higher education therefore has been recalibrated from being a nation-state building enterprise in the twentieth century to a transnational edu-business in the twenty-first century, reconceptualizing education as a private not a public good (Marginson 2011). Yet universities in the Global North have become central to the social and economic life of urban and regional communities as well as national economies. Consequently, universities often have competing roles and expectations placed on them by multiple stakeholders: government authorities, students, industry, NGOs, professional bodies, employers and local communities. Furthermore, despite the orthodoxies of NPM and rational choice theories viewing the university as the same as any other public or private organization, thereby challenging its 'uniqueness' (Deem and Brehony 2005, Gunter et al. 2016), universities still differ from corporations in that they do not have responsibility to shareholders to make a profit other than to stay financially viable (Nussbaum 2010). Even as managerialist and market logics of practice permeate through universities, their organizational form based on academic logics of practice has remarkably remained relatively unchanged, based on knowledge fields, academic tribes and governance, the structure of councils, academic boards, departments, faculties, schools and research centres (Vukasovic et al. 2012). These logics with different ideals and practices of governance or ways of organizing interact and compete (Sahlin and Eriksssen-Zetterquist 2016). The sense of uniqueness of the university and it being treated as a global business creates significant tensions between different understandings of the role of the university, a tension continuing to inform relations between management and academics.

The Australian University Sector: 'The Canary in the Field of Global Higher Education'

The nature and role of the comprehensive 'modern' university of the twentieth century, which offered a liberal education to the Global North, is significantly under threat in the early twenty-first century, particularly in the Anglophone contexts (Barber et al. 2013, Davis 2017). The Australian 'enterprise university' of 2000 (Marginson and Considine 2000) is now the entrepreneurial university, where economic ends subsume obligation to the public, which had been a central tenet of the twentieth-century social contract of education within the welfare state, to meet the needs of academic capitalism (Rhoades 2014).

The Australian higher education sector provides an exemplar of the extent, nature and impact of three decades of neoliberal reform of higher education in the Anglophone nation states particularly, acting as a warning for universities in the Global South within the context of heightened risk and the changing geopolitics of education (Marginson 2008). As a settler nation state Australia is culturally disposed towards the Global North, adopting its policy flows, particularly those of the OECD and the UK. Yet it is geographically located in the Global South on the South Pacific and Asian rim (Connell 2017) and economically dependent on Chinese education, minerals and produce markets. Australia and New Zealand sit outside the regional agreements such as the North American Free Trade Alliance, the European Union and Association of South-East Asian Nations. Both governments were quick to deregulate financial markets to gain access to global markets and adopted NPM (Olssen and Peters 2005), echoing similar trends in the UK (e.g. Kupfer 2012). As one strategy of internationalization, or Western imperialism, Australia became a major provider of curriculum, educational services and products to Asia and South-East Asia during the 1990s with education becoming the third largest Australian export earner worth $40 billion in 2019. Urban and regional economies have become reliant on educational services and international student labour, with universities contributing $41 billion to the economy in 2018 (Universities Australia 2020: 3). The 'Education State' of Victoria hosts seven of the thirty-nine public universities, with education until 2020 being its top export earner.

Due to reduced real public funding relative to other OECD countries (e.g. R&D percentage of GDP fell during 2016–17 from 0.21 to 0.19 per cent) (Howard 2020) and reliance on international student fees for research funding, Australian higher education is highly susceptible to shifts in global and regional geopolitics and economic crises, shifting student and academic mobility patterns: the 'canary' in the field of higher education as Covid-19 has shown. Australia as a settler nation, together with New Zealand, Canada and the United States, means, Gerrard et al. (2021: 1–2) argue, that systems of formal education are part of the 'mutually constituted projects of liberalism and white supremacy' and 'cannot be separated from colonial and national projects that have sought to categorise, divide, oppress, enslave, and assimilate people on the basis of race'. Capitalism's extractive project is reliant on both a racial and gender division of labour.

Three studies inform the text. The primary source is an Australian Research Council four-year project *Leadership in Entrepreneurial Universities: Dis/Engagement and Diversity* (2012–17). This focused on two key issues: disengagement with leadership as suggested in the literature due to academics not taking up formal academic management positions (Bexley et al. 2011, Coates et al. 2009); and the enduring lack of gender and ethno-racial diversity in and of leadership in senior academic and management positions in Australian universities despite equity policies and EEO practitioners working in universities over thirty years (Bell

2010, Eddy et al. 2016, Francis and Schulz 2020, Jarboe 2017, Johnson 2017). Two other studies tracked the emerging concerns about credentialism and graduate employability, critical issues for Australian universities due to the high-risk policy setting of international education due to changing geopolitics and global crises.[1]

The leadership study aimed, through institutional case studies and individual biographies, to map the scope and nature of leadership dis/engagement and lack of diversity within the wider problematic of academic recruitment and retention and the contextual constraints and possibilities impacting on academic career pathways, which shape who gets to be senior managers or professors. Three case studies representing the sector were undertaken: one of a research-intensive university established in the 1850s and member of the Group of Eight (Go8)[2]; the second a former technical institute which became a university with five other technical institutes post-1989 (Utech) to form the University Technology Network; and the third a regional university established in the 1960s (Regional) which belongs to the Innovative Research Group. These universities were selected because their histories, and that their websites, highlighted how they were both entrepreneurial with a focus on innovation, applied research, diversifying income sources and partnerships, and were inclusive of diversity and interdisciplinarity.

Semi-structured interviews were undertaken with those in formal or positional leadership in management or research and the professoriate. Snowball sampling enabled me to identify 'informal' leaders, who did not intend to apply for formal leadership, and aspirant leaders, and to include where possible a representative sample of each university's gender profile at each level of the organization. Over 150 interviews were undertaken: with policymakers in higher education and on the Australian Research Council (ARC); with, in each case study university, the Vice Chancellor (VC), Deputy Vice Chancellors (DVC), Pro Vice Chancellors (PVC), Deans, Heads of School (Head); with Directors of Research Centres and Institutes; and with academics including early career researchers (ECRs), from level B to full professor as well as post-doctoral fellows (PDF), across all disciplines.

In addition, I interviewed equal employment opportunity (EEO), now called diversity managers, union representatives and human resource (HR) managers as these positions provided a university-wide perspective on organizational issues regarding equity and workplace conditions. HR managers were expected to both implement change and negotiate enterprise agreements. Finally, management consultants and search firms ('headhunters'), increasingly used for high-level appointments in the sector as well as for leadership coaching, were interviewed. As outsiders they had knowledge of more personal aspects of managing and brought a comparative perspective with organizations other than universities.

This text focuses on the voices of senior academic managers and professors but draws on themes arising from the overarching project regarding university governance, national and institutional policies, recruitment practices, work conditions, leadership roles in research and management, family/work issues as well as policies, programmes and strategies addressing recruitment and retention into leadership (development programmes, succession planning, mentoring, search firms). The three university case studies illustrated how specific national policy framings and institutional contexts and priorities shaped leadership opportunities and how these differed by (a) discipline (e.g. social sciences, physical sciences); (b) gender, race, ethnicity and age; (c) each university's internal/external structures and cultures; and (d) the (mal)distribution patterns of research funds and resources within and between universities and within the higher education sector.

Studying leadership is one way to access how organizations such as universities are changing in the context of wider globalizing forces, and in national and local contexts according to their internal institutional legacies, logics and dynamics. The senior academics and managers interviewed spoke from a position of perceived power, many having experienced twenty years of university reform. This focus meant, first, the sample was skewed towards the largest number of positions, Heads of School. This is novel as there is little research on this role, yet they are held responsible for implementing change. Second, research is foregrounded more than teaching because of the focus on the role of the professoriate. Both samples point to dominant masculinities and whiteness throughout, which itself is indicative of the lack of diversity in both management and research leadership. Since no interviewee self-identified as other than cisgender, while retaining anonymity of the interviewee and university, it was important to recognize power/gender/ knowledge relations by indicating the role, disciplinary field and gender with the use of pseudonyms after each quote. None of the voluntary participants indicated a disability and most were older than fifty, due to my focus on senior academics and managers.

Positioning Myself

A feminist perspective provides insights into key workings of the university which are often neglected in mainstream studies that either focus only on women and leadership or ignore gender altogether. Interviewing both men and women presents differing perspectives as to the nature of the structural, cultural and social relations of gender, class and ethno-racial difference within the academy. As a cisgender woman and educational researcher who has worked at Deakin University since 1987, after fifteen years as a secondary public school teacher, I am both an insider and outsider when researching the academy. On the one hand, I experience the university from what Bourdieu (1999: 3–4) refers to as 'perspectivism', working with 'the managerialized structural realignment of lived practices, social relations and inter-subjective dispositions (especially ethical dispositions) of university work' (Zipin and Brennan 2003: 352). On the other hand, I seek to practise a form of reflexivity and 'a willingness to step back from discrete issues, and to problematize the deep structures that underlie them' (Fraser 2008: 154).

Deakin University, a regional university established in 1974 as a distance education provider, developed a culture marked by a strong presence of feminist scholars and a small professoriate without the usual historical baggage and status hierarchy. We enjoyed an unstructured research environment and form of organizing organically that was interdisciplinary. Deakin offered innovative curriculum and bi-modal course materials which constantly adapted to new technologies. Networking was encouraged and the Education Faculty was known internationally for its critical scholarship (Tinning and Sirna 2011). Subsequently, I have been a participant-observer of multiple restructurings. Deakin developed from a one-campus regional university to a four-campus urban and regional provider with a strong digital footprint, much of it fully 'in the Cloud' by 2020. The Faculty of Education went from having one school, to five schools, to three schools and then amalgamated as a School within the Faculty of Arts in 2009. Under six Vice Chancellors, seven Deans, ten Heads of School, Deakin has been rebranded multiple times with logos that have puzzled those who teach and research, signalling the widening disconnect between academic and marketing practice.

Within the field of education, I have had first-hand experience of the repositioning of educational research as a field and professional practice. When a mid-career researcher, I mentored colleagues in research after an amalgamation with two Colleges of Advanced Education in 2003, and as member, then Director, of Deakin Centre for Education and Change. As Deputy and Acting Chair of Academic Board and member of multiple university-wide committees in the early 2000s, I experienced the increasing exercise of executive power and growing bifurcation between managerial and academic decision-making first evident in 1992 (Blackmore 1992). After 2010, as a professor and inaugural director of a strategic research centre, the Centre for Research into Educational Futures and Innovation, I came to understand how the professorial voice, although I was designated as a 'senior manager', was sidelined from decision-making despite being expected to build research capacity and meet financial KPIs. As journal editor of the *Australian Educational Researcher* for thirteen years and executive member (and President) of the Australian Association of Research in Education (AARE), I was one of many educational researchers who lobbied against journal rankings, informed and critiqued research assessment policies, disputed what counted as evidence-based policy and promoted the value of educational research by co-initiating a blog (*EduResearchMatters*).

I have been simultaneously a successful academic 'in the game', encouraging others to adopt and adapt to a competitive academic habitus, both complicit in and contesting the performative aspects of academy while maintaining a clear focus on the substantive debates around socially just education and inclusive workplaces. I have been frequently contacted about applying or recommending others for positions in research and administrative leadership nationally and internationally. I declined these roles, partly out of fear of what many academics refer to as the managerial logic subsuming their former academic self. My preference has been to work outside and to disrupt the corporate framing of the university because of its failure to listen and draw on the collective and collegial practices that constitute the core work of the academy – teaching, research and service.

My feelings of ambivalence towards my university as an employer and the role of the university as a key institution in a democratic society have led me to struggle with how I position myself within an institution which has at one level done me well and to which I feel some loyalty, and in which I have invested much of my career and life. I have witnessed and experienced supportive and productive leadership practices which build collective and individual capacity as well as toxic, narcissistic and destructive leadership practices (Klaus and Steele 2020, Pelletier 2010, Samier and Atkins 2009). I have watched how top-down bullying permeates organizational practices and how those legitimated by their position are able to exert power through apparently neutral processes to cause personal and professional damage, a form of institutional bullying often motivated by the individual's own insecurities, animosities or narcissist tendencies. My experience is that these individuals always move on (and often upward) but in the context of 2021, *#Enoughisenough*, such bullying should now be named and shamed.

This ambivalent attitude towards 'the university' as employer derives from debates over who comprise 'the university', evident throughout the interviews at all levels of the academy. Like many professors so disposed to take a critical stance, my response has been to become involved where possible, speak out for others and encourage ethical and collegial practices among colleagues and students, thereby creating a relatively 'safe' place and sense of belonging at the level of scholarly practice despite the corporate ethos. Jill Jameson's (2018: 375) comment appeals as to how 'informal stoical leadership exists in the tacit knowledge of quiet critical corridor talk (CCT) shared amongst academics in a minority of dysfunctional management situations in Higher Education, hidden underneath the iceberg of what officially happens'.

It is difficult to extract my experiences of being an academic under both highly effective and dysfunctional leadership, observations from being at the executive level and listening to collegial responses to reforms from the text. Jameson (2018: 376) reflects on

> the value of a qualitative methodological stance. It is also concerned with the kinds of human variabilities and self-expressed fragilities that are as intangible and ultimately immeasurable as the uncertain creative space. It is these variabilities and fragilities that add flesh to the bones of the story. It is also about how academics seek to defend through 'creative critically' their ethical beliefs.

Adopting a critical feminist approach as an academic and researcher raises methodological and ethical questions. It involves asking practical questions which care for participants' views at the same time as seeking to challenge the same participants. This is a difficult balance to strike when one works in the same field that one is researching and therefore this is a sympathetic but critical account. Bourdieu (1999: 617–18) asserted, 'true submission to the data' demands 'practical mastery of the social logic by which these data are constructed', and it is this social logic that I explore.

As a feminist scholar, I have faced the usual dilemmas of a performative academic: how to achieve institutional demands, maintain a critical positioning (feminist theory, professional activism and inclusive pedagogy), protect oneself (from some students, social media trolls, institutional bullying) and how to self-protect against the exploitation of academics' passion resulting in overwork. As Tomlinson (2010: 195) puts it, 'Every feminist argument negotiates a dialectical relationship between undeniable risk and undeniable possibilities, between affect and reason, between situated knowledges and social change.' This text is written with passion expressed by many interviewees – a passion for research and teaching, for working with colleagues and students, and out of a sense of obligation to and responsibility for the field of educational research, social justice and education for the public good. Czarniawski (2008: 158) reflects that 'such passion is going out of fashion in universities, except when an exceptional discovery is made, one that can be measured, displayed and commercialized, and usually in medical, material or health sciences or digital technology'. Yet the passion of academics is what sustains contemporary universities and upon which universities increasingly rely because academics volunteer or 'gift' their energy and significant unpaid overtime.

While education is political, as are knowledge–state–society relations, the Dawkins reforms of 1990s had a strong policy rationale and framing of massification and equity, even though many disagreed. The current illiberal Coalition government is operating in a policy free zone with a transparent ideological agenda that continues Howard's culture wars against the academy as a critical voice and conscience. This is a worrying trend in a democracy when the legitimacy of what counts as knowledge and truth is under threat. The Coalition refused to protect universities from the effects of Covid-19. Consequently, and ironically, having tracked the vulnerability of Australian universities and precarity of academic work, I am currently experiencing with colleagues, while writing, the anger and grief of restructuring yet again in 2021. Deakin's VC has twice adopted a corporate top-down logic that has been harsh and careless in its delivery, rejecting a more collegial approach granting academics greater ownership over difficult reforms, and therefore losing the trust of staff. I have been trapped in a 'spill and kill' redundancy situation after thirty-five years of service having earned millions of dollars of grant funding, led two research centres, supervised fifty PhD completions, mentored multiple academics and accrued reputational status which Deakin happily claimed. I have achieved most of this despite, rather than because of, university management.

Organizing the Text

There is significant discussion within academic and business literature around both leadership and creative disruption. Creative disruption is seen to be when things radically change, and in so doing, creative solutions emerge due to different conjunctures of events, people and places – a contingency approach to complexity. This text takes a different stance. Disruption is both a theme and an organizer. Part I – 'Disrupting Universities' – provides a conceptual framing (Chapter 2) and the contextual disruptions driving the global restructuring of higher education (Chapter 3). Part II focuses on disruptive leadership practices with a focus on leaderism and the exertion of executive power enabled by corporatization

(Chapter 4), the communicative practices of leadership storying in change management (Chapter 5) and how these have repositioned and changed the nature of the professoriate (Chapter 6). Chapter 7 addresses the affective effects of corporatization and leaderism: disenchantment with and disengagement from academic management under conditions of overwork and work/life conflict. Part III focuses on contemporary disruptors. First, the notion of diversity as a potential disruptor of leadership practices (Chapter 8); and second, the great disruptor of Covid-19, which exposed the vulnerability of Australian universities and leadership (Chapter 9). I conclude considering the possibilities of leadership for a more sustainable university that offers a secure, equitable and safe workplace based on inclusive, collegial and critical leadership refocusing on the public good.

Part I

DISRUPTING UNIVERSITIES

Chapter 2

RE-FRAMING LEADERSHIP IN HIGHER EDUCATION

The focus of this text is on the global, national, local and institutional contexts, constituting and being constituted by the global field of higher education at a time in which there is a 'leadership crisis' (MacFarlane 2012a). This crisis is defined variously in the university: as a lack of applicants for management positions, the lack of cultural and gender diversity in management and research leadership (Bell 2010, Blackmore et al. 2016, Collins et al. 2011, Jarboe 2017), and the lack of ethical leadership symptomatic of a wider decline in trust in political, religious and business leaders (Bentley et al. 2013, Blackmore and Sachs 2007, Coates et al. 2010, Scott et al. 2010). The focus is on leadership as a lens through which to understand the nature of organizational change from the perspectives of those considered to be in formal and informal 'leadership' positions: academic managers and the professoriate.

For feminist scholars, the issue in any analysis is always whether we just adopt a 'correctionist mode of thinking', 'modifying existing socio-theoretical discourses to include the interests of women' or do something fundamentally different (Adkins 2005: 195). Unable to fully resolve this dilemma, I draw eclectically but critically on interrelated theoretical strands to analyse leadership in three Australian universities. '[N]ot content to simply to treat problems in the form in which they are given within the established frame, we [I] make the frame itself the focus of attention and reconstruction' (Fraser 2008: 155). Based on the criteria of using theories that have strong explanatory power, and a capacity to focus on social change and on social justice, I take a critical feminist and reflexive stance on Bourdieu's practical tools of analysis in higher education – field, habitus, capitals (economic, social, cultural and symbolic), doxa and hysterisis (Adkins and Skeggs 2004, Ahmed 2004, McLeod 2005, McNay 2000, Naidoo 2004, Reay 2004) and draw on critical organizational theory (e.g. Acker 1990, Benschop and Brouns 2003, Czarniawski 2014a and 2014b, Gherardi 2017a and 2017b).

Feminist theory is itself a contested field of theory and research (Blackmore 2022). Multiple feminisms (liberal, Black, queer, post-colonial, Indigenous, queer, Islamic, Asian, to name a few) address the situatedness of power/knowledge/ gender relations which have informed educational leadership research (Fuller 2021). While each adopts different politics and strategies, the shared feminist project globally is one of social justice for all women and girls and education is a key site of social change. Feminism's polyvocalism and shared purpose are drawn on in this analysis to

- consider gender as a 'structuring structure' re/constituting different masculinities and femininities in relation to each other;
- interrogate gender/race/power/knowledge relations and how these are formed through the cultural, structural and institutional arrangements;
- undertake a critical discourse analysis that questions assumptions, concepts and categories and their equity effects, for example, merit, diversity and flexibility;
- unpack assumptions, processes, structures and practices of education reform/ restructuring at global, national and institutional levels and their effects;
- foreground material and temporal conditions and division of labour of everyday life;
- illuminate how discursive, cultural, symbolic, temporal and spatial practices of organizing position individuals and social groups;
- reflect on the epistemological and ontological assumptions of research;
- propose critical leadership practices for inclusive and socially just universities.

Gender is embodied within cultural and other value systems, as evident in contemporary debates over same-sex marriage, abortion, religious discrimination and gender identity (she/her, he/him, they/their/them).

At the same time, not everything is about gender or race, as this analysis indicates, even as enduring power/knowledge relations and practices of the academy produce multiple exclusions.

Bourdieu's tools provide an additional capacity to analyse systematically shifts within and between higher education (HE) and other fields (politics, media, business, etc.), to identify emergent as well as established forms of capital (e.g. techno-administrative capital), the role of symbolic violence when it comes to diversity policy, and how the logics of practice inform being and doing leadership.

From this feminist and Bourdieuian perspective, understanding leadership as a relational and situated practice means adopting a practice-based analysis in which 'sense-making and knowing are foregrounded, and located in the material and discursive activity, body, artefacts, habits, and preoccupations that populate the life of organizational members' (Nicolini 2013: 7). Gherardi (2017a: 3) views practice as a 'process in which identities, artefacts, ideologies, rules, language, morality and interests are woven together and affect each other in a process of learning', non-cognitive and cognitive. The elements that comprise a practice are linked to each other according to Gherardi and Nicolini (2001: 38) by 'practical understanding, rules, teleo-affective structure, general understanding, and social memories', all elements that emerged in this analysis. Bourdieu (1990) more specifically argues that practice is coordinated, institutionalized, purposeful and meaningful. While practice theorists adopt different perspectives, 'most subscribe to these theorizing moves: (1) that situated actions are consequential in the production of social life,

(2) that dualisms are rejected as a way of theorizing, and (3) that relations are mutually constitutive' (Feldman and Orlikowski 2011: 1243).

Leadership as a Situated and Relational Practice

Leadership has supplanted notions of administration and management in the literature, higher education discourses and practice. Leadership research generally makes conceptual and practice-related distinctions between leadership and management: leadership is understood as being about meaning-making and purposeful practice, while management is about planning, budgeting, resource allocation and assigning tasks (Branson et al. 2018). Most studies have focused on the changing global context and external pressures on university executive managers and the increasingly interventionist and evaluative role of the state governing 'autonomous' universities, and less so on the practices of leadership and organizational change (Fumasoli and Stensaker 2013, Scott et al. 2010). Recent developments in HE research include texts offering tools for institutional change (e.g. Kretovics 2020), which tend to have an instrumentalist skills-oriented perspective, and 'utilitarian analysis of intelligences, ethics, emotions and even personality traits' drawing largely from mainstream management literature (Oleksiyenko and Ruan 2019: 407), with little discussion of intellectual leadership (Macfarlane 2012a) or leadership for social justice (e.g. Kezar and Posselt 2020). Other research focuses on the professoriate (e.g. Evans 2018, Macfarlane 2012a) or, on middle or senior management (e.g. Acker 2014, Bryman 2007, Davis et al. 2016, Hancock and Hellawell 2003) and more recently, the 'life giving qualities' of leadership rather than the 'scarcity mindset' that dominates higher education (Cherkowski et al. 2021: 158).

Often leadership research relies on leaders' self-reporting and life histories gained through interview. Bourdieu (1990: 102) is sceptical because life history presumes actors have a 'thorough understanding of the historical preconditions of their own experiences and unwittingly introduce an implicit philosophy of practice as driven by processes of reflective justification, rather than an intuitive "feel for the game"' (Bourdieu 1977: 18–19, 1990: 98–105). Self-reporting of leadership practice provides the opportunity to rehearse a coherent life project which only emerges on reflection and was not necessarily how it was experienced. Wacquant (1995: 173) refers to '[T]he kinds of "capital" that individuals draw upon to generate certain impressions; the values, themes, and interests that underpin the self-representations offered; the implicit "audience" towards which narratives are projected; and how narrativizations may reflect particular forms of "illusio" – a commitment to the field and investment in the stakes'.

At the same time, Asher (2010) (a post-colonial, feminist scholar and a South Asian, immigrant woman academic currently teaching in the US South), Showunmi (2020) (a Black feminist scholar in the UK) and Moreton-Robinson (2013) (a First Nation scholar in Australia) argue that life history narratives are often the only form of expression available to otherwise marginalized voices of leaders who do not fit the norm, for example of whiteness or heterosexuality, to enable them to build a knowledge base which depicts different ways of leading (Lugg 2017, Sumara 2021). Bourdieu's notion of social trajectory suggests a more contingent on one's positioning (gender, race, class, sexuality, ableness) and less coherent perspective that recognizes the impediments that cause shifts in direction and purpose as the individual encounters historically situated fields. It illuminates how individuals are repositioned relative to other agents in the field while recognizing 'the "generative structures", embedded both within social space and the habitus that predispose individuals toward certain practices, self-understandings, experiences, and social relationships' (Barrett 2015: 4–5) such as leadership.

Leadership habitus is constituted through political, cultural, socio-economic and material contexts and experiences in a 'recursive relationship between agency (habitus) and structure (field)' and bundles of relations so neatly put by Bourdieu (1984: 101) in theorizing the generation of practice: [(habitus) (capital)]+field=practice. It is through the workings of habitus – the doing and being of learning – that practice is linked to capitals and fields (Lovell 2000: 12). Habitus emerges out of 'historical relations "deposited" within individual bodies in the form of mental and corporeal schemata of perception, appreciation and action' connecting agents and practices through 'systems of dispositions' which are bodily incorporations of social histories (Wacquant 2005: 318). Habitus is about strategizing, improvisation and accommodation as habitus is constituted over time and space. Habitus therefore conceptually captures academic life as 'a system of shared social dispositions and cognitive structures which generates perceptions, appreciations and actions' (Bourdieu 1988a: 279). Put another way, if a field is the game, habitus is the 'sense of the game' (Kloot 2009). Having a 'feel for the game and capacity to strategize relies as much on intuition and a game sense as it does mastery of explicit activities and . . . a practical sense that is affective, intuitive as well as good sense' (Grenfell and James 1998: 15). There is also a collective academic habitus acquired through engaging with others in the field of higher education and sharing dispositions, attitudes and values as well as an individual habitus specific to one's experience (Burke et al. 2013). Some argue there is a managerial habitus, a readiness to resort to proceduralism as the default position to manage not lead when unable to read the play of the game (Carroll and Levy 2008).

Focusing on relational practices of leadership means that academics are better conceived as audiences rather than followers. Academics also enact leadership in research, pedagogy, disciplinary fields, curriculum development as well as service to the community, government, industry and NGOs, and as experts, advocates and public intellectuals (Jones et al. 2012, Marginson 2011). Perceptions matter in such relationships: 'As a leader you are the object of others' perceptions' (Nixon 2015: 11), often troubling gender norms like masculine women and feminine men (Atkins and Vicars 2016). Acting as a leader is about asserting a particular habitus both unconsciously and consciously that is recognizable to others but mediated, if not distorted, by expectations of others. In turn, these relationships impact on leadership self-efficacy and behaviour (Skorobohacz et al. 2016). How others view leadership practice and how this influences their perceptions of, understandings about and informs their own leadership aspirations and practice is central to this analysis. Leadership habitus is continually re/produced within the field through practice, displayed often as a form of 'practical mastery' of 'the logic or of the immanent necessity of a game – a mastery acquired by experience of the game and one which occurs outside conscious control and discourse (in the way that, for instance, techniques of the body do)' (Bourdieu 1990: 61). Bourdieu argued that we should not intellectualize these logics 'at the expense of the intuitive, affective, and corporeal logic of practice' (Barrett 2015: 8), but that such logics are enacted unconsciously through practice.

Leadership is understood therefore not as an inherent personal attribute, nor a set of generic 'transferrable skills', or a role. Leadership practice is purposeful, situated and context-specific, built on circumstantial coincidence of relationships, within particular discursive, temporal and material conditions, informed by different cultural, gendering and racializing tropes and norms. Leaders can often be more effective in a context where there is a shared sense of readiness to change because it is a relational practice co-constructed through interactions with and through perceptions of others within unequal power relations.

The Distinctiveness of Leadership in Universities

Using leadership as a conceptual lens enables a focus on the practical mastery displayed by individuals who are disposed towards managing and leading and who display a feel for the game and its logics of practice within the field of higher education. In the university, leadership is undertaken by many within complex systems of academic governance (Juntrasook 2014). Academic leadership in the university is widely distributed: it can be found everywhere in formal positions but more often informally – it is 'social, tacit, situated' (MacFarlane 2012a: 6). A prerequisite in promotion and job applications is to provide evidence of leadership, which is considered central to becoming and being an academic (Pitt and Mewburn 2016).

Universities, because of their size, complexity, collegial processes and committee systems, multiplicity of programmes, commercial partnerships and public roles, could be depicted from an organizational chart as exemplifying distributed leadership in which horizontal relationships work across hierarchical relationships (Jones et al. 2012, Sewerin and Holberg 2017). Critical scholars warn that distributed leadership within a corporate frame is more like delegating down responsibility and risk to individuals who are then held accountable for outcomes and circumstances often out of their control (Lumby 2013, Youngs 2017). Distributed leadership in practice occurs when individuals and groups have both the resources and recognition to change things systemically and the power to act, through collegial and deliberative processes (MacFarlane 2014).

At the same time, power is dispersed, exerted and felt both directly and diffusely, infused with implicit understandings and formal recognition of different decision-making processes and forums, forms of knowledge and levels of expertise. Multiple strategies are used to exert power in process-driven decision-making committees and in executive offices: what's on the agenda, what gets tabled, who chairs, who gets to speak and who caucused prior to the meeting. Power is exerted with or over others, can be supportive or undermining, in the unequal arrangements and intimate relationships, for example, of individual performance review meetings (Kallio et al. 2016). While many academics lead due to their experience of working with rather than over others in teams, professional organizations and community activities, those in senior management can mobilize their authority of position and control throughout the organization to inform planning, policy and resource allocation.

Viewing universities as sites of polyvocal leadership practices assumes a collective ethos, which is premised upon shared understandings of the role of the university as a site of collegial practice and criticality (Jameson 2019). How 'the university' is viewed and experienced depends on the positioning of the individual or group, coming from different disciplinary and functional positions, interacting within a field of unequal knowledge/power relations or 'perspectivism' (Bourdieu 1999: 3–4). Individual and group positioning (and sense of self) is contingent on the socio-material conditions of their work and its perceived value. The university exists in the mind of the actor and various stakeholders, and although university management seeks to impose a distinctive profile in a process of sensemaking through strategic plans and branding (Degn 2015), a profile or brand is not necessarily how various employees or students view or experience the university. While executive managers often speak for the university as if they are the university, who or what constitutes the university, given its internal complexity, international reach and external contractual relations, is contested (Shore and Taitz 2012).

Whereas Bourdieu never directly addressed institutions or organizations, viewing them merely as boundaries, mediators, and constituted within fields, feminist and critical organizational theorists see the organization as a key site where gender and racial inequalities are institutionalized, legitimated and normalized, and how the university constitutes and is constituted by the global field. There are also particular ways of doing, saying, being and relating within a particular university due to its status, location and disciplinary profiles, all of which mediate academic practices. Universities have an organizational identity at a particular time, a strategic positioning or orientation that is largely defined by the executive in the mission statement or strategic plan (Stensaker 2015). Different institutional capitals (prestige of ivy-covered walls) are mobilized within the field to manage internal and external pressures. This could be called the 'institutional habitus . . . which is more than the culture of the educational institution; it refers to relational issues and priorities, which are deeply embedded, and sub-consciously informing practice' (Thomas 2002: 431). While specific institutional contexts 'confer identity through a process of categorization and classification' (Nixon 2015: 6), institutional habitus recognizes that there is no fixed state of organizing or culture, as the effects of organizing are temporary, transient, although they may feel static at any one moment. Any structure is 'a frozen moment in organizational life', never stable, not always progressing (Czarniawaska 2014b: 15).

From this perspective, universities are more akin to networks of relationships between multiple subunits with different functions (Pinheiro and Young 2017) and a multiplicity of activities and associations. These functions are coupled, some relatively tightly through contractual relations or loosely through professional affiliation, internally linking a range of organizing overlapping and contradictory logics of practice, creating both implicit and explicit rules of the game. Management consultants recruited by executives inevitably propose restructuring to gain greater efficiencies using organizational charts with vertical and horizontal lines which do not represent the complexity of what universities and academics do. Such advice not only wastes time, money and energy but is therefore counterproductive, as it alienates its staff.

Thinking through the relationship between leadership, governance and management has rarely been taken up as 'there is little explanation of how universities perform their everyday practices on the micro level of (inter)actions, let alone face organizational change' (Blaschke et al. 2014: 712). There is a social order in terms of certain connections and actions that are legitimate and others not within an institutional habitus. For example, the transparent lines of responsibility of Academic Board committees and functional line management do not necessarily reflect key decisions being made by a small group of executive managers (Rowlands 2013). At the same time, policies and decisions articulate differently into practice in each school, programme or project. Stability of process and practice is always accompanied by change as both adapt to meet specific conditions. Organizational change is often about reinstating stability to reach the desired outcome (Czarniawaska 2014b) because change occurs constantly, is not necessarily progressive and can be regressive, for some and not others.

Social Relations of Power and Difference

The social relations of power work through the interacting externalities and internalities and networks linking micro contexts (universities, departments) to macro-social (policy, state, economic interests). Higher education as a field operates through rules that have multiple inclusions and exclusions, in which different forms of capital are circulating that inform competing principles of hierarchization – 'knowledge for its own sake and knowledge for generating income; those with scholastic capital and those with managerial capital' (Maton 2005: 690). Bourdieu (1986: 241) defines capital as 'accumulated labor (in its materialized form or its "incorporated", embodied form)'. Some individuals are situated favourably within these complex status hierarchies. Bourdieu (1986) identified three types of capital in universities: academic, scientific and intellectual. Academic capital refers to the power of control over academic resources. Scientific capital refers to research reputation and prestige based in scholarly publications (Bourdieu 1988a, Rowlands 2011). Intellectual capital is the ability to influence public opinion, usually a product of scientific capital.

Bourdieu views power and capital as 'the same thing' (Bourdieu 1986: 243), and academic and intellectual capital as opposing forms of power. Each form of capital was accumulated and derived from particular dispositions – cognitive and affective factors such as attitudes, thinking, feeling and preferences of individuals, a tendency or propensity (Bourdieu 1977: 34). Academic capital was accrued through a disposition towards managing and intellectual capital more often from a disposition towards inquiry, although both dispositions inform the academic habitus and display different forms of practical mastery. Over thirty years serial university restructurings have produced a shift in institutional power from intellectual/scientific capital towards academic/managerial capital, which has power over organizing the university resulting from the exertion of executive authority and the embedding of policies and practices of corporatization-managerialism and marketization (Rowlands 2017). New forms of techno-administrative capital are also emerging.

Unintended gendered effects of national and institutional policies and decision-making processes occur (Blackmore 1992). When universities are being reorganized according to the logic of efficiency and not equity, there is a gender restructuring as the temporal, spatial and material conditions of academic work are reconstituted based on institutionalized gendered divisions of labour, knowledge hierarchies and social practices (Blackmore et al. 2016, Brooks and Mackinnon 2001). In universities, gender is 'done' in a specific way and is 'part of the structural, cultural and procedural arrangements of academic organizing' (Benschop and Brouns 2003: 194–95). '[M]en and women socially construct each other at work by means of a two-sided dynamic of gendering practices and practicing of gender' (Yancey-Martin 2003: 343). In universities constituted by Enlightenment binaries of science/humanities, public/private, rational/emotional are premised on fixed gender roles. This dynamic has historically produced a gendering of knowledge hierarchies and internal gender labour stratification (Blackmore and Sachs 2007). The processes of re-organization are gendering in terms of who does what work (gender segmentation), who restructuring benefits (gender division of labour), what knowledges are valued (science/humanities) and how resources (time, space and equipment) are allocated. Organizational structures as represented on organizational plans are enacted as if processes of decision-making and practices of leading, teaching, researching are gender-neutral (Acker 1990, Ahmed 2004). Yet gender and ethno-racial relations inform everyday practices in terms of who does what work, who gets rewarded, how work is organized and who leads (Curtis 2016). Restructuring therefore has a multiplier effect, reinforcing existing injustices, often by default rather than intent, because a gender audit is rarely integral to any reform (Fricker 2007).

Feminist theorizing of agency and subjectivity from a range of relational perspectives (e.g. Clegg 2008) foregrounds social practice as indicative of the cultural, semiotic, symbolic milieu in which the unequal social relations of gender/ethnic/racial academic identities are re/constituted. Relational views talk about repetitively doing or performing gender (Butler 2004), saying and doing gender as a daily routinized practice (Yancey-Martin 2003) filtered through race

(Ahmed 2012) and class positionalities (Adkins and Skeggs 2004). Gender as race is socially constituted and fluid, being in a constant state of being and becoming, a performative and repetitive practice of doings and relatings which become normalized and govern behaviour (Butler 2004).

Yet the social, political and economic structures and practices of universities constitute particular gender subjectivities and fixed categories institutionalized through data collection which inform understandings of the social practices through which 'men and women adjust their ideas of themselves to fit changing socio-material circumstances' (Gherardi 2017a: 43), and, some argue producing neoliberal academic subjectivities. By contrast, notions of hybridity (Anthias 2012) and intersectionality (Atewologun et al. 2016, Collins and Bilge 2016) recognize the materiality of social relations which produces systemic gender and racial injustice and how relations between identity, context and power differ according to status, time and place. In some instances, for a Black female leader, gender is foregrounded and in others, race, whereas the whiteness or masculinity of a leader is rarely questioned or needs to be justified (Arday and Mirza 2018). Consequently, 'enduring arrangements exist that shape lives and possibilities. Gender inequalities are embedded in the multi-dimensional structure of relationships between women and men, which as the modern sociology of gender shows, operates at every level of experience, from economic arrangements, culture and the state to interpersonal relationships and individual emotions' (Connell 2005: 1801).

Gender is central to the 'relations of ruling', how power/knowledge works locally and institutionally (universities, government) and discursively through a range of differentiating practices of 'bureaucracy, administration, management, professional organization and the media . . . [and] also the complex of discourses, scientific, technical and cultural, that intersect, interpenetrate, and coordinate the multiple sites of ruling' (Smith 1990: 6). Engrained social practices based on unequal gender relations in all their complexity are linked to institutionalized power and knowledge hierarchies and capacity to acquire the necessary cultural, economic and social capitals to gain greater agency (Thornton 2008, Brown 2015, Nussbaum 2010) and intellectual and managerial capitals in the university.

The academic habitus, feminists remind us, is a relational concept fastened to different forms of capital in ways that are gendered and racialized (McNay 2000, McLeod 2005). The embodiment of 'capitals' means that pre-conceived perceptions of gender, race and class are affixed to individuals regardless of their experience, expertise or forms of capital they possess and how they are positioned within the field. In that sense, someone from a working-class background in positional leadership in an elite university may feel out of place, and an Asian woman who as a professor has the burden of being a 'double stranger' – her position defined by her race and gender within a white male-dominated environment (Ahmed 2004). Anthias (2012: 12) argues that 'you cannot invoke only gender processes to understand gendered practices or outcomes, you cannot invoke only "race" and racialization to understand racist practices and outcomes and you cannot invoke only class processes to understand classed outcomes'.

Gender also constitutes how leadership practices are represented, enacted and perceived by others. The politics of gender shape how leadership is embodied: the *hexis* of walking, looking, standing and emoting. Numerous tropes circulate about leadership. One is the discourse about women's leadership style which assumes all women leaders are caring and sharing (Blackmore and Sachs 2007). Another is that non-Anglo academics lack leadership aspirations as they are not assertive and wait to speak, for example (Mirza 2009). Both essentialize difference as if women or a cultural minority constitute a unitary group with shared histories, experiences, values, cultural meanings across diverse ethno-cultural nationalities. Such gendered and racialized expectations, norms and discourses of leadership expect all women to be caring and sharing and all men assertive, Asian women and men to be passive and quiet and damns any woman who is either too authoritarian or too caring. Feminist scholars therefore debate whether all women in leadership will be committed to gender equity as more Anglo-European women move into executive university positions and whether the onus is only on women and not men also in executive positions. They interrogate whether women executives have the feminist credentials or political will to proactively commit to changing the workplace to make it more equitable, enact a 'moderate feminism' that supports individual women where possible or totally reject feminism in any form (Tzanakou and Pearce 2019).

Post-colonial and Indigenous feminists point to how universities as 'structuring-structures' organize knowledge production in a multiplicity of ways to produce systematic and institutionalized racism, which is experienced daily (Arday and Mirza 2018, Moreton-Robinson 2004, 2013). The imperative for decolonization of the academy originates from critical post-colonial and Indigenous scholars (Coates et al. 2019, Gray and Beresford 2008, Nakata 2017, Shahjahan 2014, Tuhiwa-Smith 1999, Williams et al. 2017) largely from within the numerically feminized fields of Humanities and Social Sciences (HASS). These fields experience epistemic or cognitive injustice (Fricker 2007) due to the privileging of Western-centric modes of being and knowing, and often bear the unintended consequences of restructuring and strategic prioritizing of Science, Technology, Engineering, Mathematics, Medicine (STEMM) (Blackmore 2022).

Never named is the whiteness of leadership and the advantages accruing to white men in accumulating valued economic, cultural and social capitals that produce and realize leadership opportunities (Blackmore 2010, Earick 2018, Leonardo 2013, Sang and Calvard 2019). A hegemonic, masculine, heterosexual whiteness is the cultural norm of leadership in Australia, a bodily identity 'enscripted with dominant social norms or the "cultural arbitrary"' (McNay 2000: 36) with most VCs and DVCs not having identified other than white, male and heterosexual. While hegemonic masculinity is in a 'constant process of negotiation, translation, and reconfiguration' it also mobilizes various cultural and institutional mechanisms that act as 'tactics of maintenance through the exclusion of women' and which benefit all men regardless of their personal values and dispositions (Connell 2016: 311). At the level of the interpersonal where gender/race/class/sexual and ethno-racial dynamics of difference operate we need to avoid: 'the trap of excessive de-personalization of the nature of control . . . [recognising that] it is some people who impose control on others, an order of affairs made to the measure of their own interest and comfort and oblivious or explicitly unfriendly to the interests of others' (Bauman and Raud 2015: 98).

A shared habitus can come into being at key moments of practice: 'Habitus is most influential when in a group form, the homogeneity of self-presupposed shared norms – attitudes and dispositions – provide an opportunity for significant directive influence' (Burke 2016: 9). For example, practices of homosociability occur because individuals prefer working with, and therefore select for jobs, research projects or promotion, people like themselves (Grummell et al. 2009b, Blackmore et al. 2019). 'People like us' was a constant discourse in the data.

Fraser (2013) refers to how organizational practices circulate nationally and internationally due to the androcentric state-organized capitalism's authoritative construction of norms that privilege masculinist attributes. This study suggests there is a transnational professional-managerial class (Connell 2016) emerging that travels in the new geopolitical space of global policy communities and transnational business, professional consultants and edu-philanthropist, a class which arguably Vice Chancellors (predominantly men) benefit from, accruing the capital of transnational entrepreneurial masculinity. Even if the concept of hegemonic (white) masculinity precludes a comprehensive understanding of the lived realities of men's emotional lives, it can still provide important insights into the constructions or cultural ideals of masculinity that are most valued in a society.

Critical studies of men and masculinities (Connell 2005, Hearn 2010) argue that a focus on practice recognizes caring masculinities not as a 'homogenizing character description of the "new man"' but that there is a need to 'conceptualize caring masculinities theoretically and to open up debate and discussion around the concept of care in men's lives' (Elliott 2016: 241). Many men in this study spoke of caring for students and colleagues. The question is whether they were able to achieve leadership because of the reproductive/caring labour of partners in the domestic domain, which allows many men to do what they do and gain credit in the public domain (Adkins 2005, Angervall et al. 2015).

This points to how the social relations of gender are informed by the material, temporal and spatial conditions of academic work/life relations. The well-documented intensification of academic work infiltrating into the home has created endemic work/life conflict, impacting on academic women more than men (Bothwell 2018, NTEU 2015, Kenny 2018). The pace of the entrepreneurial university is one of accelerationism (Sellar and Cole 2017, Wajcman and Dodd 2016) and hyper-performativity (Ylijoki 2013). Yet for academic women and those responsible for care, particularly in Australia, there has been little change in the distribution of familial responsibilities and gendered division of labour of care responsibilities, thereby constraining their career 'choices' (Foster and Stratton 2019, Hassan 2017, Rafnsdóttir and Heijstra 2013, Wajcman 2010). Feminists challenge Bourdieu's conceptualization of social capital because of its masculine ontology of the social which reinstates women's role as being responsible for, and equates women's interests to, 'the family's' interests. His implicit gender division of labour and public/private divide mean the family remains as 'a crucial source and site of the accumulation, mobilization and transmission, circulation and reproduction of social capital' and therefore women's responsibility (Adkins 2005: 198). Adkins (2012: 467) suggests that the 'dispersal of productive and value-creating activities away from the bounded workplace across the entire social body . . . is, economizing domestic labour without paying for or counting it'.

How difference and diversity are understood therefore has significant implications for diversity policy in universities. If difference (e.g. gender) is viewed from an essentialist position as fixed and inherent in the individual, then the focus of policy and practitioners will be on changing the individual (e.g. training female or Indigenous academics to write better applications for promotion and grants), that is normalization. If diversity is understood as being socially contextualized and context-specific, constituted by and through the dynamics of unequal social relations, fluid identities and the socio-material conditions of work within universities, then the focus is on changing the workplace, changing dominant (white) masculinities, reconceptualizing how merit and success are understood and how knowledge is valued (Thornton 2013).

Leading, Managing and Affect

Feminists have long rejected the view that 'to be emotional is to have one's judgement affected' (Ahmed 2004: 3) because emotions are part of our being, everyday thinking, ways of seeing and doing. Emotional capital comprises 'valued assets and skills, love and affection, expenditure of time, attention, care and concern' (Allatt 1993cited in Reay 2004: 61). Feminist scholars reject gender-, race- and class-neutral notions of emotional intelligence so popular in the leadership literature which treats emotions 'as tools that can be used by subjects in the project of life and career enhancement' (Ahmed 2004: 3; Blackmore 2016, Grummell et al. 2009a). Leadership is about doing emotional labour: both managing their own and others' emotions (Blackmore and Sachs 2007, Cherkowski et al. 2021). Furthermore, emotions are gendered and racialized, with certain emotional displays possible for some leaders and not others. Male leaders can display a softer masculinity and even cry in public now, whereas women crying publicly is still considered a weakness. Emotional stereotypes such as 'Asians are inscrutable' are embedded in everyday discourses.

The 2000s saw a theoretical turn to affect. Affect as 'collective knowledgeable doing' in management and educational theory has, as practice theory, a relational epistemology with a focus on the body and socio-materiality (Gherardi 2017b: 3). Affect 'has become a major element in the organization of the way we live now. . . . Production, consumption, participation: in every case we are addressed as (and retain relevance by) being affective operators' (Sharma and Tygstrup 2015: 2). Affect is a more generalized unconscious intensity located within individualized bodies that shapes individual and collective emotional reactions and interactions. There can be a shift in the affective economies of nations to produce 'structures of feeling' which realize people's collective experience during a period in time, for example, war, terrorism and a pandemic (Williams 2015).

Organizations also have affective economies. Those in positional power can mobilize discourses and undertake practices which can at micro and macro levels create a divisive or inclusive, toxic or welcoming ethos (Pelletier 2010, Skinner et al. 2015). Organizational change is infused with emotionality. Restructuring of a university shifts the affective economy to one infused by fear, anxiety, anger, despair, which become drivers of people's behaviours. But so do everyday practices, expectations, aspirations such as metrics, and the counting and comparing of all activities shaping academic identity.

Gender, class and race differences are infused through affective economies because affect informs relations between bodies and social groups who are excluded and othered (Czarniawska and Hopfl 2002). Indigenous academics nearly always do the confronting emotional work of educating white academics on race (Asmar and Page 2009), just as feminists are held responsible for raising the emotional issues of sexual harassment and discrimination. Teaching others about recognition and respect for difference produces discomfort as individuals have significant investment in their gender, ethno-racial and sexual identities (Boler 1999), and reflection can produce resistance in the form of anger, guilt and regret (Blackmore 2010).

Academic labour is constituted through affective relations (mentoring, collegiality, pedagogy), which can create feelings of ease, satisfaction, well-being, passion, a sense of connectedness and belonging to community as well as discontent and dissatisfaction. Academic capitalism exploits this affective labour, previously considered a source of resistance to commodification and commercialization, pulling it into its instrumentalist capitalist nexus (Adkins 2005). The commodification of academics' emotional labour in the greedy institution of the performative entrepreneurial university is critical to the university's survival as it exploits academics' passion for teaching and research and their gifting of unpaid labour (Blackmore and Sachs 2007, Sullivan 2014). This contradiction is, Hanlon (2016: 3) argues, because contemporary capitalism requires us to 'sell our subjectivity. No longer do we trade technical, professional or expert skills today we sell personality.' Value is now 'located in the subject' or human capital, as our personal dispositions as well as emotions (desire, fear) are critical and part of the means of production (Hanlon 2016: 16), affecting all members of the university and how they are personally invested in particular organizational logics.

Organizing Logics of the Entrepreneurial University

With increased institutional autonomy during the latter years of the twentieth century came increased accountability and a turn to the latest reincarnation of leadership in the form of leaderism: when a leader is considered to be 'the solution' to organizational and contextual complexity (Morley 2013, O'Reilly and Reed 2010). Leaderism is about appropriating the passion of academics and gaining their cooperation for them to become agents of their own transformation, thereby moving the university forward in particular ways. Leaderism utilizes a range of strategies, strategic plans, funding mechanisms, performance reviews but relies on communicative practice of telling the story of organizational change to encourage adoption (Czarniawska 2014a: 72). But all stories or narratives, whether of individuals, organizations or nation states, are suspect in terms of a selective coherence and seeming linearity. A VC's storying may, due to the managerial capital (material, symbolic) attached, accrue value externally or within their close circle of managers, but what is said, and how it is said, will depend on their intuitive 'sense' of the audience's response.

Organizational narratives, for example, about technology are particularly suspect, despite technologies' pedagogical and internationalizing potential to change workplaces, as these narratives derive from multiple positionings and interests: senior organizational actors, the tech industry and researchers (Dawson and Buchanan 2005). These narratives are often de-politicized, deflecting attention away from competing stories of complexity and contestation over meaning and the purpose of change. Dawson and Buchanan (2005: 852) argue that 'a "compelling narrative" is more than just "a good story". It is a device for cementing a particular interpretation of events and can thus be a vital resource in the political arena of organizations where prizes include influence, status, and advancement'.

The communicative practice of storying (Czarniawska 2014a) by those who lead seeks to provide a shared narrative in the context of the contradictory logics which are re/articulated in texts (policy) and discourses, inform conditions of work, and mediate and shape everyday practices. These logics of practice are not linear but are ways of being, saying, doing and relating – interconnected, entangled with some more dominant (corporate), others increasingly evident (techno-bureaucratic) and others becoming residualized (collegial) in specific contexts.

The corporate logic is informed by leaderism (O'Reilly and Reed 2011) and has become dominant with the exertion of executive power over thirty years. The organization is identified with the leader who in turn considers themselves to be the organization. The corporate logic of practice is based on the alignment of individuals and units to the organizational goals through strategic planning and performance management as well as measurable outcomes, another evolutionary stage from NPM (O'Reilly and Reed 2011). University line management, now a decision-making space parallel to Academic Board committees, runs down from the VC and Division heads to line managers (DVCs, PVCs, Deans and Heads of School) (Rowlands 2011) who are expected to make loosely coupled networks look as if they are tied together, to reduce ambiguity and to more tightly couple individuals to particular agenda in teaching and research. In turn, academics are expected to increasingly 'align' their teaching with the priorities and predetermined learning outcomes of the School, Faculty and University and in research with university priorities and government policies, while drawing on their collegial relationships and networks. The leader/manager's role is to take up the organizational narrative that positions the university within the market and promote the story externally and internally while gaining efficiency of how they coordinate all activities for which they are responsible.

The techno-administrative logic of practice is reliant on a proceduralism, which focuses on transparent processes and standards as well as compliance and adherence to regulative frameworks imposed externally (e.g. Tertiary Education Quality Standards Authority (TEQSA), national research ethics) as well as internal administrative procedures. The expansion of 'administrative academic capitalism' results from the expanding reach of universities internationally and in partnerships requiring more professional staff who

> are integral to moves to being entrepreneurial as they increasingly have become the public interface and mediate academic relations internally and externally. They seek out partnerships, sponsors and grant applications, design infrastructure, create student programs, raise funds from philanthropists, set a vision around entrepreneurship. (McLure 2016: 516)

These professionals not only have control over budgets, but they are at the forefront of commercialization, marketing, sourcing and raising revenue and introducing new technologies.

The dominance of the corporate logic has enabled the techno-administrative logic to consolidate the third space with the professionalization of the administrative staff, themselves accruing new forms of administrative capital (Roberts and O'Donahue 2000). As administrators, their job is to coordinate and manage academic initiatives to fit with organizational priorities, reduce the messiness, handle the reputation of the university and manage processes across segmented subunits. They must provide stability and a coherent face for the organization and are therefore the administrative face of academic capitalism (McLure 2016). Neither administrators nor academics, they interact with both in professional development, data collection and research responsibilities as they populate the new organizational units on innovation and policy (e.g. learning analytics, learning management systems, instructional design, quality assurance) (Marini et al. 2019). A further significant organizer of practice is the ubiquitous technological infrastructure that has its designer's own rationale and logic shaping everyday academic and administrative activities through multiple forms of communication, data collection, pedagogies and administration, evaluating and measuring without consulting academics (Selwyn 2014, Williamson 2016a and 2016b).

The collegial/scientific logic is premised largely around the practices of critical inquiry, peer review and collaboration. Serendipity and conjuncture occur as much as planning to produce new ideas and create new associations. Collegial practices are based on a commitment to teach and research in specialist fields of expertise and for many, the aim is to make a difference and benefit others (Bacon 2014, Kligyte and Barrie 2014, Marini and Reale 2019). Collegiality of academics involves loyalty to their disciplinary field of research and to their students, not just the university as employer, a sense of belonging more to teams and colleagues nationally and internationally in a network of relationships based on trust and premised upon reciprocity and knowledge exchange (Jameson 2012). This can mean sharing ideas and supporting and mentoring students and colleagues in an international network or community of practice or intellectual collegiality – premised on academic rigour, peer review and a critical dialogic process of knowledge production which tests and reviews (Bacon 2014, Kligyte and Barrie 2014, Tight 2014). Typical of most professions, there is a strong service orientation not only to students but also to the public. On the moral continuum, collegiality is at the opposite end to collaboration, which has become the buzzword of corporate speak (Macfarlane 2017).

All members of the university manage these coexisting logics of practice, which sometimes converge and work together on a particular activity and other times compete with, if not undermine, each other, as in the case of the pressure to be more innovative and entrepreneurial. McLure (2016: 516) found that 'the institutional orientation to knowledge privatization and profit taking was largely an administrator-driven project. Efforts to promote innovation and entrepreneurship engendered some conflict with faculty members, demonstrating the possible consequences of extended managerial control over processes of production in the academy.'

The collegial logic which works through more distributed governance practices has been appropriated or marginalized over decades by the corporate/managerial and techno-administrative logics, imposing new expectations, modes of being, doing and relating. The process has been characterized by the unbundling of academic work (curriculum design, teaching, assessment) to increase efficiency, with strategic research priorities shifting the university's sociocultural goals towards instrumental goals (employability) and market-driven curriculum (Tight 2014). These factors contribute to a changing academic habitus. Individuals bring different capitals and dispositions to sites of practice. Barrett (2015: 5–6) argues:

> The habitus reflects a form of incorporated history, the durable effects of particular social environments and relationships, and how these shape individual predispositions, tastes, preferences, understandings, assumptions, bodily comportments and emotions (Bourdieu 1989: 18–20). It reflects the background set of assumptions, perceptions, and preferences that predispose agents toward certain decisions but which is always expressed in situ and with a (socially embedded) form of improvizational flexibility.

Most academic managers in the study had accrued both intellectual and managerial capital and displayed a disposition towards organizing, and evidence of practical mastery of the game. The tension articulated throughout the data was, on the one hand, how 'laws, rules, and ideologies all speak through individuals, who are never entirely aware that this is happening – and on the other hand, the individual production of practices – since the individual always acts in self-interest' (Webb et al. 2002: 15). Knowing the rules when moving into management required a repositioning, constant improvization, rethinking of positioning and values, thereby negotiating and practising an 'altered habitus' (Bourdieu and Wacquant 1992).

Academic managers come to 'feel' the formal and unspoken rules of the game with its different obligations, routines and activities. They could claim new forms of authority within the academic hierarchy and field of higher education, as their 'own histories, social conditioning and aspirations can come up against new structures of expectation' (Bourdieu 2004: 116). For recruits into management from industry without an academic background, practices of corporate management would readily translate more directly into the corporate logic of practice (Rowlands and Gale 2017: 94). But the praxis of every day making 'regulated improvisations' constituting the 'altered habitus' meant that academic managers' interests shifted to align with immediate managerial colleagues and the university, even if not initially disposed towards such interests. Bourdieu refers to this as 'taking positions', the consequence of the differing interests of academic institutions and individuals and the investments they have in the stakes and over which they struggle. Academic interests, which lie with teaching, research and their colleagues, do not necessarily coincide with institutional/managerial interests, which lie with efficiency and effectiveness of the university, as do the interests of the professional and technical administrative staff (Evans and Nixon 2015). This is the tension of and for leadership in the university.

Taking a Position

To finish on a more optimistic note regarding leadership as a situated and relational practice: leadership is not just thinking outside and beyond the frame but also using one's authority compassionately and questioning the framing of positionality with a clear sense of purpose. A feminist re-framing of leadership in higher education (e.g. Kezar and Posselt 2020) would focus on social justice, enabling others to work and learn in a safe and inclusive space for staff and students, seek to make a difference by improving the socio-material conditions globally and nurture the good society requiring criticality and with reflexivity (Jameson 2019). Taking up this challenge in the conclusion, I draw on Fraser's (2013) tools to both analyse and inform leadership practice based on her three principles of social justice: redistribution (of economic, material and temporal resources); recognition (of difference); and representation (of diversity), with participatory parity as the key criteria in negotiating tensions between race/ethnicity and gender, and meaningful change. A feminist re-framing brings a normative dimension to leadership work, despite feminist pluralism, which focuses not only on the limits of agency and activism but also on their potentialities by taking the position that leadership in higher education has a primary purpose of social justice for the public good, which is critical to sustaining democratic societies and polities.

Chapter 3

AGILE YET FRAGILE

THE VULNERABILITY OF AUSTRALIAN UNIVERSITIES

The dynamics between processes of massification, internationalization, corporatization, financialization and digitalization have reconstituted, in differentiating ways, 'conditions of im/possibility' confronting universities globally and Australian universities specifically (Ziguras and McBurnie 2015). The institutional responses to these challenges are articulated in this chapter from the perspectives of senior and middle academic managers and professorial in three Australian universities – Go8, Utech and Regional – as reform discourses shifted from a focus on quantity to quality to excellence over three decades. Global discourses, national contexts, institutional histories and cultural sensibilities informed changing attitudes towards the role of the university as an institution, towards particular disciplines and towards professional expertise (Barnett 2011). The analysis therefore interrogates 'the relationship between different scales of governance in education: the subnational, national, and supranational (above nation states) across the coordinating institutions of state, market, community, "family" and tracks the activities of funding, ownership, provision and regulation' (Dale 2005: 132).

Restructuring Higher Education and the Neoliberal Tide

Transnational policy shifts since the 1980s have re/constituted the terrain of higher education globally and informed the restructuring of national systems and universities, particularly in the Anglophone nations where neoliberal policies have dominated (Altbach et al. 2010, Blackmore et al. 2010, Deem and Brehony 2005, Olssen and Peters 2005, Vukasovic et al. 2012). Post-1945, higher education was framed by social democratic liberalism in the Humboldian tradition, as a public good worthy of investment and as a nation-building project (Marginson 2011, Pinheiro 2015). Post-1989, fast capitalism enabled by economic globalization interacted with neoliberal policies, the fall of communism and the democratizing potential of the World Wide Web and email (Rizvi 2004). Political globalization saw a repositioning of the nation state interpellating with new forms of global policy governance (OECD, UNESCO, World Bank, IMF) (Rizvi and Lingard

2010) and more malleable borders interrupted by claims for cultural recognition and sovereignty. In response, regional polities were formed, such as the European Union, initiating the Bologna process in higher education in 1999, a period marked by the rise of the evaluative state as it devolved responsibility to individual institutions while making them more accountable (Neave 2012). Higher education as a global field now comprises 'continuously expanding, multi-actor, multi-level and multi-subject governance networks' (Rizvi and Lingard 2010: 17). Universities have become transnational edu-businesses within state-managed capitalism and global governance networks, vulnerable to global economic, political, environmental and health crises (Stensaker and Harvey 2011, Ball 2012, Verger et al. 2016).

Australia, geographically located in the Global South, is historically and culturally oriented to the Global North (Connell 2006). Australia, as does New Zealand, sits outside regional economic and political bodies formed to negotiate trade agreements critical to IP and commercialization, such as the European Union, North American Trade Alliance and Association of East Asian Nations. Due to their socio-geographical marginality and dependence on export industries, Australian and NZ governments voluntarily adopted during the 1980s neoliberal structural adjustment policies of reduced government expenditure in health, education and welfare, deregulation, devolution, privatization and marketization (Olssen and Peters 2005). Public sector reform agendas nationally, informed by corporate managerialism, leaked into universities during the 1990s as the nation state shifted away from the welfarist orientation of post-war social liberalism (Marginson 2008).

The 1980s saw the first phase of the restructuring of higher education in the UK, Australia and NZ to facilitate rapid massification (Lauder et al. 2012). The Dawkins reforms post-1989 in Australia unified the sector into thirty-nine public universities by amalgamating Colleges of Advanced Education and upgrading Technical Institutes to university status (Utechs), echoing reform undertaken in the UK and NZ (Deem and Brehony 2005, Olssen and Peters 2005). While the 'new universities were designed in this single image, each a public self-governing institution … strongly tipped towards educating the professions, meritocratic, non-residential and comprehensive, with a mission that required teaching and research', some 'faced years of internal power struggle in the search for coherence' (Davis 2017: 92–3). Sectoral restructuring and federal policies enabled managerialism to infiltrate, with Vice Chancellors (VCs) opportunistically appointing Heads of School and Deans instead of them being elected and state legislation increasing business representation on University Councils.

While Universities Australia, comprised of VCs, became the peak lobbying group in 2007, competitive pressures encouraged differentiation between universities in domestic and international markets. Subgroups formed based on universities' distinctive histories – the Group of Eight (Go8), the older mid-nineteenth-century sandstones, sought to retain research-intensiveness; the Australian Technology Network universities were strong in the material sciences and the arts; the six regionals established in the 1960s and 1970s became the Regional University

Network, while the Innovative Research Universities comprised seven post-1960s universities. Deakin, modelled on the UK Open University, as others, was stand-alone (Marginson and Considine 2000). Observers would see the 'sector characterized by fairness and comprehensiveness', but insiders saw the sector as diversified and 'vulnerable to disruption, whether by design or market forces' (Davis 2017: 10).

By 2016, Australian university executives were rethinking their university's positioning within global and national education markets. Academic managers and professors in the three case study universities, named funding as the foremost pressure transforming higher education, followed by a volatile policy environment and new competitors due to privatization and Asian expansion in the sector. The professoriate, while recognizing these external pressures, were also critical of the internal pressures of managerialism and marketization; competitive research funding; the audit culture and high student-staff ratios, many attributing this to poor leadership (Enders and de Weert 2015, Stensaker and Harvey 2011). 'I don't think we've got many leaders. I think we've got a lot of managers and not many visionaries' (Rosanne, former DVC). How academic managers addressed the dynamics of external pressures and internal tensions remains a source of contestation between academic managers and academics.

'The Perfect Storm': Funding, Funding, Funding

Higher education reform in Australia in the 1990s aimed to massify the sector to 'skill up and fuel the knowledge economies' (Lauder et al. 2012). The trebling of student numbers while only doubling staff was followed by a similar expansion in 2000s, then repeated in the 2010s (Norton and Cherastidtham 2018). Addressing the tension between equity and massification, the Higher Education Contribution Scheme (HECS, later HELP) enabled graduates to reimburse government through the tax system once their salary reached a minimum level, a similar scheme adopted later in the UK (Hillman 2016). Block funding of teaching and research and numbers negotiated in a compact during the 1990s gave executives significant discretionary capacity to build research capacity, and funding of academics was based on workloads approximating 40:40:20 for teaching: research: service. The shift to earmarked funding for Commonwealth Supported Places (CSP) which could be capped later was performance-based funding (e.g. graduations, employment outcomes, publications) and teaching-only funding (Norton 2021). Research funding became a national competitive scheme after 2001, in which individual academics competed for funds from the ARC and National Health and Medical Research Council, which are similar to national funding bodies in the United Kingdom and the United States. Research infrastructure funds also had to be won back from the ARC, encouraging university research to be cross-subsidized from teaching income. While public funding reduced, private income increased from post-graduate and international student fees, particularly after 2014 (Norton 2021).

In 2008, the Bradley Review of Higher Education in Australia warned that higher education was 'undervalued and underfunded' and cited emergent threats to the sector 'challenging its 'long-term viability' and the 'renewal of the academic and research workforce'(Bradley 2008: xiv) because of low participation rates of 18–24-year-old, Indigenous, rural and regional students and those from lower socio-economic backgrounds; quality assurance; underinvestment by government; cross-subsidizing of research from teaching; international student concentration in a few subjects and from China and India. Bradley (2008) recommended widening the student intake, establishing a regulatory body to monitor quality, greater accountability for equity outcomes, demand-driven funding, increased funding per student for teaching, regular re-accreditation of universities and pathways into universities from an expanded vocational and education and training (VET) sector.

The Labor government (2009–13) instituted demand-driven funding which stimulated a rapid increase in enrolments from 2013 until CSP were capped in 2017 by the Coalition government. Executives resolved funding by over-enrolling fee-paying students, recruiting academics at lower levels and increasing international student intake to increase research productivity (Norton 2021). Research infrastructure funding from ARC grants was reduced in real terms after 2016, which affected the research-intensive Go8 universities most (Howard 2020: 24). Overall, Australian R&D funding reduced from 2.2 to 1.8 per cent of GDP from 2008 to 2020 (Howard 2020: 23–4). 'For such a large sector of the Australian economy [higher education] does not always attract the policy focus and public interest that might be expected. . . . Funding per place for Commonwealth-supported students reflects political rather than educational factors' (Norton 2012: 2).

An acute sense of vulnerability filtered through most interviews with academic managers and professors in all three universities. Arthur (Dean, Go8, STEMM) explained the politics of attrition: 'The vice-chancellors were persuaded that the only way they were going to survive is by going along with successive governments and allow the number of students to increase disproportionately to the funding. With less and less money per student, staff have had to absorb it.' Over decades there have been 'more students, more research, more teaching, more whatever' (Diana. A/Professor, Go8, STEMM). The implications, Roy (Professor, Regional, STEMM) argued, were that 'If teaching subsidizes research and teaching gets relatively cheap and partly online and partly remains local . . . the liberal disciplines may disappear.' Monica (Dean, Regional, HASS) warned about 'volatile exchange rates, things like SARS and Asia spending up big on its own universities. What happens if the international students don't keep coming in the same proportions?'

The funding model affected each case study university differently according to location and history. The research-intensive Go8 had asset investments because of being located in urban centres, with large alumni, endowments and a strong science research base favoured in policy shifts prioritizing STEMM. Even then, Rob (Research Director, Go8, STEMM) explained, pure medical research relied heavily on external 'soft' funding requiring a 'balance between philanthropy, commercial dollars, research, government support, federal and state'. At the Regional, Kurt (Head, STEMM) exclaimed: 'we haven't got those problems. We got no bloody money at all. If you don't have a hundred years of earning capital you're very exposed to the vagrancy of policy' although Regional is 'relatively protected by its geographic monopoly'. Another professor (Lawrence, former Universities Australia) concluded that reduced funding overall impacted on how 'the humanities and social sciences . . . have been increasingly compromised by heavy teaching loads. . . . Research funding is heavily skewed to the high-cost sciences. HASS are more individual scholar driven and been squeezed out'. Frank (management consultant) encapsulated the key dilemma for university managers in 2018:

> The perfect storm after twenty years of progressive defunding. There's a fantasy that universities operated in a fully commercial market, but it's not. It's radically rationed with turbulent and perverse funding. You couldn't run a commercial organisation like that. . . . At a university executive level, you can't predict from one year to the next and [there is] the managerialist pressure on performance measures.

The VC of Utech agreed that 'the increasing investment in research is by virtue of student numbers but not better support for those students'. Lauren (Dean, Utech, HASS) pointed out the catch-22 as Deans and VCs had to claim they have the 'best university or faculty' in the country or globally, while at the same time argue that they were underfunded and quality was threatened.

Policy Volatility, Ideology and an Australian Cultural Sensibility

Successive changes of government over three decades have created a context of policy volatility creating, according to Nicole (DVC, Go8) 'the intellectual challenge of coping with constant change and trying to better performance' making planning impossible and creating frustration because 'ideology, not evidence drove policy'. There was confusion over governance, with state governments responsible for universities, state schools, TAFE and course accreditation. The federal government, responsible for universities and non-government schools, could intervene through funding, immigration and visa policies, targeted programmes and national regulatory bodies. This complexity produced contradictory demands and mixed messages, particularly in professional disciplines. Monica (Dean, Regional, HASS) explained that 'on one hand you've got the federal government wanting to increase access and equity and then on the other hand you've got state politicians in teacher education focused on inputs, outputs, quality based on anecdotal evidence, telling us to do different things to the national'.

Higher education is also highly 'path dependent': 'heavily influenced by national, cultural or institutional peculiarities and history' (Stensaker and Harvey 2011: 8). Australia's cultural sensibility towards higher education is informed by a historical disposition for the 'practical' (Forsyth 2014) and vocational (MacIntyre 2010), an instrumentalist view of international education (Stier 2010), and an economic growth model when compared to the traditional model of a liberal education, as in the United States and Nordic states (Nussbaum2010). This culturally engrained instrumentalism, which encouraged treating education as a private or positional good (Marginson 2011, Naidoo and Williams 2015) shocked Karl (Head, Regional, STEMM) coming from South Africa where 'higher education is viewed as a common good. . . . The Australian system sees education as a commodity and a trade. Academics are not very comfortable with this overriding Anglo Saxon culture.'

Despite discourses about STEMM and innovation, there was general agreement that both major political parties did not support the sector. Tanya (DVC, Go8) lamented: 'there's no strong political support for universities. . . . This lack of respect felt by leaders and academics alike from government is undoubtedly linked to government positioning HE as a cash cow and the absence of creative thinking and generative policy for the HE sector.' Jay (Dean, Go8, HASS) considered that 'we've got a really serious gap in the way the political system is thinking about the knowledge economy. We're struggling to keep up investment and participation, the flexibility, the capacity to innovate, teaching and research, increasingly being constrained and bending us all out of shape.' NTEU representative, Kellie, saw Coalition government policy as both practical and ideological, with deep contradictions between seeing the university as a place of high-end research and as a 'tool of social policy and indeed social engineering, or a "degree factory" and largely vocational, market driven by commercialization and privatization'.

Others agreed government attitudes were merely articulating an Australian historical legacy or cultural sensibility, even an anti-intellectualism. Carla (PVC, Go8, HASS) believed that 'a bigger challenge in Australia is that there's no respect for tertiary education by government or the community. If the community was really passionate about its importance then so would the government be. We have failed to shift the government away from the agricultural and resources economy. The economic perspective absolutely dominates.' Professors from overseas considered social policy complacency was the norm in a natural-resource-driven economy and in a society which Karl (Head, Regional, STEMM) depicted as 'incredibly homogenous. We talk about multiculturalism, but it is a relatively narrow minded European/English cultural setup.'

The capacity of Universities Australia (UA), to lobby government as a united sector was limited by internal frictions and, depending on the stature of the elected chair, the UA's positioning with government changed as did the way VCs cooperated. Lawrence (former UA) recalled: 'Universities would not share knowledge other than in their network. Getting collective activity out of them to contribute, for example, to good practice guidelines in any area: student safety, internationalization, sustainability. Each thought initiatives gave them a competitive advantage and you couldn't give away commercial secrets.' UA's divided interests were evident, with the Go8 group often lobbying government separately, for example, to mandate higher entrance scores. This penalized regional universities and forced the VC at Regional, Heather (DVC) recalled, to 'remind the big guys that if they invite interference by the government . . . is that what they want?'. In the tension between regulation and autonomy, VCs preferred autonomy.

Usefulness?

Australian policymakers and university executives were particularly susceptible to, but selective of, travelling policies such as OECD discourses of the knowledge economy (Rizvi and Lingard 2010), UK research assessment (Blackmore 2009b) and US industry-university research partnerships (Campbell and Slaughter 1999). The Chief Scientist described the knowledge economy as 'the new social contract for science . . . linking education to intellectual property rights and innovation' (Rawolle 2013: 3). In the Australian context, science and innovation have been narrowly construed in both policy and popular understandings to be science, technology, engineering, mathematics and medicine (MacIntyre 2010). This differs from European understandings of 'science' as incorporating all forms of systematic knowledge production inclusive of the Humanities, the Arts and Social Sciences (Forsyth 2014).

Most of the HASS scholars interviewed referred to the privileging of STEMM in the policy texts, political and popular discourses, thereby entrenching knowledge hierarchies, explaining why 'the social sciences are really undervalued and underfunded' (Jeanette, Professor, Go8, HASS). Historically, the social sciences as a discipline in Australian universities had not been well-established, faced by the long-held view that the university's role was to train for the professions (law, medicine, agriculture, social work, journalism) (Forsyth 2014). MacIntyre (2010: 4) suggested that the 'scientific endeavour to build a comprehensive understanding of society [social sciences] through the establishment of systematic and empirically verified principles collapsed before it was realized in Australia, so that we inherited a variety of specialized disciplines and quasi-disciplines that are more restricted in their reach'. He attributed this 'lesser regard for the social sciences internationally to increased international trade in knowledge intensive products and services; economic growth through commercialization; and the government research policy prioritizing STEMM' (MacIntyre 2010: 5–6).

The Howard Coalition federal government elected late 1995 exploited this instrumentalist sensibility. De-industrialization, increasing inequality and progressive social policies had created a disenfranchised populist base that elected the conservative governments of Thatcher, Reagan and Howard, all imposing neoliberal reforms. HASS were particularly suspected in the US and Australian contexts of inculcating Marxism and promoting left-wing activism (Davis 2017: 74). Howard instigated the culture wars, positioning universities as hotbeds of feminist, post-colonial and poststructuralist theory originating in sociology, gender and cultural studies. He referred to Indigenous claims for historical recognition as the Black Armband History, while calling for a return to the canon in schools and universities, depicted by critics as white male and stale.

A 'new right' alliance of interests comprising 'market liberals and social conservatives' who were 'anti-welfarist, free market orientated and socially authoritative' (Olssen et al. 2004: 134) and supported by right-wing commentators in populist Murdoch News outlets, attacked identity politics. Gary (Dean, Go8, HASS) characterized the Howard government as being about 'disinvestment, the breaking of the unions, contracts being changed, more competitive and more business focused'. Coalition ministers intervened in the ARC's international peer review process by rejecting eleven Humanities projects in 2017–20 (Jayasuriya and McCarthy 2021). One professor, Rick (Regional, STEMM), saw the lack of feedback on ARC grants as 'ministerial arse covering . . . the minister can axe grants and not have to explain himself'. This politicization of research promoted further distrust among academics towards government about the lack of consultation, the influence of invisible policy advisors and the fairness of research allocations (Barry 2019).

A Learned Academies of Humanities and Social Sciences report in 2014 confirmed that the national capacity for HASS disciplines was 'highly contingent upon short-term strategic policy settings, relatively autonomous institutional and sector-level funding decisions, and fluctuations in student study preferences' (Turner and Brass 2014: 1). While 65 per cent of the workforce had HASS degrees, HASS received only 16 per cent of national research income, yet contributed 44 per cent of Units of Evaluation in the 2012 ERA rankings, produced 34 per cent of the research outputs and generated 22 per cent of research income from industry partnerships (Turner and Brass 2014: 1). HASS was excluded from strategic research initiatives or tax relief for R&D, yet business and commerce contributed to the bulk of international student income. This signalled 'critical issues for the sustainability of the workforce: unbalanced staffing profiles, declining career opportunities, the feminization of casual and part-time staff cohorts, and an ageing academic workforce' (Turner and Brass 2014: 2).

The devaluing of HASS, often by default due to prioritizing of technological and science, was not peculiar to Australia (Coleman and Kamboureli 2011, Lightowler and Knight 2013), with austerity cuts in HASS in the United States and the United Kingdom (Belfiore 2015, Morgan 2016). This is despite the cultural and economic value of the arts and HASS for understanding societies and social change, promoting a 'good society' and the democratic benefits of a strong citizenry (Small 2013). But prioritizing STEMM met with little opposition within the wider Australian community because, Eric, VC of Utech argued, there was a lack of political and popular understanding as to both the high quality of Australian research and the necessity to have strong Australian-focused research typical of HASS. He commented, 'It is worrying when you hear people saying "in Australia do you need to do research at all given we're just a small population". As I say to political people why should anybody else in the world be focusing on Australian issues if we don't do it?' Given this deep-seated instrumentalism ingrained in political and popular attitudes regarding the role of the university and the value of research, the corporatization of the sector went unnoticed and unchallenged outside the academy, with few defending the liberal education of a comprehensive university leading to an 'associated narrowing of the base values' (Dale 2005: 121).

This instrumentalist sensibility and reduced funding fed into government pressure for industry partnerships, quantifiable outcomes and commercialization, the third mission of universities. Policy discourses linked interdisciplinarity to innovation and research managers sought to nurture cross-faculty conversations. Academic debates centred on differences between inter-disciplinarity, multi-disciplinarity and trans-disciplinarity (Hellström et al. 2018). Martin (Professor, Go8, HASS) commented: 'It's an endless discussion . . . the move here was to develop centrally funded interdisciplinary research institutes which would address complex social problems and fit our mutually beneficial triple helix of research/engagement/social impact agenda all in one. Everyone claims to be interdisciplinary without knowing what it means.'

At Utech, the disciplines of history and sociology no longer existed in the faculty structure after an earlier restructure. Sociologists and historians were embedded into largely science/health research centres. Most professors argued that a loss of a disciplinary base impacted on the capacity for interdisciplinarity. According to Jeff (Professor, Regional, HASS), 'you actually have to have a disciplinary base for something to be interdisciplinary or trans-disciplinary. Becoming an academic in a given field is a process of prolonged socialization and cultivation. Doing away with those structures is problematic.' Furthermore, while interdisciplinary activity occurred through doctoral supervision, most professors felt that management, research assessment and reward systems did not address interdisciplinarity well. Cross-institutional or cross-faculty interdisciplinary research centres created particular problems about distributing funds fairly, the location of the work, the ideas and naming, and when rewards (monetary and reputational) are allocated only to individuals within and not between competing units: 'There can only be one first author and one last author, after all . . . when it comes to promotion and tenure time' (Stephan 2012: 230). Individual metrics counted most.

The Metric Flood: Quality, Reputation and Ranking

The dilemma for Australian university executives and government has been how to provide evidence that the Australian higher education sector is high quality to attract international students yet achieve world-class status for a few elite universities. University priorities had shifted away from quantity in the 1990s to quality of research output in the 2000s. Multiple reviews focused on governance: *Our Universities: Backing Australian Universities* (Nelson 2003) established Australian National Governance Protocols to increase the 'independence' and corporate nature of University Councils, reducing their size and academic and student representation and increasing industry representation similar to the Dearing report in the UK (Vidovich and Currie 2011: 47). Various standards-driven bodies established focused on quality: Australian University Quality Assurance (AUQA) scheme in 2002 aimed to audit universities on the basis of fitness for purpose;

the Australian Institute of Teaching, Standards and Learning (AITSL) funded innovative teaching programmes; and the Tertiary Education Quality Assurance Agency (TEQSA) in 2011 focused on outcomes based on the Australian Quality Framework (AQF) which specified standards for all levels of qualification across the education sector including vocational education, producing multiple layers of external mechanisms of standardization.

The most significant shift towards quality after 2005 was triggered by global university rankings (Jing Qua Tong, Times Higher Education, Quacquarelli-Symonds). Commercial firms were creating the 'emoscape' (Shahjahan et al. 2020), transforming the transnational field with rankings acting like 'engines of anxiety' (Espeland and Sauder 2016). Rankings indicated 'the increasingly and genuinely international and competitive nature of our industry' (DVC, Utech, female) particularly as they informed international student choices of study destinations (IDP 2019). Universities and disciplines are ranked globally on multiple indicators (publications, reputation, teaching according to regions, age, etc.) with little transparency on how the rankings had been achieved (Ordorika and Lloyd 2015, Stack 2016). With research reputation central, 'all the measures used to assess quality and construct rankings enhance the stature of the larger universities in the major English-speaking centres of science and scholarship and especially the United States and the United Kingdom' (Altbach 2006: 1–2). Furthermore, comparing Australian with US and European universities, Brett (PVC, Go8, HASS) argued, was 'questionable benchmarking as international universities had quite different funding sources, huge endowments, or not the same teaching load, even at the Go8 compared to Harvard or Stanford' and different communities to serve (Crossley 2021). Yet rankings were at the forefront of every Australian Vice Chancellor's mind and a key performance indicator in their contracts. The Go8 VC wished to be 'world class' and invested significantly in branding. High global rankings were emblazoned on websites, walls, footpaths, trams, T-shirts and emails (Drori 2016). Paradoxically, student satisfaction measures indicated lower satisfaction in teaching in research-intensive universities because rankings encouraged reputational research games with less emphasis on improving teaching (Norton and Cherastidtham 2018) because 'it is the global rankings that – with the explicit aim of differentiating institutions according to hierarchies of excellence – have done more about institutional convergence' (Nixon 2015: 8).

The quality agenda underpinned by a return-on-investment discourse moved policymakers' focus onto research assessment (Besley 2010, Currie 2008). A trial of a Research Quality Framework during the 2000s was modelled on the well-established Research Assessment Exercise in the UK (Blackmore 2009b, Oancea 2019). The first Excellence in Research for Australia (ERA) exercise in 2010 was based on the aggregate of active researchers to be submitted for assessment in each field, and not a select few star academics as with the RAE, catching out some university's anticipatory strategies of recruiting star researchers (Blackmore 2009b). As Roger (Professor, Go8, HASS) commented: 'Much of what we do is directed by what we think the government wants and how we think the government is going to control the ARC. . . . The government is pulling back funding so the universities have to get funding by second guessing what's going to be commercially successful . . . we are unfree to pursue their own research agendas.'

The first ERA round had mixed and unpredictable results due to lack of clarity as to criteria, poor data management and mapping by universities, and institutional and disciplinary gaming (Henman et al. 2017). An additional problem in assessment according to Rick (Professor, Regional, STEMM) was Australia's small academic community: 'Your work is much less likely to be assessed by an expert in your field compared to North America or Europe. . . . Consequently it means external assessors often rely on performance metrics which are imperfect.' Each iteration of ERA has led to increased centralized management, data analysis and strategic selection of disciplinary fields, with executive interventions reducing internal gaming to create the most advantageous storyline (Martin-Sardesai et al. 2017). ERA also saw more academics redefined as teaching-only so that 'they did not count' and counting in of research-only casual and contract academics (NTEU 2018b, Probert 2014) as well as additional administration. Aaron (Professor, Regional) considered 'a great deal of the university's money is sunk into basically shuffling papers around between Fields of Research Codes for ERA'. ERA is another 'example of an immense amount of reporting required for a relatively small pool of money' (Lawrence, former UA).

In turn, ERA had differential effects within each university. Karl (Head, Regional, STEMM) reflected: 'We got ERA 4s and 5s, but only this school. Now the university realizes that it's got to protect its reputation. . . . But we're being drained because we can't pay for our research and have great difficulty maintaining academic excellence.' Professors in HASS saw ERA's focus on metrics as imposing a science model on fields such as economics and the humanities whose focus was largely Australian. The RQA pilot on journal rankings was questioned because the rankings were so arbitrary. Furthermore, Adam (Professor, Regional, HASS) observed, 'most Q1 journals in education are American and don't want to publish Australian or international papers.' Despite this, ERA radically changed academic practice. 'Academics within a short period moved from considering relevance of publication outlet, audience and citations to ranking of journal. . . . Senior academics argued it would lead universities to specialize and encourage hyper-performative cultures among academics' (Hughes and Bennett 2013: 350). Metric creep has meant journal rankings are now embedded in ERA in 2020, in performance reviews, promotions, workload formulae and included in ARC applications. This individualizing drive of metrics is both self-referential and self-fulfilling but also means 'you get what you measure' (Kallio et al. 2016: 687) in the production of the neoliberal academic subject.

Executive responses to ERA results also had significant institutional impact. On the one hand, ERA justified executives putting pressure on 'non-performing' disciplines, closing-down disciplinary areas, forcing faculty amalgamations and creating redundancies even though most senior academics strongly believed ERA failed to capture quality. Colin (Head, Regional, STEMM) stated defiantly: 'ERA is another thing I got really angry about. The process is opaque. Our discipline had high productivity in good journals and was ranked One. I got very harsh words from up above saying your discipline is not worth keeping.' Many professors interviewed argued that ERA should be treated as a performative exercise and not translated into organizational restructuring or funding, and most HASS scholars saw ERA exacerbating existing epistemic injustices favouring STEMM (Curtis 2016, Fricker 2007, Walby 2011). June (Professor, Regional) considered that in HASS it was 'crazy not to be nervous in the short term or maybe they will just slash and burn. I think we're vulnerable. Other people in this faculty feel vulnerable. Arts and social sciences are particularly vulnerable. It's all very reactive'. On the other hand, ERA encouraged a focus in strategic planning on high-performing fields. All three universities had a strong science profile, but this was equally problematic. At Regional 'science has the enormous research profile, the strength of the university. This Faculty owns the brand but we can't afford to do what we're doing. It's difficult to expect other parts of the university to pay for us' (Keith, Dean, STEMM).

A typical response to ERA was to identify strategic research priorities at the university level, recruit star researchers and establish strategic research centres to promote 'the brand'. Todd, Director of a Research Institute (Go8, STEMM), explained, 'For the first couple of years the goalposts were constantly changing. The university wasn't sure what they wanted and I wasn't sure of what I should be doing.' As a research director Jim (Regional, HASS) also was expected to be self-funding in three years: 'It is the science model imposed on as measures for the social sciences. We're given freedom as long as we're increasing research productivity.' These Directors had 'freedom to lead' with many Institutes located physically and organizationally outside Faculties, reporting centrally to a DVC Research on predetermined KPIs (external income, doctoral completions and publications) that were ratcheted up annually as 'aspirational' targets, while the Faculties lost research leadership. ERA also encouraged recruiting star researchers, which by default devalued teaching:

> ERA is driving the behaviours we don't necessarily want. It's changing HR practices. We're employing for one end of the spectrum. Before we might have allowed more of a teaching-only profile. Now we're shopping around, buying profs in. Not all universities can afford that game. The Sandstones can. But regionals struggle . . . it's driving a change in the way funding is distributed. (Larry, Head, Utech, STEMM)

The affective effects were a sense of collective vulnerability and anxiety. A high-performing research professor in STEMM at Regional Rick could ignore such pressures because 'my position is not marginal and so I have some freedom'. But he worried about early career researchers being 'pushed in the wrong direction and not guided by the discipline'. Paradoxically, the counterproductive effect of research assessment was to focus on h-indices and journal impact ratings rather than work with policy-makers in government, industry and NGOs (Papadopoulos 2017, Peseta et al. 2017). Crucially, as Wilsdon et al. (2015: 1) concluded: 'some of the most precious qualities of academic culture resist simple quantification, and individual indicators can struggle to do justice to the richness and plurality of our research. Metrics hold real power: they are constitutive of values, identities and livelihoods.' While metrics enable comparison between the incommensurable, circulate easily and induce academic anxieties, quantification ignores the assumptions embedded in the numbers, deletes the complex social processes of their production and has significant impact because of what is left out. Difficult 'things' to quantify are the relational and social aspects of academic collegiality which create the cultural conditions conducive to teaching and research.

Internationalization and the Asian Century

University management's primary response to underfunding and widening participation was to increase international student intake. Academics, traditionally disposed to work internationally, experienced after 1989 an up-scaling and speeding-up of multidirectional flows of people (students and academics), goods (curriculum, credentials), ideas (research, patents), images (DNA helix) and technologies (online learning, AI). These flows in the 1990s favoured Western nations, creating a 'brain drain' from the Global South and a 'brain gain' for the Global North (including Australia) (Huisman 2011, Welch and Zhan 2018). While the concept of internationalization incorporates the policies and practices which integrate international and intercultural dimensions into teaching and research (internationalization-at-home) (Knight 2012), Stier (2010) argued after Bologna in 1999 that 'internationalization' in policy was informed by three ideologies. The instrumentalist ideology of the knowledge economy is where HE was about marketing education, building partnerships and useful knowledge. The educationalist ideology was about learning for its own sake as an intrinsic good, capturing the OECD lifelong learning discourse of inclusive pedagogies and twentieth-century skills of critical thinking, teamwork and intercultural competencies. The idealist ideology was about producing and exchanging knowledge for its own sake, about education as a right and the universities' role being to 'foster' good, morally conscious citizens, and, for example, promote UNESCO's Sustainable Development Goals. He concluded that policy framing internationalization in the Anglophone states was 'instrumentalist, about entrepreneurial and innovative processes, sustainable development, economic growth and profit' (Stier 2010: 343).

In Australia by the mid-1990s, internationalization was in every university mission statement and managers' KPIs, incorporating all educational, idealist and instrumentalist ideologies uncritically, despite each having different assumptions about pedagogy, partnerships, institutional and research relationships. By 2010, the Australian national policy context had moved from 'aid to trade', and from soft power to knowledge diplomacy (Knight 2015). International student fees funded domestic student expansion and research, trebling student to staff ratios (NTEU 2015) together with 'accelerated marketization' in China (Mok 2016). At Regional, Jeff (Professor, HASS) argued that 'the middle class in Asia can double . . . we've got to be open to the possibilities'. But the United Kingdom, the United

States and Australia, the primary provider countries in the international student market, were acutely aware that China and India, their primary sources, as well as Singapore and Malaysia, were becoming competitors (Jones et al. 2018). The global field of HE was changing with new international, local and commercial players in the game as Nancy (Dean, Go8, HASS) observed: 'We've got much more competition from other institutions in the knowledge economy than ten years ago, grounded locally but global in reach. . . . Private institutions have taken up space. We laughed when McDonalds said they had the university and Donald Trump owned his own university . . . India and Indonesia have thousands of so-called universities.'

The mid-2010s was more about 'brain circulation' with China encouraging a return diaspora to achieve 'brain gain' (Welch and Zhan 2018). Australian universities were increasingly aware of the emerging 'Asia Century' (Rizvi 2012), shifting away from the previous deficit post-colonial view that positioned Western curriculum and pedagogical practice as the norm to which international students aspired (Jones et al. 2018). A more nuanced understanding emerged, first, 'internationalization at home', that is, inculcating cross-cultural sensitivity and open mindedness to others among domestic students (Knight and de Wit 2018), and second, recognition that Asian middle-class families, in choosing a Western education, were highly strategic and well informed by university rankings in terms of study destinations that would enhance their children's social, cultural and economic capital and their employability.

Nationally, Australian policy such as the *National International Education Strategy 2025* (Minister of Education 2016: 2) continued to view international education as an export service and industry to extend Australia's reach internationally without government investment. Other than the New Columbo Plan initiated in 2015 (Knight 2015), policies neglected the benefits of international students, gained through cultural exchange, as employees in urban and regional communities, or the soft power of the return diaspora of Australian graduates, which could enhance Australia's position in the Indo-Pacific region even though international students had become a major source of skilled labour through migration (Tran 2016). While the link had been broken between student visas and permanent residency in 2012, many international students undertook post-study work visas, often leading to permanent residency (Gribble and Blackmore 2012, Tran et al. 2019). Graduates returning to their home countries were experiencing difficulties readjusting to local labour markets and employer expectations (Hao and Welch 2012, Tran et al. 2021) and the global financial crisis of 2008 had destabilized employment with fewer 'opportunities for upward social movement' and increased 'positional competition'(Mok 2016: 51).

All three case study universities were early players in international education, with the Go8 most heavily invested in international students. Internationalization was critical for every Dean and HoS, particularly in business faculties as a large proportion of students went into accounting (Blackmore et al. 2014). Senior academic managers and faculty representatives in designated 'global engagement' roles travelled constantly promoting their university, recruiting students, identifying source regions and developing partnerships with highly ranked international universities (e.g. joint degrees). This multi-level activity led to a proliferation of cross-institutional agreements, most not developing beyond paper unless there was a critical mass of academics involved in teaching or research (Proctor and Rumbley 2018). But Hannah (A/Dean, Regional) noted, 'none of those things have ever come to fruition. It's a big MOU signing then nothing. It's got to happen between people.' Most professors agreed that cross-national partnerships had to be built from the bottom-up and based on collegial relationships in teaching and research, not centrally driven.

Heads of School responsible for management of staffing, support and evaluation of these programmes, expressed concerns, as did Jeremy (Regional, STEMM), that the focus of internationalization was 'just getting more students . . . rather than teaching the students once on campus' without considering 'the moral question' in terms of the public interest and ethical responsibilities not only to their local community but also internationally. Most of the professors raised issues regarding the quality of social and economic supports available to international students, many who struggled with English even having met IELTS requirements and managerial pressure to pass international students (Cook 2019). The doxa about the economic benefits of internationalization competed with academic discourses about an ethics of care, fostering intercultural relations and valuing the student experience, while media representations of international students, often mobilized stereotypic cultural tropes of 'the other' (Sidhu 2006: 178).

Diversifying and Partnering Up

The second executive strategy to remedy the funding deficit, and encouraged by government policy, was for universities to seek alternative funding sources and improve knowledge transfer to industry, community and government. *The Australia 2030: Prosperity through Innovation Report* stated 'linkages between business and the research and education system in Australia are reported to be some of the weakest in the world' (Innovation and Science Australia 2017: 2). Promoting partnerships with industry for commercialization assumed that private sector investment was the primary funding source of innovation. Yet in the United States, pure research in universities is 60 per cent government-funded and then commercialized through private firms (Stephan 2012). Furthermore, structural arrangements in Australia differed from Europe and the United States. The failure to convert pure research into commercial ventures was explained by Bruce (Professor, Go8, STEMM) who had successfully commercialized patents in Australia and in partnership with US companies: 'In Australia we don't have the big pharmaceutical companies in the same way as the US' because there is 'global concentration of financial institutions, multinational corporations and strong government and philanthropic traditions of investment in research in the US'. Furthermore, Howard (2020: 18) argues:

the Rand D system fails at the organizational and institutional intersections between industry, research organizations and government. These institutions are fundamentally different in terms of mission, objectives, and routines. Perhaps reflecting an Australian short-term transactional culture, there has been a reluctance to seriously invest for the long term in building capacity and capability for business, university, and government institutions to engage efficiently and effectively.

This disjuncture was in part because of the mismatch between what research is done and where industry is concentrated. As summated by Tim (DVC, Utech): 'Australia lacks a high industrial sector which collaborates in research in a significant way. We have very large industrial sectors in the resources, in primary industries and infrastructure, but most research funding is in the life sciences. . . . Our research and academic priorities are different to national economic priorities.'

At the same time, multiple university–industry partnerships existed in health and medicine, engineering, education, the Arts and IT. Hospitals on-campus and adjunct professorships enabled clinical research which, if commercialized, benefitted universities, industry and government. Health faculties were 'heavily dependent upon adjuncts because universities have got no money. Even if we did have the income to pay for the academic salary, the industry person that they're seeking to recruit has a market value that's twice that. So health is investing in the health workforce, not education investing in the health workforce' (Patrick, Dean, Utech, STEMM).

Despite these contextual and policy constraints, university strategic plans and reward systems focused on building industry partnerships and advancement units were established centrally to act as administrative intermediaries managing academics (McLure 2016). But the playing field was uneven, as elite universities could call on alumni networks and prestige to attract partners. Ken (Head, Go8, STEMM) commented: 'Philanthropy is a cultural change that's happening in Australian universities which Go8 will benefit from.' Greg (Dean, Utech, HASS) saw his biggest challenge as 'looking for new ways to earn money to do the things which are at the core of undergraduate teaching and research'. Diversification of funding sources was more difficult in HASS fields which relied more on government sources for external income (Howard 2020). The focus on STEMM means it is easier to build a hospital than to pull down the slums which created the problems of poor health and well-being, educational and social inequality, which is where HASS is so important.

Deregulation, Vocationalization and Credentialism

By 2016, all three university executives recognized that the post-graduate market for universities had collapsed, and Australian universities had failed to make inroads into the doctoral market internationally. A DVC at Utech listed 'multiple disruptive innovations': the rise of the professional bodies and the private providers in the graduate space; the decline in domestic fee-paying students; Open Universities Australia doubling their market share in post-graduate online provision; and professional bodies like CPA Australia doubling their professional courses (Blackmore et al. 2018). He lamented that 'we're quite arrogant or at best very conservative with a supply side mentality. We create a new course, run it and people don't come'. Phillip (Head, Utech, HASS) foresaw 'fewer people doing formal postgrad qualifications and more packaging of degrees'.

With TAFE moving into undergraduate degrees (e.g. teacher education) the issue became whether to collaborate or compete. Some universities had become dual providers incorporating TAFE, radically tilting the governance structure and academic culture towards the vocational. At Utech, Dennis (Head, STEMM) cautioned: 'We work closely with the TAFEs knowing that we're not playing in each other's space. Once they're in our space offering undergraduate degrees, will we not be so willing to work with them'. A deregulated vocational education and training sector (VET) with high levels of casualization had expanded exponentially since the 1990s due to the influx of private providers, often overseas-owned, catering for predominantly international students in the profitable areas (hospitality, hairdressing and English language training) in city centres. These Registered Training Organisations (RTOs) undermined the dominance of publicly funded TAFE Institutes who also serviced the unprofitable regions.

Deregulation without strong accountability led to multiple market failures and corruption in the VET sector. After a review in 2012, the link between student visas and Permanent Residency (PR) was broken without forewarning to the university sector which 'made it very difficult for universities financially. The VET sector has blown it' (Heather, DVC, Regional). Australia's competitive advantage internationally was restored only after post-study work visas were instituted in 2014 (Tran et al. 2019). With access to CSP and more agile modes of operation, the remaining RTOs were 'able to do what we're not able to do because they're small and fleet of foot. They identify a niche and provide very high-quality targeted instruction using modern technology in ways that we can't, because of our size' (Veronica, Head, Utech, HASS). By 2016, there were an additional 140 higher education providers to the forty universities, 'the high-water mark in terms of funding' to both private and public providers (Edward, DVC, Utech).

Overall, university post-graduate provision was fractured. All three universities sought to improve their fee-paying domestic and international post-graduate capacity as 'the whole post grad space will change universities' (Dennis, Head, Utech, STEMM). Identifying niche or new markets was the response. Dana (Dean, Utech, HASS) responded: 'We built a corporate education business which enabled us to design programmes, award and non-award, for organizations in the private sector, not-for-profit or government sectors, to get closer to companies and build relationships'. But the workplace was changing with the Big 4 management firms – themselves graduate employers, HE providers and change management consultants offering 'apprenticeship'-style professional courses. Other professional fields were following. 'In the law space people are learning on the job. Law firms are going out to clients as part of their business development and running programs' (Kristina, Dean, Utech, HASS). She reported that she developed an 'applied law program for a niche client group'. This unbundling of content and re-packaging of courses into smaller units to satisfy niche markets was expected to feed students into Master and PhD programmes.

Graduate employability in a context of labour market volatility had become a priority. Employability was also a key factor in international and domestic student choices of study destinations (IDP 2019): government funding was determined by graduate employment outcomes (QILT 2019); professional organizations were increasing regulation of qualification standards; the Tertiary Education Quality Standards Agency (TEQSA) after 2011 required all degrees including PhDs to include vocational requirements; and employers viewed work experience, volunteering as indicators of employability (Blackmore and Rahimi 2019). Work-integrated learning (WIL) was less onerous for professional disciplines such as nursing, education, engineering with decades of practicum experience but added to academic workloads in other fields. For international students, finding internship placements and employment was difficult as visa policies required employers to recruit those with PR or sponsor the applicant to gain PR, both expensive and time-consuming (Blackmore and Rahimi 2019).

For universities, their major concern was maintaining the value and distinctiveness of the university credential as a form of institutionalized capital. A DVC (Tim, Utech) argued: 'the value proposition of the university is content and certification. . . . Assessment and accreditation are what universities have held onto but chinks are appearing' due to online provision, proliferation of providers and micro-credentials. On the demand side, studies found that in Australia, India and China, with cultural variations, the credential signified technical knowledge (Blackmore and Rahimi 2019, Tran 2020). Employers then looked for enhanced social capital or 'employability capabilities' such as intercultural awareness, English language communication, teamwork, critical thinking and interpersonal capabilities. Any show of initiative or social responsibility or an agentic disposition (e.g. travel, volunteering) added value. But crucially, the final criteria were local knowledge and then 'best fit' with the team, the firm's culture, and being 'people like us', enabling racial and gender discrimination (Blackmore et al. 2016, Tran et al. 2021). Universities can assist students becoming employable but not guarantee employment.

The wider concern was how to make courses more relevant while claiming the university credential enhanced cultural and economic capital because of its theoretical and research base, and therefore being distinctive from other providers. A Dean (Lauren, Utech, HASS) argued: 'Research underpins it. We are scholars, self-accrediting, basing it on research, deep knowledge and reflection. It is why you would come to us and you don't just go to consultants.' University legitimacy rested on this form of symbolic capital. But a DVC, Vanessa, at Utech summed up the problem: 'big chunky qualifications are not necessarily the way of the future . . . personalization is the key. Just in time. Just for you. Just enough' for student-centred learning.

'Just in Time, Just for You, Just Enough':
Personalizing Student-Centred Learning

In 2007, iPhone, AirBnb, Twitter, Facebook and Netflix were viewed optimistically for their democratizing potential in the digital economy (Williamson 2016b). The discourse circulating was about the changing needs of the digital student as articulated in the policy doxa of the global citizen-worker's 'soft skills' and employability (Beetham and Sharpe 2007, Brown et al. 2011). Most respondents agreed with the need to identify what students wanted to engage with given 'the burst of the internet and competing private providers' (Ruth, A/Dean, Utech, HASS). The doxa of the digital generation having different preferences for how they studied, centred academic managers' discussions on the mix of on-campus and online provision (King 2012). Massification and internationalization had diversified the social and academic mix of the student population, and student life/study/work conditions had altered. Rising domestic fees and full-fee international students meant many students worked twenty hours a week, an issue made worse by lack of affordable rental accommodation. This impacted on study modes and course offerings as an A/Dean (Ruth, Utech) reflected: 'we are now delivering things probably at more compressed times or stretched out . . . most kids have part-time jobs and do not move out of home.' Melinda (A/Dean, Utech, HASS) agreed that 'in postgraduate courses "people who have been out in the workforce earning good wages are seeking a different educational experience"'.

How they conceptualized the student impacted on the strategic thinking of university executives regarding the online/on-campus mix when setting new strategic plans and budgets. Historically, distance education by regional universities was well developed in Australia because of its geography, but the widespread integration of blended learning varied between and within each university. Open Universities Australia, an alliance of eighteen universities established in 1993 and offering online units and degrees, was rapidly expanding. Massive Online Open Courses (MOOCs) in 2012 had caught most Australian universities by surprise and were viewed variously as originating from elite US universities with mass international potential; a 'diversion from an integrated, scaffolded degree or diploma' (King 2012); 'a fad with emotional attraction' (Dennis, Head, Utech, STEMM); or 'as a de-bundling process where cheap high-quality Americanizing course can be a substitute for teaching on expensive inner-city sites' (Vanessa, DVC, Utech). For most, MOOCs offered a potential marketing strategy to add value 'with which we potentially brand ourselves' (Patrick, Professor, Regional, STEMM) or another factor in the changing competitive landscape 'whether it's Stanford offering course work or professional associations doing post-grad course work' (Heather, DVC, Regional).

A DVC (Tim, Utech, STEMM) considered Australian universities had been too complacent about the potential of online provision for commercial and entrepreneurial activity: 'We missed the professionalization of graduate education and now will miss the online revolution.' All interviewees agreed the online environment had potential for different students and universities, leading to greater differentiation between universities based on the balance of online/face-to-face experience. While regional universities were long-term players in distance education (e.g. Deakin, Charles Sturt, University of New England), other universities sought to capture specific aspects of technological innovation such as gamification and AI (e.g. the University of Melbourne's eLearning Incubator partnered with Coursera to develop learning analytical techniques) (Boys 2015: 149). Overall, the IT infrastructure in universities, because of uneven development, size and complexity, was clunky and not fully integrated compared to commercial providers, such as SEEK (an online employment service), offering adaptive modes of learning and micro-credentials.

Approaches to online provision in each university were linked to the doxa about the need to change academic pedagogies and engage students, recognize the role of the visual and the virtual, and better utilize the affordances of multimodal learning. While many interviewees felt 'too much was invested in the physical space', there remained apparent confusion as to what 'online delivery' actually meant: 'People think they've got online but it's light compliant . . . put up your unit guide online' (Nick, DVC, Utech); or it's just a technical issue on how to use learning management systems and not a pedagogical issue because 'content is king' (Adam, Head, Regional, HASS). How management approached any moves towards online learning was therefore critical. At Regional, 'we jumped into online teaching with no resources and no clear direction. You guys will figure it out. They're treating it as just another income stream with no strategy behind it or training. All universities are trying to do it. A "me too" strategy' (Gerald, A/Head, Regional, STEMM). An A/Dean (Hannah, Regional, HASS) said surveys indicated students wanted to be able to 'flip in and out of internal and external modes' but 'Regional will remain primarily an on-campus experience moving towards blended learning'. Yet in health, online provision had already advantaged Regional by 'distributing medical education across thousands of kilometres . . . in a vast geographically distributed, technologically enabled, mode'. But Regional 'had less of the third of the resources on every other equivalent campus in Australia' (Justine, A/Dean, Regional, STEMM).

In administration, the challenges and opportunities of technology were evident with significant moves towards datafication bringing in new forms of digital governance (Williamson 2016a and 2016b). Universities were slow developing interconnected databases responsive to the multiple tasks of recording, reporting, measuring and comparing, resulting in onerous duplication for academics responsible for uploading: student assessments; publications into digital repositories; students' academic progress; invoices into financial systems and ethics; and OHS and professional development modules. All professors agreed that online delivery and digitalization of administration was time-consuming, required professional development and just-in-time support to keep up with a new skillset and a user-friendly technology infrastructure, most of which was unavailable.

Spatial Marginalization

Aiming to attract the digital student, the three universities by the mid-2010s had invested significantly on bespoke architectural edifices to transform the campus into an innovative learning environment designed for the digital century (Beetham and Sharpe 2007, Boys 2015). 'The quality of classrooms in Australian universities is awful and everybody wants to do something that's distinctive' (Adam, Professor, Regional, HASS). Both academics and academic managers considered students preferred an on-campus experience that online delivery disadvantaged many students. At Regional, Damian, a Head in STEMM, considered that 'parents want their kids to come somewhere. Online is hard to design, hard to resource, hard to engage students'. For Go8, on-campus life meant enjoying the cultural capital of ivy-covered sandstone signifying an elite university. The face-to-face experience was 'what sets this university apart' (Bill, Professor, Go8, HASS). Others considered many students 'don't want this holistic immersion into the university world' (Martin, Professor, Go8, HASS). Despite this, place was considered key to distinctiveness. 'They'll want good places and spaces and a rich exciting environment which may not be the classroom. More in social learning areas or libraries to pick up people and socialize' (Vanessa, DVC, Utech). The built environment symbolized both a traditional and forward-looking public image, offered community facilities (e.g. conference centres) and another revenue source. At Regional, one aim was to 'contain fixed maintenance costs' by moving all buildings on-site but also have a 'striking building at the gate' (Monica, Professor, HASS). These purpose-built buildings, informed by both architectural and educational theory, offered spaces for flipped classrooms, work integration and social spaces for learning anywhere and anytime because it is 'the pedagogy of what you do with the space . . . not just the PowerPoint', which 'flips the lecture content on its head' (Connie, A/Dean, Utech).

The redesign of the material and virtual space signified changing relationships between intellectual, managerial and administrative capital as well as for students and academics. The VC, Eric, (Utech) had been 'bemused when returning after being a bureaucrat to see the emotional waste of time that could be devoted to staff clubs'. But clubs and staff rooms have disappeared in redesigned spaces. Many professors voiced frustration that the new buildings failed to recognize the significance of academic sociality and sense of belonging to a discipline. Organizational restructuring usually meant disciplinary restructuring and reconfiguring the use of space, which fractured productive social arrangements. Jessica (Head, Go8, HASS) narrated a typical tale of spatial mismanagement:

> They've moved us without consultation. History went from a building with purpose-built bookshelves. 28,000 books were moved to rooms without bookshelves, only whiteboards. With bookshelves, the rooms shrank. We were told under false pretenses that these rooms were big, not boxes. The fine arts people who moved into our previous rooms needed very good lighting and projection for slides. They moved from a high-tech building to nothing. Mathematicians who need whiteboards moved into their high-tech space. The economists went off-campus. We are not with English, politics, history . . . a natural fit for humanities to chat. We feel beaten up, eaten up, restructured. It's cost cutting or managerial but it does not protect the discipline.

Research institutes were often located geographically distant from faculties and away from their primary discipline base because of agreements with external funders or the desire for a symbolic presence in a city centre. A director (Jim, Regional HASS) lamented that 'they've even divided the research leaders. We used to go past each other's offices clustered together. Now two colleagues are upstairs so we have to make an effort. We don't come in. We're supposed to build capacity with the schools which we've further separated from'.

These were re-occurring stories across the three case studies. Purpose-built environments designed for innovative pedagogies had welcoming student spaces with coffee bars, couches, pods and digital walls displaying researchers, yet academics felt spatially marginalized and physically uncomfortable. At Utech, Larry, a professor, commented on the symbolic capital accrued with 'all the propaganda about wonderful new pedagogical environments . . . for me, it's the worst office that I've had to endure'. Spatial allocation represents the academic hierarchy symbolically. While professors were allocated small and cramped offices, the rest fought for a hot desk in 'flexible' open-plan spaces with no access to students or colleagues without a security card. Everyone sat with headphones disallowing discussion, noise issues discouraging the serendipity discussions which would generate ideas. Meetings with interviewees had to be booked in glass spaces lacking privacy. Not surprisingly, many academics preferred to work at home when possible as they found any productive work was impossible on campus; they came in only for meetings, the laboratory and teaching.

Differentiation and the Decline of the Liberal Comprehensive University

Overall, as successive governments reduced funding, they increased demands for accountability through quality assurance regimes, assessment of quantifiable research output and student experience evaluations. Privatization, deregulation and outsourcing had converted potential partners into competitors, particularly in the post-graduate field. Ranking has fuelled the race to be a 'world-class' university and international education has become a priority, with new Asian players competing with Western dominance. Multinational organizations exercise influence from a distance (rankings, publishing, technology) or close-up through consultancies and outsourcing of services (Hogan et al. 2015, Mansell 2016). Now higher education has become even more critical to national and regional cultural life and economies, skills development and innovation. 'All happening at the same time. It's head spinning at the pace and without the resources . . . and greater differentiation' (Adam, Dean, Regional. HASS). The multi-university now has multiple stakeholders all with different agendas while academic managers' interests lie in institutional survival.

Higher education has been converted from an autonomous social field to a heteronomous one. Now a transnational social field of edu-business, academic work includes time-consuming tasks of building partnerships, accessing new funding streams, attracting and retaining international and domestic students, their relationships with each other and their students 'destabilized by market encroachment' and value shifts and changing practices (Campbell and Slaughter 1999: 312). The values of the intellectual habitus (e.g. professional autonomy, collegiality, academic freedom and knowledge production) have been gradually sidelined relative to managerial and market imperatives resulting from cross-field effects of the penetration of edu-capital, the media and politics. Academics feel they had lost some ownership over their teaching and research and that 'our working conditions have deteriorated' (Kupfer 2012: 6).

Although not mentioned in academic managers' interviews but a condition enabling universities to be 'nimble' and 'responsive' was the casualization and intensification of academic work, increased bifurcation between research and teaching, and the burgeoning administration undertaken by academics. In 2016, 47 per cent of FTE staff were teaching and research, 20 per cent faculty support, 19 per cent central (buildings and grounds, etc.), 9 per cent learning support (libraries, etc.) and 5 per cent in student welfare (Norton and Cherastidtham 2018: 35). ERA had encouraged differentiated recruitment of research-only, teaching and research, and teaching-only positions with 60 per cent of all staff casual for over six years (Norton and Cherastidtham 2018: 37). The university workforce was now highly diversified.

The academic managers and the professoriate agreed that intensified competition, the technologies of comparison and the search for distinctiveness was increasing the differentiation between universities, between disciplines and between academics and managers. Adrienne (VC, Regional) cited 'hyper competition is part of this – amongst universities and other providers – but also for the dollar'. Adam (Dean, Regional, HASS) reflected on how 'If you're not differentiated one way or another you're stuffed'. Branding was critical as was location, as Adam (Dean, Regional, HASS) reported: 'We are who we are because of where we are . . . we look north rather than south.' All interviewees worried that higher education required increased familial investment 'and how much more [can] families bear . . . with a fracturing of the system' (Nick, DVC, Utech).

Most saw ERA achieving what no policymakers were prepared to do upfront – a three-tier system: research-intensive; teaching and research; and teaching-intensive universities. Adrienne, (VC, Regional):

> the big old ones have prestige having existed happily for a century and built their reputation and research infrastructure. Those at the other end will survive if clear about what they do and where they do it and who they do it with and [if] they have community loyalty. Then the mass in the middle is going to struggle among themselves.

The balance of on-campus/online delivery was seen to create greater differentiation between universities. Nearly all academic managers and professors worried that restructuring would make them 'less comprehensive. A lot of cuts will come from law, business, creative arts, and arts education, social sciences . . . issues around public good and servicing this region' (Aaron, Regional, HASS). A Dean (Regional,

HASS, man) agreed: 'We need to be as comprehensive as we can be but we can't do everything.' Martin (Professor, Go8, HASS) queried:

> What's happening to the role of universities as a repository of liberal culture? When you de-bundle the comprehensive conglomerate university with its multiple roles, its multiversity character . . . one of the causalities is the liberal civilizational role because that role is held together by combining teaching and research. Once you de-bundle those things or cheapen them radically and that role is no longer subsidized, it's in trouble.

For elite universities, Brett (Professor, Go8, HASS) considered the 'humanities and the social sciences are a very important marker of Go8's distinction and what gives their status and role in the world. It acknowledges their claim. It's their cultural core.' Academics argued that 'we need comprehensiveness because a university is a socially responsible institution, but business managers view it very differently' (Karl, Head, Regional, STEMM). For many professors, universities had lost their sense of mission and were rapidly becoming what Clark (2004) characterized as the entrepreneurial university, with a strong steering core and leadership structures; an expanded developmental periphery linking-up with external organizations and a diversified funding base. The struggle was now over Clark's notion of an academic heartland receptive to adopting more enterprising orientations in an integrated entrepreneurial culture seeking a distinct organizational identity and market reputation. The professoriate not in management continued to argue that the university should have three 'public' purposes: promoting the public good, providing public benefit and acting in the public interest (Dawkins 2019)

Part II

Disruptive Leadership

Chapter 4

THE LEADERIST TURN AND CONTESTED
LOGICS IN HIGHER EDUCATION

Universities have become complex multinational corporations, with on and offshore campuses, international and national partnerships with industry, philanthropists, NGOs and other universities, resulting in often contradictory objectives and obligations to multiple stakeholders (Lokuwaduge and Armstrong 2014: 816). Part of the Global North, Australian public universities have been tightly linked to the national interest since the 1990s as in other Anglophone nations (Marginson and Considine 2000). They have been increasingly constrained by external shifts in funding, national research priorities, migration and industry policies and with an ever-tightening focus on quantifiable outcomes based on income earned, graduate satisfaction, completions and employment and global rankings. This performative regime of managing by numbers continues to shape everyday management and academic practice (Sellar 2015). While universities have expanded rapidly in size and reach, the accumulation of executive power has been justified by the need to be 'nimble' and 'adaptive' in this rapidly changing context (Blackmore 1992, Blackmore and Sawers 2015, Pinheiro and Young 2017, Rowlands 2019, Shepherd 2018). Perceived poor performance across the public sector means universities are told by consultancy firms to be more businesslike (EY 2020, Barber et al. 2013). Serial organizational restructuring, funding and policy priorities have allowed managerial capital to exercise greater power over academic or intellectual capital (Blackmore and Sawers 2015, Pinheiro 2015, Rowlands 2011, Wright and Shore 2017) while academics have seemingly 'largely accepted the erosion of their power to govern the university' (Brown 2015: 198).

The contemporary doxa of university management is littered with talk of leadership, the brand, the market, the student client, partnerships and intellectual property. Despite this emphasis, research on leadership and leadership development and its effectiveness in higher education has only developed recently (Bryman 2007, Gentle 2014, Lumby 2012, Middlehurst 2013, Oleksiyenko and Ruan 2019, Shepherd 2018). Leadership training has largely been informed by management consultants, is fragmented and theoretically weak and fails to adequately address the different characteristics and complex set of roles, accountabilities and stakeholders of universities compared to a profit-making enterprise (Coates et al. 2010). The paradox is that higher education as a knowledge industry 'has a relatively poor record of investing in studying its own effectiveness', with a focus on individual leaders and not leadership as distributed, with little evaluation of leadership programmes (Dopson et al. 2016: 8). Most academic managers (VCs, DVCs, PVCs, Deans and Heads of School) in this study learnt on the job, having displayed to others a disposition for or practical mastery in management. Yet 'time and again, those with recognized strengths in other significant aspects of higher education activity (particularly in research) are promoted to positions in which effective leadership is critical, but for which they are arguably given insufficient support' (Gentle 2014: 3).

The processes of corporatization (managerialization, marketization and privatization), organizational restructuring and recruitment practices have altered how universities are led, resulting in a 'leaderist turn' (Morley 2013). Leaderism, invested in the persona of the VC, has become central because institutional autonomy under conditions of policy volatility and heightened geopolitical risk, requires universities to be both agile and accountable. Executive attention in the three Australian universities in this study was largely focused on the policy space due to 'a responsibility to make sure the government settings are sympathetic as possible', although currently 'the government settings are the most unhelpful they've been in my entire life of an academic' (Brett, PVC, Go8, HASS). Leaderism aptly depicts the contemporary nature of university executive management with its focus on strategic thinking and management as a generic practice. Originating in public service reform in the UK, leaderism is the 'next evolution of managerialism', a 'social and organizational technology', aiming to refocus the public sector towards the consumer-citizen and 'leading transformational, system-wide change' (O'Reilly and Reed 2010: 961). Carla (PVC, Go8, HASS) was frustrated with the politics restructuring the HE field in which

> new public management is how the government thinks. It's indifferent to what the enterprise is. So you get lay peoples' 'off the top of the head' ideas about what would be a good way of managing things and what would be the things to measure that often have no regard for the complexities and the time and opportunity costs that they create on the ground.

Leaderism exists in this 'endemic situation of competition, survival and progress', which requires 'social co-ordination' to be achieved through 'single or small groups of specially gifted and/or positioned individuals who lead' and who 'use particular moral, intellectual, interpersonal, cognate, material, or politico-cultural resources in order to achieve social co-ordination' (O'Reilly and Reed 2010: 963). Wayne (DVC, Utech) saw continual uncertainty required adaptive and forward thinking of university leaders, a new level of reflexive activity of an entrepreneurial leadership habitus: 'We've got to be in the game. We don't know where it will end up. We don't know how much of our business in the long term. You've got to be transitioning, experimenting, innovating with programs.' These leaders, it is argued must be given 'sufficient room to manoeuvre – the "right", or authority, to lead' – in order to benefit all involved (O'Reilly and Reed 2010: 964).

Yet with leaderism, old habits survived; 'the emphasis is on the power of personality and the individual agency of the transformational leader who is parachuted in and overcomes all opposition to lead successful organizational change' (MacFarlane 2014: 2). Hence, 'managers talk about me and leaders talk about we. Too often the university is equated with management. It's the hero vice chancellor narrative' (Rosanne, former DVC). As governments and executives steer from a distance, while placing them in a pre-eminent role, leaderism is 'composed of a series of inter-related ideas and beliefs' which are articulated and seek to include all agents to become 'authors of their own reforms' (O'Reilly and Reed 2010: 962), both differing from and enhancing managerialism. Leaderism requires effort and commitment from others, and academic cooperation is to be achieved through contractual relations and multiple often contradictory technologies of governance (Rawolle et al. 2016).

Forever Restructuring

Bourdieu (1988a) refers to academic and intellectual power that dominated the field of higher education as two forms of cultural capital which have oppositional power regimes as players struggle to monopolize capital in relation to the field and other players. Academic or managerial capital is 'obtained and maintained by holding a position enabling domination of other positions and their holders' (Bourdieu 1988a: 84) and 'founded principally on control of the instruments of reproduction of the professorial body' (Bourdieu 1988a: 78). It is linked closely to the institutional hierarchy and power distribution, and its legitimation relies on the social hierarchy and internal stratification being sustained. Intellectual capital depends on processes of legitimation in the knowledge hierarchy and global field of higher education. It relies on the autonomy of the scientific and intellectual order, for example, scientific prestige arising from external measures such as citations and peer review and is built on international and national networks beyond the university. Intellectual capital is accumulated through the ability to play this particular game.

Bourdieu (1988a) identified a shift in power within the academy from intellectual capital to academic or managerial capital (Rowlands 2013), achieved through and exertion of executive power and serial organizational restructuring, the usual corporate response of VCs to the challenges of massification, internationalization, commercialization and unsympathetic and uncertain policy contexts (Geschwind 2019). Often recruited to reposition the university nationally and internationally or to resolve a budgetary crisis, VCs were disposed to leaderism in which 'certain subjectivities, values, behaviours, dispositions and characteristics can strategically overcome institutional inertia, outflank resistance and recalcitrance and provide direction for new university futures' (Morley 2013: 116). VCs sought to redirect and control, often on advice of consultants, on what they could internally (Deem et al. 2008). Jeanette (Professor, Go8, HASS) reflected: 'There is a tendency for the incoming VC to come in with a plan, turn everything round, restructure, leave, next one comes in. It's a very public service or corporate model, the CEO supposedly imposing their will. Constant change but the university's core business never changes.' Post-1992, VCs had opportunistically with system-wide unification accrued greater executive power drawing on NPM practices as VCs did in UK and NZ universities (Blackmore 1992, Deem and Brehony 2005, Olssen and Peters 2005). As justified by Edward (DVC, Utech): 'The early 1990s saw a monetary shortfall. We became more nimble and commercial and moved into international education. Of all the global university sectors, we are very resilient. We've got a good brand.' To Drori (2016: 175–6) this meant '[F]or academia, brands became . . . an intra-university organizing principle . . . masked as a mere marketing tool challenging the legitimacy of expert knowledge. . . . Brands construct higher education as a commodity, academia as a quasi-market, and universities as modern organizations.'

Academic practices of collegiality were intertwined with corporate logics and practices of planning, strategizing, partnering up, outreach, HR and financial management. At Go8, a professor, Gary, recalled the VC in 1992 'began to structure the university around notions of management and leadership – a new terminology – with more committees and administration. Now it's not academics playing those roles, only managers'. A PVC at G08, Carla, referred to 'high level of management continuously bringing about disastrous restructures driven not by pedagogical or educational concerns, purely managerial. Their own little people who live up there think: its neater to tighten up all these things.' Also, at Go8, Ken (Professor, STEMM) confirmed there was 'a kind of relentless turning of the public university into a private corporation and part of global neoliberal capitalism . . . implicating the micro-practices of everyday academic life'. At Regional, Jeremy (Head, STEMM) agreed: 'Regional has increasingly become like a corporate organization. The scholarly activities and environment are disappearing and the pursuit of knowledge is diluted. . . . Effort is focused into recruiting overseas students where your cash comes from and we spend a lot of time marketing.' Others saw corporatization as the systemic failure of governance in Australia more generally compared to Nordic universities with their strong collegial governance, and the UK which is 'a long way behind Australian universities at being corporate' (Patrick, Dean, Utech, STEMM). In the EU, Wright and Shore (2017: 3) argue, universities have been partially protected by Bologna whereas 'Australia lacks overarching collaborative structure or corporate-pluralist arrangements of Bologna and greater partnership in decision-making of student and academic unions, alternative models which protected academics from the harsher elements of corporatization'.

A professor (Rick, Regional, STEMM) represented widespread cynicism among academics when referring to 'a constant state of change with respect to teaching missions, restructuring of classic course offerings nonstop and fancy, gimmicky and multiple restructures. We've renamed and repackaged and remarketed our school frequently. . . . This isn't what breeds success, there is a cost'. Each restructuring was justified as repositioning the university internationally, bringing greater efficiencies with larger faculties, achieving better 'alignment' to organizational aims, meeting market needs as well as gaining flexibility in curriculum and staffing. Few were evaluated as to whether these aims were achieved before the next restructure.

Accounting for What?

Associated with the processes of corporatization was increased external accountability. Academics from international university systems were surprised at the audit culture and level of compliance and 'much greater bureaucratic accountability' than US universities (Rick, Professor, Regional, HASS). A Head Phillip (Utech, HASS) argued: 'Not a single business in Australia would run on this business model adding levels of bureaucracy and not putting any more frontline people.' Dual accountability to state governments with legislative authority and federal governments providing funding meant 'government funding withdrawal from universities requires universities to raise new income sources resulting in a new range of financial accountabilities and managerial controls' (Lawrence, former UA).

The introduction of the Tertiary Education Quality Standards Authority (TEQSA) federally significantly added to administrative work, as explicated by Adam (Head, Regional, HASS).

> As government gets more involved in higher education it is micro-management. We deal with the state bureaucracy, then TEQSA. We hired somebody to fill out a forty-seven-page questionnaire on each partner and each program. Administrative ratios are blown out. One bureaucrat for every person doing research or teaching. So we're teaching more with larger class sizes and look at students as income streams.

These external accountability measures cascaded down, overwhelming academics with techno-administrative logics of compliance deflecting everyday administrative work onto academics, creating antagonism towards administrators: 'They require researchers to fill out the time sheets. They think we are all sitting here twittering our thumbs' (Rick, Professor, Regional, STEMM). These regimes of accountability were both 'an instrument and a goal', initially aimed to achieve clarity of role and responsibility but increasingly were converted into 'value for money' (Stensaker and Harvey 2011: 9).

While facilitating steering at a distance, accountability regimes conveyed the image of good governance and trust (Considine 2006). When replicated institutionally they became micro-practices of management experienced by academics as increased surveillance, reduced autonomy and by implication, a lack of trust (Vidovich and Currie 2011). Power (1997) argues that professional exchange relations through these practices changed from a tacit and normative to an explicit and rationalistic audit, a key aspect of market contractualization of everyday relations in the form of workload formulae and codes of conduct (Rawolle et al. 2016). This instrumental-rationalist view of trust is based on people acting according to the consequences arising from procedural control mechanisms rather than normative versions where relationships are based on strong expectations of collegiality which are internalized (Stensaker and Harvey 2011: 11–12).

Leaderism was both a driver and effect of these regulative frames, as executive academic managers sought to gain social cooperation through a range of levers (incentives) and mechanisms (performance management). While appearing to decentralize decisionmaking to Faculties and Schools, each restructuring was 'installing a centralized system of senior executive operational and resource control' with decision-making 'driven more by senior executive command', strategic initiatives imposed upon faculties and divisions, and revenue generation. While 'derived from school level activity', much of the resulting revenue was diverted to 'strategies, subunits and projects directly controlled by the senior executive' (Parker 2002: 609–10).

Executive Fetish with Ranking and Branding

By 2010, global rankings had been foregrounded in senior managers' thinking and strategic planning, invigorating marketing and branding initiatives (Dowsett 2020, Pusser and Marginson 2013, Stack 2016). The penetration of the brand society is closely linked to world university ranking acting as 'engines of anxiety' (Espeland and Sauder 2016, Stensaker 2015) and international student preferences based on research reputation and graduate employability (IDP 2019). This reflects 'the tension in universities between capitalizing on their heritage and the legacy of the institution, on the one hand, and projecting contemporary relevance on the other hand' (Drori 2016: 184, Molesworth et al. 2011). At Go8, Brett (PVC, HASS) recalled that 'the VC had this idea of being like the elite universities in US and UK and therefore smaller. But because of the shortage of money, bigger was the way to go. But Go8 is planning to stay inside the top 50. This faculty wants to be in the top 20'. Despite the desire to move up the rankings, most recognized, as did Rosanne (former DVC), 'that ranking's reputational value is so capricious. Change the criteria slightly and you get a different ranking . . . going down 20 rankings doesn't mean that the quality is different. The international ranking stuff is an enormous distraction but that is the VC focus'.

Significant resources were directed towards media promotion on and offline, recruitment of star researchers, partnering up to universities higher on rankings, to gain and maintain reputational uniqueness (Delmestyri 2015, Hearn 2015). This focus facilitated the 'power of the branding profession to traverse the boundaries of the university' at considerable cost (Drori 2016: 177). International marketing and management firms were used and drew on their wider corporate, product-based and sales-driven knowledge of consumption', promoting a 'best practice' of an 'all-purpose, non-specific model across sectors and across countries' while claiming to be sector-specific through customized online services (Drori 2016: 177–8). The repositioning of marketing as integral to the university was evident in the marketing division head being on senior management committees and the rise of faculty marketing and media divisions seeking to 'manage' academics' media activities and profiles. Deans were criticized for allowing academics to 'pollute the brand' on Open Day by printing Faculty versions of the university logo on T-shirts. Roger (Professor, Go8, HASS) recalled having to borrow a high-end digital projector to teach from Faculty Marketing. He mentioned this indicated a shift of resources away core business which 'is teaching, research and engagement . . . as marketing is not core business' to the Head of Marketing, and 'she was surprised'.

The language of the market permeated university profiles, mission statements, strategic plans and into academic discourses and practices, with students referred to as clients, student 'satisfaction' surveys, academics as providers not educators, pedagogy became delivery, Vice Chancellors renamed as CEOs (Molesworth et al. 2011). Marketing infiltrated academic CVs and social media profiles with academics expected to become marketing promoters, authors of their own re/invention, by wearing branded clothing and sending emails or presentations with the university motto and 'good' world rankings emblazoned along the bottom (Clark et al. 2019). Academics referred in this study to their own university's relative positioning or brand. Some felt it accrued certain professional capital and status for themselves. Many Go8 academics were clear that their university was 'a cut above the others' and 'deserved the ranking' (Bruce, Research director, STEMM). Alan (Professor, Go8, STEMM) agreed: 'how many Harvard's in Australia can we have?'. Ranking measures favour older established universities with strong STEMM faculties: 'You've got to have some independent measures of quality of research and teaching and it's a competition. The people who do it best will survive and those who don't do it so well won't do it. Dollars have to flow with quality' (Bruce, Research Director, Go8, STEMM). What constituted quality in the hunger games was not questioned.

The capacity of the VC to undertake this promotional work of the university as well as internally drive reform was critical. At Regional there was agreement that 'the VC has more successfully leveraged some of the unique things we have to offer in terms of how we market ourselves' (Roy, Professor, STEMM). At Utech, Kristina (Dean, HASS) commented: 'Utech is very aspirational and is looking at where it ranks, particularly at research. It's us versus the Group of Eight and in particular the local one. Our leadership is quite competitive.' While VCs were promoting a clear brand externally, internally the capacity to 'manage academics' was more complex. The executive's mission to be distinctive in the market produced what most interviewees considered to be a dominant corporate storyline in each university and an ethos marked by competitive-collaboration (MacFarlane 2017). Academics were exhorted to collaborate internationally to improve university ranking and citations yet excel as individuals to survive. For academics, the risk is of becoming what we measure rather than being, doing and relating what we value.

Enculturating Corporatism and Embodied Leadership

While most academic managers recognized that the diversity of disciplinary interests academics bring to the academy is critical to its survival, there was also a desire to promote a coherent if not singular view of the university as an institutional identity. Leaderism required gaining integration through designed change captured through alignment of individual academics with university strategic plans. But universities are complex organizations comprising a multiplicity of subcultures, networks of relationships, despite the official narrative represented in mission statements, and executive discourses as the values underpinning this narrative are not necessarily shared (Kezar and Eckel 2002, Czarniawska 2014). Nor are the patterns of inter/action of individual agents or groups necessarily replicated on organizational charts (McRoy and Gibbs 2016). Organizational 'cultures' are about meaning-making of a particular time, are not unitary and are 'discontinuously continuous', a particular configuration of 'rules, enactments and resistances within which gendered relationships and assumptions are embedded' which change at particular 'junctures in time…[due to] an occurrence of events' in which a 'series of images, impressions and experiences come together to give the appearance of a coherent whole' (Mills 2010: 25–6, Degn 2015). Organizational culture as a social construct can be 'understood as crafted out of aspects of a discursive field … that influences what is and what isn't discussed; what is and what isn't important; and what purposes or concepts play or do not play' (Mills 2010: 26) and therefore the significance of values in change management.

While every interviewee referred to the dominant 'corporate identity' of their university, many professors expressed ambivalence about the public representations of and expectations that they promoted and adhered to 'the corporate brand' (See also Gore 2015). If organizational change is viewed as a sensemaking process for academic managers, changing the 'culture' requires a link between enactments (e.g. senior management speech acts) and drawing on the shared experience of individuals, and their sense of self and academic identity, therefore involving emotions and a search for meaning. Academics are particularly 'difficult' to manage because of shared understandings of what it means 'to be an academic' constituting the academic habitus (Reay 2004). Senior academics expressed strong views about the role of the university, academic values and their multiple allegiances beyond the university to their discipline, to their colleagues in and outside their university, to professional organizations and to the public (Evetts 2009). This 'contested logic multiplicity' meant that social coordination of leaderism relied on 'initiatives and cooperation from actors situated within different logics' as each negotiated their paradoxical effects (Sewerin and Holmberg 2017: 1291).

Furthermore, each university's institutional habitus (Reay 2004) had formed over time out of its historical local and global positioning, location, alliances and ways of organizing which unconsciously mediated everyday relationships, patterns of behaviour and individual subjectivities. Summarized by a former DVC, Rosanne: 'Universities from a technical institute background retain a strong engineering/science culture. The original universities or sandstones are old and conservative, self-referential, a bit smug. The regionals more closely connect to community, are younger and fast-moving.' Bill (Dean, Go8, HASS) argued: 'universities have different amounts and types of social capital' with the Go8's stronger professoriate able to mobilize collective 'capital'. The younger universities were considered by most interviewees to have become more corporate in their struggle for position because they didn't have, as the traditional university, a history of self-management (Marginson and Considine 2000).

Academics agreed across the three universities that the 'corporate culture' as understood by the executive meant it could exert power through strategic plans and funding, creating expectations, implicit and explicit, that academics align with institutional priorities. Even at Go8, Brett (PVC) commented on the demise of distributed leadership: 'It was previously run as faculty meetings where people were voting and committee structures all going up to university senates. It's now just driven from the top like a company, a big corporation . . . I like the VC but he can be very tough.' At the same time, there was unanimity regarding the strategic role of the VC in articulating a particular set of ideas about the university, as having the positional authority, and the political, cultural and economic but not always the intellectual capital upon which to draw. An Associate Professor, Carmen, at Go8 (HASS) commented: 'I actually think the VC's fabulous . . . impressive. He talks, promotes what we do and makes you feel like we're very scholarly and that we count as much as the professor of medicine. . . . You feel supported. Yet at times it's tough, like the Titanic moving towards an iceberg. It is a great university . . . I love it.' This VC drew upon his intellectual capital to promote a sense of shared mission. 'It's a pretty good place to work, a good community and the VC sets that tone. He knows people, is very out and about and that flows through the organization' (Brett, PVC, HASS).

Utech stood out with constant referencing of interviewees across all levels and disciplines regarding the 'strong' corporate culture and that Utech is 'entrepreneurial' and 'going places'. Utech is an ambitious, cautious, highly conservative corporate university (Dennis, Head, STEMM). Veronica, (Head, HASS) agreed: 'You've got to jump on the train cause it's going pretty fast' as did Vanessa, (DVC): 'Utech's ambitious, encourages innovation but is still quite bureaucratic, which the VC is trying to address'.

The VC of Utech was a constant physical presence observed on-campus building relationships with staff. Most middle managers agreed that executive leadership overall was in 'very good hands' and they shared the mission. Kirsten (Head, STEMM) stated: 'He is a very dynamic VC doing a fantastic job. He's got a vision and communicates that clearly. We read the blueprint regularly. The DVC Research is a mover and shaker and very strategic. Utech is a fantastic place to work. I love Utech . . . great people and good resources.' Greg (Dean, HASS) agreed: 'It absolutely comes from VC, a person's person. Other deans and heads, generally good people. Your culture comes from the top. It is about how you treat people, there's a sense of collegiality and jointness to our mission.' A DVC (Martha) acknowledged that while 'we're probably seen as being more corporate than many universities . . . fairly agile in terms of being able to do things and move, we're not stuck in old ways. So we look at innovation, new ideas and the younger universities have all got that. Very collegial, egalitarian'. Executive leadership was understood to be about relationship building through communication, being approachable, having a material presence embodying leadership and gathering supportive leadership around them (Ford et al. 2017).

For those close to the VC, there were gender subtexts (Blackmore and Sawers 2015). Tina, a Dean at Utech (HASS), knew she had to negotiate difficult gender relations because 'the VC is a bloke, loves boy things'. She was positioned due to men's greater valuation of men and preference for men's company outside the 'boys' network' (Grummell et al. 2009b). She strategically spent time persuading the VC to retain her faculty because 'the size of our Faculty was scrutinized, with the possibility of being subsumed elsewhere' with a restructure, a fear confirmed by the VC. With fewer well-established professorial interests, good interpersonal and communicative practices made the corporate ethos more engaging. But Brad (Dean, STEMM) identified the paradox of desiring both diversity of ideas and a strong corporate identity:

> I think we're grappling with diversity and a shared vision. In our striving for research intensity and a huge ambition we're finding that our own ambition and the context is driving us down one particular vision path. We have a strong sense of an unstated institutional mission that typifies the way we seek to be an entrepreneurial university. That means that the people that come here are the people who want to come here. We are all seeking high performance but we're seeking Utech high performance. And we probably promote people that perform well the Utech way, and recruit people that look like they could be well mentored by people that perform well the Utech way to become like them.

The statement 'become like them' was echoed by other senior managers and academics. The message was clear at Utech, if academics were not happy aligning with the corporate mission they could leave. Hearn (2010: 245) sees the pressure for all to fit a dominant narrative leads to 'cultural cloning: the tendency to reproduce more the same (leaders) by gender, ethnicity, organizational culture, tradition'. Patrick (Dean, Utech, STEMM) therefore felt enabled to use restructuring to offer voluntary redundancies to facilitate generational renewal: 'to get rid of fifteen academics which we needed to get rid of anyway', a turnover contingent on expelling those who could not keep up with the pace, who were not agile or ambitious. Despite such culling, the Executive considered the high level of staff retention was an indicator of staff satisfaction. Others saw this pressure to comply had long-term deleterious effects. 'Just because people felt very positively about working for Utech, they still question. People are doing the collaborative collegial thing because it's the right thing to do. How many will question in 10 years time?' (Dennis, Head, Utech, STEMM).

At Regional with a relatively new VC, consultation over a new strategic plan was underway producing some incoherence as to the message. A DVC, Heather, commented: 'I think the VC has done what she was asked to do in terms of developing a niche in a marketized higher education system. . . . She's very external facing and builds relationships with politicians', a view also held by Rob (Head, STEMM) that 'at the most senior level the VC is a very effective in terms of national profile and distinctive mission'. Despite his concerns for HASS, Adam (Dean) considered that 'in comparison to other universities, the executive engage, the VC is very active, walking around talking. The senior committees have a good dialogue down to the faculties and schools . . . always seeking responses from staff'.

Others drew on gendered discourses and the usual tropes about women and leadership, positioning the VC as either 'very ambitious pushing a big restructure' (Keith, Professor, STEMM) or being influenced and 'giving into things . . . she means well but she should never have gotten involved in this restructuring nonsense' (Phillip, Head, HASS). The timing and scale of restructuring was of concern for some but not all. For George an A/Dean (STEMM): 'Our faculty is incredibly strong, half the university' but institutionally there is 'lots of waffling around and restructuring has stalled'. Another A/Dean, Liz, expressed concern that 'the VC's frightened and worried about her reputation . . . is it worth disassembling the existing structures or is it just better trying to fix central administration and reduce costs?' All agreed that Regional had challenges in attracting and growing leaders. But June (A/Dean, Research) recognized that 'the senior DVC . . . a tremendously intelligent person never had leadership training and never thought about managing. The VC is high profile and never here. It's very unlikely you'll have a robust structure internally.' Each academic manager, in 'taking positions', had as academic managers a 'specific investment in the stakes' (Bourdieu 1993: 76) of institutional survival while recognizing and negotiating the paradoxical relations of organizational reform.

Paradoxical Effects of Serial Restructuring

Each of the three universities had gone, or were in the process of going through, major internal restructuring, seeking competitive advantage over both local and international counterparts against which they constantly benchmarked. Clear trends were evident with each move.

Exerting Executive Power

The sector-wide restructuring forming the Australian unified system in 1992 allowed Vice Chancellors to exert their authority to reconfigure university governance. DVCs, PVCs, Deans and Heads of School were appointed on contract and not elected. Legislative changes to university councils increased external business and reduced staff representation. While Academic Boards varied significantly in terms of their composition and power across universities, newer universities often had a weaker Board, sometimes chaired by the VC, as at Utech, with academics increasingly outnumbered by ex-officio managers (Rowlands 2015a). The Go8 universities had Academic Boards or Senates dominated by the professoriate and most academic managers also had research backgrounds (Rowlands 2017). A former Chair, Romaine (Go8), argued that 'this university still has the view of governance and management that senior academics are in these leadership roles. There are no deans who are not quite significant scholars . . . Professors' seniority, their permanence, and their fearlessness makes the Board a very strong part of university governance'. That is, intellectual capital was still valued across the university.

Academic Boards are 'key sites for the intersection between executive management and academia, and are, therefore, symbolic of the struggle between the multiple roles of universities as entrepreneurial businesses and places of intellectual endeavour' (Rowlands 2011: 1). But Boards have over time, Rowlands (2019) argues, been reduced to being responsible for the domestic labour of quality improvement and assurance. In the three universities, with some variations, parallel decision-making structures of Academic Board and line-management existed (Rowlands 2011). The key policy and financial decisions were made by a small executive (VC, DVCs) and a university-wide planning committee including senior managers (DVCs, PVCs, Deans, Heads of Divisions), then communicated down to Heads of School, academics and professional staff through strategic planning blueprints, budgets and policy supported by HR and financial administration. The role of Academic Board had become 'largely symbolic and performative as responsibility actually rested with senior management . . . responding to the demands of the risk society by using academic boards to protect their academic reputations and financial positions' (Rowlands 2013: 142).

While the Chair of Academic Board was on the VCs Planning Committee at Go8 and more recently at Regional, a Dean (Brad, STEMM) commented that at Utech 'there is more of the tradition of this separation of senior staff from academic staff'. Bryan (Head, Go8, HASS) associated the Board's marginalization with its feminization:

> The vice-chancellor doesn't attend . . . that says everything . . . It was a boys' club but is now mostly a girls' club. It's been marginalized because it doesn't involve people who have management responsibilities. It's now people who have a certain view of the university and are aware Academic Board has been stripped away from things and now replaced by other women in professional areas.

The numerical feminization of particular sites (the Board, disciplinary fields) signalled a shift in power institutionally.

This weakening of the role of Academic Board was confirmed by Eric, the VC at Utech, arguing that 'In the place of parliamentary theatre of Academic Board, I have campus briefings every year . . . I speak for 15 minutes and take questions', campus meetings being a leaderist strategy to gain cooperation through an embodied presence and persuasive communication (Ford et al. 2017). Management determined the rules of consultation on their terms and academics lacked any alternative decision-making structure through which to provide input or feedback, other than annual surveys instigated by HR. Not surprisingly, many academics viewed Academic Board and its subcommittees, such as Faculty Boards, as 'rubber stamping' and no longer considered to be sites for academic debate (Shattock 2017).

Game Changers

With the increasing scale and breadth of activities in each university there was a proliferation of Deputy and Pro-Vice Chancellor positions to address every new issue – internationalization, engagement, commercialization, graduate employability, internships, digital innovation, advancement, etc. A professor, Jeanette (Go8, HASS), described the burgeoning administration of the VC's office as being 'the size of a medium size country'. Each senior academic manager was expected to lead change in their portfolio, supported by integrity officers to manage risk and ethics, policy and data analysts, media and marketing units (Shepherd 2018), burdening academics with multiple, often contradictory policies and protocols to integrate into their teaching and research.

An increasingly normalized practice, due the pressure to commercialize and develop industry partnerships, was to recruit into senior management non-academic experts with an entrepreneurial disposition and connections to industry and government. Morley (2013: 118) points to a similar trend in the UK: 'Traditionally, research leaders, with accrued academic capital, have been thought most appropriate for organizational leadership. Now, it has been expanded to include mobility across different occupational sectors, as well as organizational roles.' In a high-achieving HASS Faculty at Go8, Carla (Professor) considered academic expertise was devalued when consecutive Deans without disciplinary or research background had been appointed: 'We're meant to be research led, bullshit. Our dean's background is not in the field, no research and does not believe in participating in peak organizations. . . . Leadership is not proactive, its retroactive, haphazard and ruthless under the guise of assertive bonhomie.' At Utech, a male Dean with industry expertise and connections but no research, replaced the female acting Dean. Professors in both instances questioned whether similar 'out of field' appointments would occur in STEMM, frustrated at constantly having to justify intrinsic value of HASS (Small 2013). While the 3 VCs and most of the 150 interviewees had worked outside the academy in government, industry or a profession at some stage of their career, all had intellectual capital gained through research. A former DVC, Rosanne, considered the generic manager was problematic: 'If they come into an academic role like DVC research. . . . They don't understand how research gets done, the diversity of research or research reporting and the requirements of government for compliance. If you stuff up ERA, the reputational damage is very high.' Put bluntly by Arthur (Dean, Go8, STEMM): 'generic managers can run an airline, an opera company next; management is management, but not in universities.'

From an executive perspective, external academic appointees (often recruited from the VCs former university) into key positions were considered better change agents as without interests other than loyalty to the VC. The cumulative effect of these strategies, Vincent (Head, Go8, STEMM) noted, was that

> the greater percentage of senior management who are professionals don't have an independent existence separate to the person who appointed them – the Vice-Chancellor. The executive don't have anyone responsible for teaching which is 80 percent of our budget. Most have not done teaching or research for twenty years nor had research management experience and show no interest in that. The heads of advancement, engagement, the chief financial officer- why are they in Executive?

Once in the role, these executive leaders often become 'overwhelmed by their workload and disconnected from the academic and administrative community they supposedly lead' (Parker 2002: 610). Many of the professoriate and Heads consequently considered the Executive lacked the intellectual capital yet exerted considerable power without understanding core academic values and practices.

Epistemic Injustice

Serial organizational restructuring led to larger faculties under executive deans claiming to produce administrative efficiencies. Most often this structural repackaging meant collapsing the social sciences, arts and humanities (including education), predominantly feminized fields, into one faculty (Blackmore and Sawers 2015). By default, this clumping of HASS fields effectively reduced epistemic diversity in senior management decision-making fora particularly as STEMM faculties dominated at all three universities. This consolidated prior epistemic injustices embedded in academic practices and priorities about which knowledges were valued most and evident in how men dominated journal editorships even in HASS (Langmann et al. 2011) which in turn leads to gender biases in peer review within/against feminized fields of research (Fox and Paine 2019). At Regional, the under-representation of HASS voices on key committees during restructuring was indicative of, according to June (A/Dean Research, HASS) 'a general feeling, that humanities and social sciences are under threat', a concern also expressed by Andree, a professor at Go8 in HASS, who noticed the loss of voice of HASS scholars in decision making: 'I think humanities are under threat. You need active representation. We've had that in the past but unfortunately it now depends on the whim of certain senior people in executive roles.'

Strategic planning that informed restructuring priorities as well as demand-driven funding of teaching and research led to a focus on prioritizing research strengths with implications for specific disciplinary fields and curriculum comprehensiveness. At Regional, a management consultant presented a scenario that 'the next decade will herald in the exit from disciplines in which universities cannot be excellent'. This fear was realized at Go8 when Jessica (Head HASS) saw 'the new course structure is a very generic model so specificity doesn't fit. HASS is about context. The restructure is a very science orientated model'. At Utech, new Faculties were created in order to develop a real-world connection to industry because, Melinda (Professor, HASS) explained, 'Utech decided they didn't want to do humanities anymore. So a massive restructuring and lots of people lost jobs'. Sociology and humanities were rebadged to become handmaidens to service interdisciplinary research centres. This was described by the DVC (Vanessa, Utech) 'as a balancing act between being viable but not losing the mission'. Courses that did not have 'use value' or were low in demand were dropped and languages being particularly susceptible.

To remain viable meant many research professors in HASS felt frustrated when told to find corporate sponsors and profitable lines of marketable products (Lynch et al. 2012, Hancock 2020). Romaine (Professor, Go8, HASS) argued that this commodification of the humanities denuded it of substance. During a faculty restructure, consultants were looking at our 'commercial orientation' and 'came up with the distinction between education/arts that will be vocational and the others would be recreational . . . the death nell. Even parts of this university high-up think arts makes you a good cultural citizen but not employable'. This mantra that HASS graduates do not get jobs is countered by student experience surveys undertaken six months after graduation which shows Arts graduates have similar employment rates to, if not better than, science graduates (QILT 2019). Yet HASS academics were constantly defending the relevance of HASS to society, cultural vibrancy and political life.

Debates over HASS raised issues about the idea of the university. Many considered Go8 universities were obliged to offer HASS as it was more difficult for other universities to fund. Jay, a Dean (Go8, HASS), was shocked that 'another Go8 closed down its humanities because of numbers. For a Go8 where you've got a concentration of scholars, students and post grads who pride themselves on being international and global'. Research assessment had exacerbated any disposition to pick winners in terms of how research was done, with whom, where academics published, remaking professional identities, redeploying or making them redundant because 'their research fails to match their department's "research direction"' (Priess 2012, Hughes and Bennett 2013, Rowlands and Wright 2020). Picking winners reduced the capacity to gain the momentum to nurture a new field or excluded, as Cynthia (A/Dean, STEMM) argued, a social perspective in public health at Utech. Her proposal was 'knocked back because if doesn't fit anybody's benchmarking'. Cynthia argued that decisions should be made on the basis of 'the way that we conduct ourselves, our research, with a social responsibility to health, social responsibility for the environment . . . and the people who are most disadvantaged'. Other HASS disciplines such as Business, able to attract large cohorts of international students, were expected to share the benefits of bringing in significant income but sought to protect their interests. Prioritizing STEMM endangered each university's ethical or social responsibility to its community by not realizing how the humanities and social sciences as powerful knowledges are necessary to create a better society (Nussbaum 2010).

Re-instating Gender Injustice

Epistemic injustice articulated into gender injustice, as HASS fields are numerically feminized (Thornton 2015). Yet women remain a minority in research leadership (Fitzgerald 2014, Jarboe 2017). Numerical measures indicated incremental improvement of women's representation in senior management with women in 2016 comprising 31 per cent of DVC positions, 25 per cent of Vice Chancellors and 44 per cent of DVC teaching and learning, 31 per cent of international DVC, 36 per cent of DVC Research and 21 per cent of administrative heads (Universities Australia 2016). But analysis of senior management across the sector indicated that men (twenty-eight of thirty-nine DVC Research) continued to dominate the high-status work of research, as well as internationalization, finance and technology with women (twenty-three of thirty-nine DVC) (Teaching and Learning) positions, doing the domestic labour of teaching, quality assurance and organizational change (Blackmore and Sawers 2015, Morley 2013).

Furthermore, there was disciplinary domination of STEMM in research with all but three of the thirty-nine DVC (Research) from engineering, science and health. Of the thirty-nine DVCs in teaching and learning, fourteen of the twenty-three women were from Humanities and Social Sciences (HASS) while the remaining sixteen male DVCs were from STEMM. As noted by Justine (Head, Regional, HASS), 'even though there's two women PVCs and a VC, our hierarchy is very gendered. It's very male dominated'. Research was still considered a masculinist enterprise (McManus 2018), particularly at the Go8 universities where Jeanette (Professor, HASS) noted, 'there's never really a balance or been a woman in executive positions'. In this context, 'concepts that are key to organizational life such as competence, leadership, effectiveness, excellence, rationality, strength, and authority (among others) are moreover conflated with the practicing of gender in ways that differentially affect women' (Yancey-Martin 2003: 343).

This vertical gender segmentation in executive, policy and planning committees meant STEMM dominated the mindset in decision-making, with the feminized fields of HASS and teaching under-represented (Thornton 2015). Furthermore, HASS scholars viewed Excellence of Research in Australia (ERA) as imposing a science model of research onto HASS disciplines, exemplified in using journal rankings and citations as a proxy for quality (Blackmore 2009b, Currie 2008), a move which favoured larger Anglophone countries and fields of research and 'ignored important specialist journals in minor areas such as gender studies' (Hark 2016, Spongberg 2010) and for Jessica (Professor, Go8, HASS), 'very demoralizing' as their research was devalued (Analogue University 2019, Boden and Rowlands 2020, Deem et al. 2007, Martin-Sedesai et al. 2017, Metz et al. 2016). Restructuring also had unexpected consequences. At Utech, a new disciplinary structure by default changed the gender profile of each School in STEMM, leaving one School dominated by male professors with its Head, Dennis, worried that women in lower levels not 'pushing professorships' as they were 'struggling to get the next tick in the box'. Undertaking restructuring without a gender lens had long-term equity effects in leadership.

Implicitly, this gendered division of epistemic labour produces a particular mindset about what counts as quality and research and what constitutes research leadership, the latter believed to require a particular 'scientific' disposition and form of intellectual capital. A senior manager in the ARC, Deborah, stated that science skills are 'necessary for research leadership positions such as DVC' as this discipline is 'where numerical and analytical skills are developed' and a person 'gets their head around difficult concepts' whereas 'humanities people are not exposed to the same level of research activity as people from the sciences'. This 'masculine normative framework' is reflected in the academic output of theories and publications and who dominates the gatekeeping role of journal editorship (Langmann et al. 2011, Mauleón et al. 2013, Metz et al. 2016) but also in the often technically rational disembodied way in which knowledge is rewarded. Even in feminized fields such as education with faculties or schools in most Australian universities, Cutter et al.'s (2017: 2) analysis of ARC funding found

> a significant correlation between an academic's gender (as lead chief investigator or project leader) and their university grouping in obtaining ARC funding in education. Male academics at Go8 universities have the most success, whereas women who either work at Go8 universities or have no university grouping are less successful . . . this signals a significant metropolitan-regional divide.

Gender Inequality Is Both a Structural and a Cultural Issue

Administrative Brokers

The proliferation of DVC and PVC positions, 'the managers and brokers of engagement and impact', has meant these academic managers have become 'field players in the evolving set of sectorial relations' as they seek to capture private wealth and public resources for the university (Vogel and Kaghan 2001: 359). Their roles were mirrored at faculty levels with Associate Deans to manage international students, internships, engagement, alumni and philanthropy. Each new management portfolio meant additional work for Heads of School 'where everything intersects' (Rick, Head, Regional, STEMM), with these escalating demands then downloaded onto academics who became 'actors in their own reform' (O'Reilly and Reed 2010). Furthermore, the expanded scope and scale of the academy with cross-institutional partnerships, internationalization, industry partnerships, the integration of digital technologies and a new focus on data-driven decision-making led to burgeoning numbers of 'third space' professionals (Gordon and Whitchurch 2010). Policy advisors, data analysts, instructional designers, engagement and advancement units operated in the 'interstitial units' or spaces between faculties, the university and external worlds (Rhoades 2010: 41, Gornall et al. 2015). Part of a wider reconstitution of the academic/professional interface (Marini et al. 2019), these administrators now brokered academic relationships with multiple stakeholders, negotiations formerly undertaken by academics. Carla (Professor, Go8, HASS) criticized the costs of 'a parallel universe with this increasing group of people who are running universities for the sake of administrative god knows what because the core business of the university remains teaching and research but they're concerned about something else'.

While this administrative explosion was in part due to 'compliance accountability that's imposed by the government', Nancy (Professor, Go8, HASS) agreed that 'there's a kind of internal logic that's fed on administration as an end in itself . . . compliance measures and structures that are imposed internally for no reason . . . they've got degrees but they've come through administrative training and so they have proliferated and just become more and more senior'. Evident here was the emergence of administrative-academic capitalism, where 'administrators are empowered and granted extended managerial control, while faculty members-and their role in institutional governance is marginalized' (McClure 2016: 526).

In this arrangement, academics extended their work hours to capture external income which was then extracted back to the centre through the mediation of administrative brokers.

The professionalization of university administrative staff meant many had acquired academic credentials, including PhDs, some of them women seeking respite from academia, but most gained these positions through professional development courses or in-house experience (McClure 2016), thus creating new forms of techno-administrative capital. The tension between intellectual and techno-administrative capital was evident at Go8 regarding the role of Academic Board during the restructure over who controlled academic policy. Hilary, the Academic Board Chair, explained that with the multiplicity of policy actors due to the growth of management 'senior management people want to be doing things and are thinking up things to do'. A university-wide restructure over years required a separate policy unit to deal with some matters previously done by the Board. Hilary had a 'robust discussion' with the University Policy Officer who had made minor changes after policies had gained Board approval. 'They can't do that . . . it's about power.' She argued that 'the Board brings to bear the scrutiny from across the institution on proposed changes and draws in senior and expert voices to consider what changes imply across the institution' imparting 'control of academic policy. Not just management control'.

This 'difficult line' arose because the PVCs and their administrators 'have the same aims as academic board'. Hilary saw the encroachment of management into the academic domain was primarily individuals 'near the top of management who consider excellence is their job'. They could not understand academics' role in approval processes for major course changes, selection procedures, teaching and learning development and therefore the Board's role. 'I don't think they sympathize with it as they don't see the university as a very distinctive and unique form of business organization.' This Chair refused to define the roles of Provost and DVC (Academic) relative to the Board because they expected 'there won't be any overlap. But it's messy and they like neat with owners of policies in a diagram'. This professor felt responsible that 'the contribution of senior academics to how a place runs [should] not be diminished by making it visible and justifying it'.

Corporate and techno-administrative logics aligned but often jarred against the collegial logics of academic practice due to different assumptions and priorities. Hilary, as other professors, argued that professional staff had gained an elevated position in managing academics because they work beside senior academic managers making academic decisions. Administrative staff's equivalent status was confirmed by senior academic managers who now shared interests to get things done. The Chair considered the problem lay more with upper-middle administrators 'working in a hierarchy, wanting to innovate and make things operate more efficiently to meet their KPI'. Academic administrators saw the messy, non-linear and dialogical ways of academic work and collegial decision-making as problematic because it was process driven and time-consuming. Nuanced discussions were seen to be 'precious' and impediments to getting things done. But debating knowledge claims and peer review is the essence of academic work.

Tensions also arose because university governance was 'increasingly intertwined with technologically informed innovation' such as learning analytics, data visualization, predictive analytics, learning management systems, financial management and accounting systems that added to online data repositories, assessment tools, evaluation surveys and compliance training modules, all designed with little consultation with academics (Williamson 2014, 2016b). Disputation occurred over responsibility for administrative tasks, how online financial and HR systems were not user-friendly (Waring 2007, 2015) and how automated communications reconstituted pedagogical relations. Caught up in this technologically infused managerialism, Roy (Professor, Regional, STEMM) cited how post-graduate supervision had gone from being a supervisor-student pedagogical relationship, while open to some abuse and needing quality assurance, to being micro-managed:

> Per student, it's a volume of material and work. But the measures, bureaucracy, compliance and statistics and TEQSA produce so much paperwork, it just strangles the process. The students are so attuned to 'I have to get this in and this is?' They forget it's the thesis they should be worried about and the research, not ticking a box. And layers of administrators to deal with the compliance of ethics . . . each form gets bigger and everybody has their bit in there.

While all agreed for the need for explicit and professional principles of ethics, standards and integrity, many professors saw the logics of how institutionalized ethics processes were enacted as overly more about risk management than ethical practice, about knowledge management and not knowledge diversity (Fricker 2007).

Adding to the procedural stress on academics was that universities sought to speed up higher degree by research (HDR) completions to recuperate federal funding. Research managers, held accountable for outcomes, constantly checked on progress using traffic light systems. Automated reminders were sent to students regardless of their circumstance, heightening anxiety. Roy (Professor Regional, STEMM) commented: 'historically it's created a new class with new practices and it's the tail wag the dog . . . administration for its own sake.' Most professors considered this standardization and accelerationism ignored the nature of research supervision that was not just intellectual work but also building relationships of trust and support for students managing jobs, health issues and caring responsibilities. Micro-management reduced the professional autonomy to be flexible and nimble to meet student needs, requiring constant justification for their decisions. Consequently, it is no surprise that 'policies demanding consistency and compliance are therefore not well regarded if there is no strong evidence base or rationale. Hence a sense of disenchantment with the change processes mobilized by management exists, even at the professorial level' (Evans 2018: 24), particularly when the means becomes the end.

Leaderism: To What End?

With the leaderist turn in higher education in the context of competition, survival and progress, those academics moving into management came to develop a leaderist habitus as a 'product of the internalization of the structures of that world' and of the specific work situation of universities with competing objectives (Bourdieu 1989: 18). Often beginning as 'amateur managers' they had the support and socializing influence of 'a cadre of specialist full-time professionals with their own agendas' (McNay 2012: 162). As senior academic managers, they were positioned with the authority and freedom to shape organizational structures and processes due to their control of 'human', economic and material capital. But the selection and development processes for higher education leaders offered little assistance to do other than adopt the corporate logic with which they had already displayed a disposition towards and practical mastery of. Their recruitment and professional development were often unrelated to the daily realities of their work as Scott et al. (2010: 5) concluded: 'the nature and focus of leadership development programs don't always address the capabilities that count, and that the central role of university leaders in building a change capable culture is either unrecognized or misunderstood'. Succession planning had not been a management priority, despite difficulty recruiting into senior positions (Loomes et al. 2019).

Certainly, academic managers referred to how they became aware of how their interests or illusio shifted away from their disciplinary loyalties and affiliations as they were expected to be fair, understand and defend university-wide portfolios (Clift et al. 2015). Adrienne, the VC at Regional, did not see it as moving from being an academic to becoming a manager, but rather 'at every stage of career there's a different perspective, it's a different lens. . . . You get to triangulate the knowledge that you have about what academic life is like or general staff, professional work . . . I've worked in professional operations and managerial work . . . none of it's perfect, and none of it's evil.'

At the same time, academic managers' interests lay with meeting predetermined KPIs linked to the university strategic plan. A positional role meant reorienting their practices to utilize the authority and status associated with managerial and not just intellectual capital, which provided both the right to control *and* the capacity of controlling. They were Reich's (1992) symbolic analysts who determined the objectives of work, how work is organized, who does it and who benefits and the 'neoliberal ideology certainly gives our Australian managers a feeling of solidarity with business people in the metropole' (Connell 2016: 291). VC salaries being equivalent to the corporate sector indicated their entrée into the transnational professional-managerial class (Boden and Rowlands 2020, Connell 2010), while relative to other professions and their managers, academics were losing commensurability (Welch 2012).

Despite this, many of the DVCs and PVCs argued they had little power, that exerting power did not work with academics and that they relied on persuasion through communicative practices and consultation. A few admitted to enjoying power, as did an entrepreneurial Dean, Dana, at Regional who claimed she transformed a School from a 'cottage industry into a business' and used this as evidence of leadership for promotion. But managerial power was exerted indirectly, steering from a distance through the tools of metrics, performance management, funding and contractualized relations (Piattoeva and Boden 2020). Examples were provided of executive power being exerted both directly and indirectly to punish. Roger (Professor, Go8, HASS) commented: 'Power in the university is very complex . . . most practices of power are very conservative and extremely hidden.' Roger recalled the VC punishing a professor (and therefore the Faculty) by 'gutting his program' after the professor 'refused to withdraw an invitation to a well-known environmentalist to speak. The head of a mining company, a mate of the VC, had said this person had to be stopped'. All Deans, Heads and professors were aware of this capacity to exert executive power, and most moderated their behaviour accordingly.

Four subtle manifestations of 'soft' or 'subtle' power identified by Lumby (2019) in her UK study of senior university managers were mobilized. One was impression management, the performative exercise of being seen as a material presence, knowing everybody and being contactable, as was the case of the three VCs in this study. The paradox is, as the evidence argues here, 'leader-managers are possibly more effective both when highly visible and sometimes "hands-off" as the occasion demands it' (Jameson 2019: xxv). A second was by shaping discussion and decisions, achieved through putting out consultation papers, tabling documents which others had not had a chance to read, withholding information or merely determining who spoke when talking with others. This capacity to control agendas and exclude issues was obvious in Academic and Faculty Board terms of reference and agendas, executive policy and planning meetings and the use of blueprints when restructuring. A third power move was to trade interests and negotiate a transactional agreement prior to or after meetings, a common practice among 'boy networks' excluding women academic managers. A fourth strategy was to appoint and promote individuals who would remain aligned to your interests out of loyalty and with like dispositions and values to be change agents, a pattern increasingly evident in Australian universities (Grummell et al. 2009a).

Certainly, senior academic managers interviewed indicated an emotional toll involved to bring about what they argued were necessary changes, such as closing-down disciplines, forced redundancies or changing behaviours through performance management. A common response was to distance themselves physically and psychologically from the consequences of such decisions, a defensive mechanism of psychic splitting as a survivalist strategy and made possible for those at executive level working in the self-affirming 'corporate bubble' (Baker and Kelan 2019), while relying on the comfort of corporate and techno-administrative proceduralism as being 'fair'. Gentle (2014: 3) explains how managers default to top-down imposition of change rather than collegial practices because they 'find it more intuitive (and sometimes politically convenient) to resort to well-defined (and frequently critiqued) management roles and associated toolkits for implementation. They find it much more difficult to engage with their own identity and that of their colleagues as leaders'. They were not confronted as were Heads of School, by the daily realities of casualization, overload and work/life conflict, nor by the ethical dilemmas experienced by academics when a budget blow-out leads a Head of School to order an academic to teach a course. It is the academic who then tells casual staff they recruited that they are surplus and bears both the additional work and guilt (Zipin and Brennan 2003).

While more women were now senior academic managers, they were ambiguously positioned as doing the 'detail' of the affective labour of quality, teaching and learning, 'massaging the psychic economy', both 'queen' and 'worker bees' adhering to the tasks in hand (Morley 2013). Accessing seniority was not transgressing the social categories of gender because as individuals they were merely re-embedded 'women' in new socialities, 'thus individualization may not be emptying out gender but creating new lines of gender demarcation and domination' (Adkins 1999: 136). For many women 'the transformation to a managerial subject position is as much about relinquishing the love of teaching as acquiring cherished identifications, or more complexly, the recruitment of a skilled emotional praxis for the treacherous work of professional, educational, and/or institutional restructuring' (Hey and Bradford 2004: 706). Becoming an academic manager could 'represent vertical career success or it can also mean incorporation into unhealthy and undesirable masculinist, managerial practices and incarceration in an identity' (Morley 2013: 116). At the same time, some women in management showed that

> the ability to distance oneself from one's immediate emotional experience is the prerogative of those who have readily available a range of emotional options, who are not overwhelmed by emotional necessity and intensity, and can therefore approach their own self and emotions with the same detached mode that comes from accumulated emotional competence. (Illouz 1997: 56, cited in Reay 2004: 63)

The performative culture driven by KPIs and performance management did not allow for any personal insecurities or identity crises to be manifested or voiced. Instead, managers fantasized leadership success through quantifying their achievements which were more often the aggregation of subordinates' work.

Significant tensions and conflict therefore existed between academic managers and the professoriate over the role, direction and governance of the university. Thornton and Ocasio (2008: 100) remind us that 'institutional logics shape rational, mindful behavior, individual and organizational actors have some hand in shaping and changing institutional logics'. The clear message from the professoriate was that university management had been too receptive to implementing shifts in government policy, failed to protect academics from the vagaries of external demands, uncritically translated policy externalities into internal structural and cultural reform and work organization, undermined collegial governance and allowed the casualization of academic work. With 'system imperatives as drivers, [management] tends towards dependency and an agency role, with low-risk strategies and a culture of centralization, conformity, compliance and control, reflecting a perception of the external policy environment, with an assertive interventionist and regulatory state' (McNay 2012: 163).

Many, but not all, of the professoriate in this study rejected the increasingly explicit assumption that they must perform in particular ways and be loyal to their university (paternal contract), as this loyalty was not reciprocated in terms of employment (market contract) or reciprocity in which flexibility was balanced by employment security (psychological contract). Executive management was losing their intellectual authority and considered to no longer represent the core functions of and breadth of organizational and disciplinary knowledge comprising the university and 'where managerial decisions inhibit good academic work, there's a real ethical dilemma for academics' (Lawrence, former Universities Australia). Executive managers had lost the key element of leadership-trust. The shift towards managerial capital devalued intellectual capital, re-positioned academics as technical experts within their specified field and less so as critical intellectuals and advocates for their field as they had been in in the twentieth century, suggesting a process of de-professionalization is underway (Brint 2001, Slater et al. 2008, MacFarlane 2012a). Lorenz (2012: 617) aptly argues:

> The unrelenting organizing of reorganization – and splitting up professional jobs into processes that can be managed, measured, and controlled – has therefore become the quintessential specialization of management. The fact that reorganization is also the easiest means of disconnecting employees from former faculty rights – such as shared governance, tenure, and academic freedom – adds to this managerial drive, furthering their organizations' flexibility.

But the corporate template was an uncomfortable 'fit' for the complexity of the contemporary university which 'works best when the collegial enterprise is the norm' (McNay 2012: 162–3). In contrast, the corporate and techno-administrative culture 'often derives from a lack of institutional confidence, perhaps linked to lack of felt competence in senior staff. It leads to a lack of trust in colleagues and a closed system where, despite pressures for open accountability to the outside world, there is poor communication inside, and strong control over data' (McNay 2012: 163). While framed and restrained by external pressures and policies (Oleksiyenko and Tierney 2018), university managers had the opportunity and capacity to articulate internally less standardizing practices and more normative academic values recognizing the importance of professional autonomous judgement to achieve the same outcomes but lacked the inclination (or competence) to do so. Lea (2011: 835) argues that the uncertainty of the future requires those 'of the administrative/managerial class with greater moral fibre . . . to do what is appropriate', such as reassert the academic or intellectual values over managerial and market values but cautions that increasingly 'we cannot rely on this scenario as there is now little to distinguish between them'.

Chapter 5

LEADERSHIP STORYING, CHANGE MANAGEMENT AND ACADEMIC 'LINE DANCING'

Contemporary policy narratives view universities as being critical to knowledge economies, to sustain economic growth, to provide solutions to increasingly wicked problems as well as provide quality education to the next generation of global citizen-workers (Lauder et al. 2012). Business narratives argue that universities should be more entrepreneurial and commercial or become redundant (e.g. EY 2020, Barber et al. 2013). Spurred on by global rankings as 'engines of anxiety' (Espeland and Saunder 2016), universities have been restructured, with narrowed teaching and research priorities, and marketing themselves as a brand (Amsler and Bolsmann 2012, Delmestri et al. 2015). In this context, academic managers mobilize a repertoire of leadership practices – sometimes resorting to executive mandate – using the communicative practice of storying to persuade academics to become 'agents of their own reform' in ways that meet the needs of the university (O'Reilly and Reed 2010: 961).

While universities work within competitive student and academic markets, multi-levels of governance, limited funding, policy and regulative frameworks, university executives are 'free to decide' due to a high degree of internal autonomy. Executives seek to re-position their university advantageously (Marginson 2011) by portraying a unified public face or brand backed by an internal logic in which strategic plans act as a normative glue, discursively representing the university as an uncontested whole. Yet the traditional university has been re-formed into an increasingly complex multinational corporation with multiple, often contradictory, aims and obligations. Universities are fragmented entities, differentiated by multiple positional and disciplinary hierarchies. They have a complex politics of ascribed status, seemingly neutral structures and processes and competing discourses and practices, which simultaneously integrate and disaggregate understandings of who and what comprise the university. Everyday interpersonal relations occur within unequal power relations informed by hybrid arrangements and relationships arising from 'interactions of individual habitus, collective stories, and management-engineered programs of change' (Parker 2002: 2). Unable to manage external disruptions, executive academic managers seek to control what they can internally – people, plans, priorities and budgets – to achieve alignment between individual, institutional and government priorities. In this way they create metanarratives across disparate fields of activity.

Change Management through Storytelling

Narrative knowledge is the main source of organizational knowledge and leadership narratives, a primary mechanism of organizing change and the production of a particular institutional identity (Czarniawska 2014). Storytelling is a mechanism by which executives direct change from a distance in large organizations to influence others to be receptive to and adopt the managerial repertoire of policy, strategic plans and budgets. It is 'a management tool, a marketing tool and a communication tool' (Czarniawska 2014a: 72, 2015). As a management tool storytelling appears in mainly two versions following management fashions of time: the corporate culture advocates were interested in narratives that create stability while the learning organization generation (Senge 1990) were 'interested in narrative knowledge for enabling (planned) change' (Czarniawska 2014a: 72). Managers cannot create or assemble an organizational culture but can articulate and spread a particular storyline about and within a cultural arena about a university, department, individual to capture interest. Knowledge management is when stories are used as repositories of knowledge and for invoking managerial competence, or in Bourdieusian terms, a manager's accumulation of knowledge through experience to achieve practical mastery through saying and doing. Storying is also a communication tool where 'communication' is usually a euphemism for controlling' (Czarniawska 2014a: 72). Aiming to create a sense of inclusion and belonging, storying seeks to tap into the affective dimensions, the last source of productivity in knowledge economies. As a marketing tool, storying is most evident in the mobilization of the 'brand' and what makes the university distinctive (Molesworth et al. 2011).

Leadership practices cannot be separated from their institutional contexts or from the field of higher education. Universities internationally confront a multiplicity of conflicting challenges that are transforming the academy, among them massification, internationalization, digitalization, commercialization and privatization (Williamson 2014, de Wit and Altbach 2020). The literature charts how universities survive in fast-moving contexts and volatile policy settings with intensified competition for mobile students and academics, rising expectations of personalized multimodal learning, development of industry partnerships and cross-national alliances and negotiation of regulative accountability frameworks and reduced funding (Altbach et al. 2010, Stensaker and Harvey 2011, Proctor and Rumbley 2018, Verger et al. 2016). The dominant storyline mobilized by VCs to justify radical restructuring is the discourse of survival under conditions of uncertainty requiring changes in the positioning, priorities and practices of academics (Kauppi 2015).

Narratives provide a particularly compelling and powerful tool not only for communicating meaning but also for establishing the hegemony of a particular interpretation of, or perspective on, a sequence of organizational change events. As such, the storytelling skills associated with constructing a compelling and convincing account can be viewed as another power base that may often overlap with others, for example, in the use of expertise, and as such, is an effective political instrument for influencing others (Dawson and Buchanan 2005: 854.) Equally, the inability to provide a convincing story reduces trust in leaders (Jameson 2012).

O'Reilly and Reed (2010) argue that leaderism is about framing metaphorical narratives that in an endemic situation of competition, survival and progress require social coordination. This social coordination is best achieved through small groups of specially gifted and/or positioned individuals who lead, those with the practical mastery and with the positional authority to develop and disseminate metanarratives. For the VC, generating and translating a storyline requires unqualified commitment by DVCs, Deans and Heads and draws on their capacity to gain cooperation of others to adhere to the corporate storyline throughout the organization. Ironically, universities whose core work is teaching and research, lack the organizational means to capture and mobilize their staff's collective energies and ideas (knowledge management) and knowledge practices (e.g. critical thinking) (Szenes et al. 2015) through horizontal organization or cyclical feedback across fields to learn about organizational change.

There are few moments when VCs, or even Deans, talk face-to-face with staff, with occasional opportunities for storytelling such as university-wide campus consultations and faculty or school planning days. But stories about and by leaders and failed change proliferate within the academy. Academic managers, in moving around the university, use backstories about the everyday practices of leadership work, recounting anecdotes about of exemplars of 'good or bad practice', often universalized to justify change. They use autobiographical stories about how they came to be a leader to explain their actions (but not necessarily their values). Regarding technological change, the management story tends to be oversimplified and positive, assuming a linearity of how change will occur, sanitizing the political nature of organizational and technological change and competing stories. 'Anecdotes and stories are often used to support ready-made solutions in which political process is often down-played or ignored' (Dawson and Buchanan 2005: 846).

Various tropes and stories circulate among academic managers and professional staff about particular academics or disciplines: that professors are ego-driven, academics are difficult to change and HASS academics are always critical. Institutional memory about previous reforms and leaders and their effects is accumulated and passed on through storying by senior academics (institutional memory) and then forgotten or ignored by new managers. Academics use storying as a way of mentoring and supporting each other in corridor talk (Jameson 2018). Sharing stories is a communicative practice central to women in leadership networks. Storytelling is central to academic practice. In promotions, it talks about contribution to knowledge in research grant applications, impact and engagement exemplars in ERA and online academic profiling and making research accessible to the public and other users (Pitt and Mewburn 2016). Storying also is also a form of performative work, as academics work on themselves as a project of becoming and being an academic informed by technologies of the audit culture (Bansel and Davies 2010, Cheng 2011). In that sense, telling stories is a management tool, which depending on the content, both indicates the state of the organization's health and also 'enables individuals to convey information, and assists individuals in ascribing meaning to, and making sense of their organization' (Kjeldal et al. 2005: 432).

Czarniawska (2014a) warns, for every management story there is a counter-story, often acting as a form of resistance or indicating a dissonance between the meta- or narrative (corporate) storyline and how organizational life is experienced in practice. These counter-stories are also important within the context of an institution such as a university, which expects debate in which knowledge is valued, as feminists have argued. Felski (2000: 226) states:

> Stories often play a decisive role in this regard because they can convey experiential truths with force and clarity and emotional involvement, they help persuade their audience that certain things matter . . . storytelling is linked to the demand for recognition, but it can also gesture towards transformation and redistribution, by forging new links between the moral and the aesthetic spheres.

Storying can be a catalyst for cultural change of gender-based discrimination, harassment and violence (Kjeldal et al. 2005). In 2017, women sharing stories of sexual abuse and publicly naming perpetrators in the #MeToo movement highlighted systemic discrimination and hegemonic 'toxic cultures', potentially creating a reputational problem for universities who seek, for example, to be badged as good equal opportunity employers as a form of affective solidarity (Hemmings 2012). Finally, Jameson (2018) talks about the significance of 'critical corridor talk' which is treated only as 'gossip', but which can be a form of resistance as well as information exchange, creating stories of despair and hope, but also building relationships of trust and informal leadership (Bosetti and Heffernan 2021). Such stories are often where hearts and minds are lost or won as academics tell recognizable 'stories from the field' to each other regarding unethical situations in which they find themselves being compliant (Zipin and Brennan 2003).

Managing Change or Changing Management?

The higher education literature (as distinct from the critical organizational literature focusing on higher education) has largely failed until recently to theorize change, and yet fundamental organizational change has been undertaken (Scott et al. 2010). The literature has multiple variations on change: political focusing on contestation of interests; 'biological' or un-planned change; and teleological models (planned change), which produce generalized change strategies. Cultural theories illustrate complexity in showing 'the ambiguity, context-based nature and human aspects' of change and 'comprehensive change theories . . . focus[ing] on how change alters values and belief systems' (Kezar and Eckel 2002: 437). All are pertinent to understanding change in Australian universities.

The emergent field of leadership and change research in HE (e.g. Su et al. 2017, Evans 2014, 2017, 2018) includes stories by Deans (e.g. Clift et al. 2015) and Vice Chancellors (Davis 2017), professors (e.g. Macfarlane 2011, 2012a, 2014), women's stories of leadership challenges (e.g. Fitzgerald 2014) and 'how to lead' texts (e.g. Kretovics 2020). There has been little research theorizing organizational change in universities. Instead, Australian universities have uncritically adopted 'the tools of a trading corporation: branding and promotion, business planning and programme budgeting, line management and performance appraisal, benchmarking and review, in a continual quest for improvement' (Macintyre 2010: 8). These 'broad change strategies are presented as uniform, universal, and applicable' across all campuses presuming that 'nuance and context do not much matter' (Kezar and Eckel 2002: 435). Macintyre (2010: 8) agrees that 'the character of any university strategic plan is the lack of historical depth', being both 'generic in their striving for excellence' and 'impoverished by their inattention to context'. Andre (Research Director, Go8, STEMM) commented that 'most people in universities pay no attention to the literature on leadership or organizational structure'.

Instead of executive managers investing in long-term change-management processes developed internally, they pay highly for management consultants as coaches or change managers to provide a solution to 'the problem' (Gherardi and Nicolini 2001, Drori 2016). The consultants' corporate logic and change narrative assume leadership is invested in the executive and the individual, that academics are invested in the brand, that leaders can change organizational cultures and that universities are not distinctive. They utilize organizational charts which do not display academic practice, focus on changing structures, procedures and roles, and often fail to reduce the budget other than in the immediacy because they do not understand how universities work nor how to motivate changed behaviour by addressing academics' understandings or values (Czarniawaska 2014a). For example, Kirkby and Reiger (2015: np) analysed the Organizational Implementation Strategy at one Australian university designed by corporate consultants.

> University structures are reinterpreted through 'a narrative of separation, internal division and unification', so that 'the university' becomes senior management and it is left unstated just what the disciplines and programs are. Where 'the faculty' fits is subject to a further slide insofar as it becomes largely responsible for its own fate in inadequately supporting 'the university' financially. . . . The narrative positions the faculty both as actor and its management as victim of circumstances, yet the authors of the document are not named and the passive voice camouflages any possibility of responsibility. In terms of curriculum planning, . . . there is ambivalence about disciplines and the separation of academic staff from planning of teaching and learning, and from the entity called 'the faculty' . . . there is a seemingly 'baffling lack of interest in . . . the nature of "the market"': students too are outside the 'university' as consumers,

whose shifty allegiances occasion considerable anxiety, but little, it seems, effective research and analysis.

Such shifting of blame is a dangerous game for executive managers. It ignores how 'in managing change, leaders make it wanted; managers make it happen; academics, administrators and ancillary staff make it work' (McNay 2005: 56). From an outsider perspective, a change consultant at Go8 (Frank) attributed his success to having been an academic when a Deputy Dean told him: 'You're the third consultant and they've all been nuff-nuffs in suits and you've got a suit but you're not a nuff-nuff'. Change-management theorists refer to feedback loops in a learning organization (knowledge communication) and the necessity to draw on the practical mastery of those who do the work prior to developing a plan (knowledge management), and not one based on corporate logics designed by non-academics (Czarniawska 2014a).

Storytelling as a Managerial, Marketing and Communication Tool

Storytelling is also a methodology which facilitates examination of how university managers un/consciously use storying to articulate the necessity, nature and intended outcomes of structural reform and organizational change. University executives in large and devolved organizational structures seek to direct, coordinate and influence by engaging with and converting academic dispositions and intellectual capital to align with the university's mission through a variety of behavioural approaches. These include persuasion, incentivization and sometimes punitive measures and entanglements of accountability and performative mechanisms based on contract-like arrangements such as targets, KPIs, performance reviews, student evaluations, publication metrics and workload formulae (Rawolle et al. 2016). Universities utilize an array of data about the relative performance of individuals, research centres, schools and faculties with regard to student preferences and retention, research income from high stakes grant bodies as well as diversity of funding resources (government, NGOs and philanthropists), graduate employability outcomes, global university and subject rankings, ERA rankings, publications and citations (Piattoeva and Boden 2020). These measures are all included in the co-ordinating strategic plan which the three universities in this study called 'the blueprint', from which the corporate storyline is developed, strategies listed and targets for individual academic managers developed. As Rosanne, a former DVC, commented: 'The Vice-Chancellor has to set the vision but most strategic plans, they're pretty much the same with local nuances.' Frank, a management consultant, saw strategic plans as 'mainstream management leadership stuff: what's our primary purpose, are we aligned to it, have we got the structures to do it, have we got the relationships to be able to talk about it'. But work conditions, relationships and the psychological contract of reciprocity underpinning strategic plans have been neglected as the focus is on the strategic plan and structure and communicating down rather than building relationships and discussing what the university should and could be as a place of learning and research.

Writing the Storyline

Structural reform, as organizational theory and the following stories show, does not necessarily lead to the intended cultural reform. All three of the VCs in this study were change oriented leaders. Nicole (DVC, Go8) considered the culture in the inner executive circle had altered towards thinking that the university modus operandi is about constant change, not about continuity and then the occasional crisis. Consensus was often achieved through recruitment of like-minded line managers, or gentle persuasion of existing managers through a planning process over months. The universities – Go8, Utech and Regional – had undergone major structural reforms to 're-brand' over the previous decade as had the sector. Tim (DVC, Utech) commented, 'being in time with the context' meant 'we needed to respond to the changing context quickly. Universities are inherently conservative institutions and tend to be slow moving, but the world outside was moving faster than we were'. The acceleration of external change produced a sense of urgency, reverberating through the discourse of survivalism (sometimes triumphalism) mobilized by leaders to justify change, while often ignoring the time needed to realize and accommodate large-scale change (Wajcman and Dodd 2016).

Each university adopted a similar approach given the complexity of change within a university with multiple layers of committees, decision-making sites and devolved governance to faculties. Developing a coherent and clear storyline by the executive and the senior management usually emerged out of a consultation process, explicated by a former DVC, Rosanne, as 'the green paper, white paper process. Everything was evidenced based . . . I would go out and test ideas, work with consultants, give presentations for transparency and accountability, I'm here to listen while developing a common story about the university and you know consult, consult, consult'. The narrative was then communicated through the strategic plan and cascaded through Faculty strategic plans to Schools to gain reluctant acceptance if not consensus.

Importantly, many change managers fail to recognize whether there was a condition of readiness for change within the university, to understand the dynamics of discursive struggles over layers of meaning regarding organizational circumstances, identities and practices. Roseanne considered that 'there was a readiness at her university, people knew that it had to change and so there was a sense that things could happen'. At Utech, Vanessa (DVC) felt that communication of the message was critical to creating such conditions during the third iteration of the blueprint: 'We go out and do the road shows. The reframe project is about being very collaborative and has engaged a lot of people. That might not be the same everywhere'. It was simultaneously a process of shifting the rules of the game and priorities (i.e. what is valued here and how we work), aligning individual academics, research institutes and schools with faculty and university-wide policies. The aim was to change academic habitus or 'feel for the game' by presenting the individual unit or academic with the notion that their interests were 'out of sync' if they did not align, and a process many professors noted, of creating exclusions (about who and what is not valued). Each university had developed a distinctive storyline: Go8's blueprint informing a major restructure a few years earlier was to be in the top fifty globally and align with North American and European systems; Utech had undertaken fundamental restructuring a decade ago and the blueprint was being 'tweaked' (Eric, VC, Utech); Regional was in the middle of an overall restructure to reposition itself under a relatively new VC and was 'testing' a new blueprint focusing on its regional positioning.

Thriving

At Utech, the storyline of being relevant with close ties to industry and experiential learning developed ten years earlier, required only minor 'tweaks' to be a university 'for the real'. The current VC was astutely aware of the symbolic nature and role of the blueprint, which he said had 'to be readable and doable: the latest versions are shorter with a limited number of objectives. The moveable feast in it is what "real" means . . . but everyone believes in it and talks about it'. Certainly, most interviewees at Utech referred to the blueprint. A DVC (Martha): 'Everybody knows, recognizes, and accepts the blueprint . . . we've had three iterations. When the VC developed it he had campus meetings and gained really wide acceptance. It was a matter of time and place, we were ready, a new VC and only a slight change of direction.'

Discussions were then about the balance between on and off campus, online and face-to-face teaching, ramping up international students and to become a more research-intensive university. A professor (Patrick, STEMM) liked the incremental approach and 'the kind of leadership of being able to just standstill for a moment and think about what the landscape is going to look like in five or ten years' time based on trends, considering whether our traditional research paradigm is sustainable'. Ruth's (A/Professor, HASS) characterization of Utech was representative of academic responses across all faculties.

> Our motto is relevance and that's true. We've got lots of good and bad things but Utech rewards ambition and activity no matter what age or gender you are. If you are doing things, Utech is there for you. We are audacious, in your face, ambitious cause we are young and never going to be a group of 8, and don't want to be.

While the corporate storyline was widely accepted, equally, another storyline that was clear to all interviewees that those who did not adhere to it: leave!

Striving

Regional was in the process of consultation to develop the storyline and work out how the blueprint would be operationalized, creating a sense of uncertainty. A consultancy firm had developed four scenarios, but a Dean (Keith, STEMM) felt that 'the VC already has the answer because the answer is in the assumptions: it's about lining up your ducks first and getting your story right and from my perspective the journey is crystal clear to me'. For Regional, the VC on arriving had decided that the university meta-narrative was to return to its original warrant as a regional university to service the north and capitalize on its research strengths. Linking institutional identity to location also tapped into the shared academic sentiment that Regional was distinctive as explained by Connie (A/ Dean, STEMM): 'Every university in the country is fighting for differentiation or you're stuffed and no university is more differentiated than Regional.'

With a DVC responsible for the blueprint's development, consultation and implementation, the VC's job was to talk up the storyline. 'Her state of the region papers has been circulated. She spoke to our school and we're all waiting to hear the outcomes' (Hannah, A/Dean, HASS). But Monica (Dean, HASS) considered that the multiplicity of agendas was only loosely related with no clear process even for those at the centre:

> The VC will tell you the grandest story. . . . But everybody struggling with curriculum refresh has a whole list of things that have to go in including the regional agenda. We've hired new leaders, putting in applications for laureates, developing alumni groups and creating a college for our adjuncts. Budgets are very, very tight. We've got multiple review teams . . . business operations, Ernest and Young looking at admin and a consultant writing scenarios, all happening together.

She referred to the provocations circulated about the role of the university focusing on the public and private good, East and West relations and how to position the university as 'the conversation starters as to who we want to be. Then you decide what stays and what goes. All at a head spinning pace at which external pressure comes without resources'. Additionally, the faculty was struggling with the regulatory environment (TEQSA and ERA) while redesigning their teaching.

With the regional focus outlined, the potential organizational restructuring created anxiety in certain disciplines. Some saw the regional focus as a 'very clearly defined vision and opportunity', while others considered the storyline privileged STEMM fields due to their international research reputation rather than the more community-oriented HASS fields. Gerald (Professor, STEMM) stated: In global rankings over the last ten years, Regional actually outranks Cambridge, Yale, Columbia . . . now it's even more strategically focused'. The new strategic focus had attracted key staff in the social sciences, as the new Research Institute Director in HASS recalled, because 'the conceptualization just brought a whole lot of things together to me – and a young faculty who had terrific potential'. Another professor George (STEMM) saw the focus fitted well with the future of the region and internationally because 'Northern Australia is going to be very much a growth area over the next twenty to fifty years . . . we're well placed to service that if we can align ourselves and have the expertise in developing areas. . . . The leadership is certainly trying to engage much better with the region.'

For others the strategic focus was problematic, particularly where expertise was not clearly aligned with place. Many felt they were 'suddenly having to change objectives' (Jeremy, Head, STEMM) depending on whether the regional story was 'a focus or a filter' (Keith, Dean, STEMM). A filter, with perceptions of the blueprint as a knowledge management tool, meant restricting disciplinary activities inside this frame, which was perceived to be difficult for the generic engineering and law disciplines. Evelyn (Head, HASS) saw the blueprint's storyline together with ERA as threatening her School: 'The Dean thinks that we might be able to save some stuff if we develop an Asian focus. I'm not convinced that students will respond to imposing an Asian focus. We have to have integrity, that requires resourcing, or else you just package something a little bit differently and underneath it looks exactly the same.' The ethical dilemma for her was that the strategic plan's brand required her to reconceptualize her teaching in ways that were not student-centred and which felt like fabricating the course profile to fit the brand. Others treated the storyline as just a marketing tool, a performative exercise with little impact on what they did.

Those in positional roles responsible for implementation sought to massage the message, arguing that the priority was a lens that did not require change in content. Hannah (A/Dean, HASS) argued it was returning to the original rationale for the university, which appealed to most academics: 'It's just about the community, who we are and where we are.' She argued the storyline evoked 'just a different sense of place, a different way you have to network and a good way to talk about the importance of place'. Similarly, Adam (Head, HASS) argued that you should not think 'geographically but if you think of it more as a state of mind and how people might sort of interact with an environment we really focus on regional and rural, and remote, so that's one pillar'. Many felt that the regional focus would occur anyway by default because of lack of money and reduced course provision, although most interviewees felt the university should remain a comprehensive university for the region 'as we have a very strong equity agenda and a richly diverse group of students and to step back from this commitment would mean we just become a science institute, a huge loss to community' (Monica, PVC, HASS). The lack of clarity meant that HASS scholars feared a restructure as Monica stated:

> The blueprint showed that the university is schizophrenic. In some areas (STEMM) we're some of the top research in the world with ERA 5s. But because we're a regional university you have all the professional schools, otherwise this region would not get professionals. So it's hugely political about how we are redefined. You can do both, but we shouldn't try and make all of them fit the same size and that's the tension. . . . The social sciences are particularly nervous because we are the smaller faculty bringing in less money. Some will get amalgamated.

A strong social justice subtext emerged as many academics saw the university had 'quite a commitment to rural, regional, and indigenous and issues with low SES' (Karl, Head, STEMM). A restructure could therefore change core values.

Excelling

Prior to this study, the Go8 VC on his appointment had sought to upscale and position his university globally, aiming to be in the first fifty universities ranked globally. The storyline articulated widely at all levels was about research excellence and the quality of the on-campus experience at an elite university. Brett (PVC, HASS) recalled on arrival the VC sent around

> a very personally written account of the history of the university. . . . It was very smart, very academic, well argued. It ended with questions: Where are we in this, and what does the future hold? It was bleeding obvious that he was going to lead us down that path of graduate school or North American model, exactly what I wanted.

The restructuring took many years with rounds of redundancies and a reorientation of all courses, despite initial opposition from both academics and students. But the storyline of excellence globally was coherent and consistent. The blueprint was implemented by the Provost but relied heavily on the VC's authoritative voice. 'Being Vice Chancellor is about selling the organization . . . you are the CEO and the prime advocate' (Bill, Dean, HASS). Brett (PVC, HASS) explained how the VC gained cooperation by mobilizing his intellectual, moral and political capital or leaderism: 'The restructure was his idea. But a sophisticated consultation process went on with the university community before the final design was communicated. He might have known all along what he was going to do.' This professor recalled how the VC displayed a 'really expert consultation practice showing how different views had been evaluated and making sure he included comments that the people who had written them could see. It was very, very skillful, upfront, clear what he was trying to do but clearly no plan B'. This practice suited the ways in which academics worked. Martin (Professor, HASS) saw the VC as 'having a great communicative skill and a good sense of what's needed to get the message through to the troops . . . very persuasive'. He was both 'quite laid back . . . yet managed to be on top of a complex institution, trusting people to do their job so he doesn't micro-manage' but 'always there at the critical times, especially for Council, external appointments, the budget and the main game changes'. Although memories lingered as to the emotional effects of distress and grief at the changes, there was strong agreement among interviewees that restructuring had been successful as the university had raised it rankings. Indeed, many academics remained at Go8 because of the prestige factor that accrued for them intellectual capital, despite high levels of casualization and a highly competitive promotion system.

These examples of change management analysed through storying showed the need for: a process of intellectual and affective engagement with academics; both consistency and coherence in messaging; a capacity to identify blockers requiring personal intervention; and recognition of how change took years.

Relay(er)ing the Corporate Storyline: Power, Persuasiveness and Persistence

Storying was a key mechanism for managers to engage organizational actors in change. But the success of any storyline relied on conditions of readiness and receptivity of multiple audiences. The strategic plan defined the various roles of the actors and the script they are expected to act out. Reissner et al. (2011: 418) argue:

> Story is the prime means for the construction of social reality . . . and for the creation of meaning. . . . Its strength is its ability to establish coherence and causal relationships between different actions and events by means of a plot. . . . The plot adds meaning to the actions and events told by a story . . . ; this meaning is subject to interpretation by the audience. . . . It is this ambiguity of meaning that allows for multiple readings and differing interpretations of the management of organizational change. While ambiguity of meaning can encourage more creative approaches to organizational change management, it can also be problematic for practising managers as diverging interpretations may lead to fragmentation among organizational actors.

The DVCs and PVCs were responsible for developing the plot to be enacted by Deans and Heads. Their authority rested with their capacity to influence largely through symbolic capital and some budgetary power, the latter particularly wielded by the DVC Research. The DVCs and PVCs argued implementing the blueprint was about persuasion and persistence rather than power, minimizing the importance of their positional authority and the underlying pervasive mechanisms of measurement and accountability (workload formulae, performance management, metrics, etc.) making compliance in the individual's interest. Persuasion was key, Martin (Professor, HASS) argued, because the distributed committee systems, multiple leadership roles and disciplinary enclaves required particular strategic moves:

> We have a unique cultural asset . . . the academic and professional workforce who really buy into this idea that it's a collective effort. People own and operate the institution . . . When you decide to go to fix problems or get change, you can't use conventional methods or a command-and-control system and nor can you use incentives. They're very rubbery in our game. So you have to get people on board, talk to them, give them a chance to influence and shape the proposal, move at a speed that the average person accepts, be incredibly persistent with consultation. Typically, it takes a year to get anything really big done and probably two or three years to land results . . . different from non-universities.

The most powerful stories tapped into the affective economies, whether by projecting a discourse of institutional survival (fear), service (love) or excellence (desire), with the survivalist discourse dominating: 'As a leader one of the hardest jobs you've got is to persuade people about what's coming. I'm preparing our colleagues, not about tomorrow, but ten years out in more competitive ways' (Tim, DVC, Utech). For Monica (Dean, Utech), it was 'first about the lack of money and we have no choice . . . the TINA effect . . . and keeping market-share'. Adam (Head, Regional, HASS) argued that 'we have to change . . . try and distinguish ourselves in a number of different ways, change the way we teach'.

The mechanisms of relaying the story down were through the multiple committees, upon which academic managers and academics sit, global emails and occasional campus meetings of staff with the VC. Significant investment in the storyline is required by key positional actors such as Academic Board chairs, Deans and Heads upon whom responsibility for operationalizing the blueprint and developing the plot is devolved and who are linked to the strategic plan through individual KPIs. Many did not need such incentives. Rick (Dean, Regional, STEMM) enthusiastically adopted the storyline: 'We are who we are because of where we. We've got a terrific vision across four themes. . . . Our story is spectacular. I cannot imagine this university changing even if the VC left, you could not change the vision of this university. . . . Our best researchers are our best teachers, and they 'need to come onboard with the story'. His strategy was to select advocates (change agents) who as leaders would work with the storyline to inform practice, recognizing the importance of ownership of change. Such commitment was not always evident, even at the executive level. Liz, an A/Professor (Regional) commented that a newly appointed DVC had arrived with the blueprint written: 'I don't think she feels a huge amount of ownership of the blueprint because she started late. She is more comfortable with the learning and teaching plan she wrote.'

In large organizations, there is no monolithic culture other than shared understandings about academic practices and disciplinary ways of doing, seeing, saying and being. Individual academics, when necessary, re-invented themselves to appear to accommodate with the corporate logic in grants, promotion and institutional demands – a performative exercise. Each disciplinary field had different readings of any blueprint. High-performing academics or disciplines had the economic, cultural and social capital and more leverage than others and were able to block imposed reform, with individual academic's options of exit, loyalty or voice. Dana (Head, Utech) had to persuade staff to 'do more funded research . . . collaborate externally and engage not just locally but internationally, which a lot of business schools traditionally haven't'. But in Business and Law, 'keeping academics onboard is a challenge because they can go out and double or triple their salary' – exit not loyalty. Recruiting and retaining talent was the key issue.

The challenges for academic managers varied considerably in multi-campus institutions. Regional had responsibilities in remote areas off-campus across a wide geographical region, requiring cross-subsidization by the wealthier faculties, an accepted responsibility of the university 'because it's part of us contributing to the social fabric of the region' (Adam, Professor, HASS). Liz, the director of a university-wide teaching and learning unit at Regional visualized herself as centre of a learning hub with spokes out to the associate deans of teaching and learning whom she met monthly 'to decide what are the key things that we're driving forward' and breakfasting with the DVC and Heads 'as they want leadership'. She wrote a charter of responsibilities for teaching and learning and ran activities to embed it and to inform staffing decisions because 'at the operational level it's about networks, relationships with people'. Liz sent out communiqués fortnightly about 'just in time' policy issues while 'scrambling in terms of operational requirements and envisaging a newly structured unit going forward'. She undertook performance management of all staff, HR and budgeting without support and adapted to sudden executive shifts in the reform language used by the executive – one being the mantra we're 'one university, two countries, three campuses' to '[now we are] harmonizing and have practices that talk to each other but not one aligned vision'. Liz's focus was on communication of an open-ended storyline able to accommodate shifts, while bringing multiple stories into existence by listening to staff about what choices each had and wanted to do. As a middle manager she had to adhere to corporate agendas, be responsive, adapting to the changing storylines while keeping focused on what it meant for academic practice.

A recurrent storyline that emerged from among the professoriate was that there needed to be 'room for debate' in recognition of the nature of academic work and expertise and 'for the institution to negotiate that shared space' (Bill, Professor, Go8, HASS). Bill talked about the ambivalence he had: '[in a] leadership team you're never in the business of wanting to remove debate but you're often in the business of wanting to very actively debate and negotiate how it is that the consensual self-determining qualities of the academy get mobilized positively for a change agenda'. He agreed that academic managers were 'afraid you might spoil that kind of narrative of change' with negative feedback. The dilemma for management as stated by Jay (Dean, Go8, HASS) was that 'I can't imagine a really high performing academic outfit that isn't incredibly empowering for its high performing academics'.

The process of change was often described as a metaphor which 'carries over meaning from one domain to another . . . and can open up new ways of thinking and acting' (Reissner et al. 2011: 417). Academic managers talked about identifying niche markets (like luxury brands). Tweaking the blueprint at Utech meant 'never throwing the baby out with the bath water' (Vanessa, DVC, Utech). A restructure was likened to an earthquake in which there is settlement after disruption, 'steering a large ship to change direction' or 'herding cats'. Alan, a research director (Go8, STEMM) saw his role was to find catnip (a research project) to which academics 'became addicted'. Metaphors foregrounded affect and the ambivalence towards the corporate agenda with frustration among professors directed at 'too many chiefs and not enough Indians' (Jeff, Professor, Regional) (Skorobohacz et al. 2016). Kristina, an Acting Dean at Utech tried to redirect the debate from management's 'knee jerk reactions' to a long-term challenge: 'from the game being a 20/20 cricket match and more a test match' requiring 'stewardship statesman . . . making sure that we are positioned in society as relevant for the public good'. Implicit in these metaphors were ways of thinking about organizational change – whether an organic, self-adjusting system; or cyclical process moving from centralized to more decentralized decision-making organizational structures, but less so about what motivates people to change: political stance, prior experience, passion for social justice, status, sense of agency or money. All agreed change took time.

As a heuristic device, storying as a leadership practice provoked considering about whether and what is the problem, opening up capacity to ask others about alternatives, before taking a particular decision. In each instance, the three storylines linked to the blueprint identified to their institutional histories: Utech's story of relevance echoed its origins as a former Institute of Technology and countered images of academics in ivory towers; Regional's storyline reinstated its research strengths based on its origins to serve the northern regions. But the messaging was confused. 'It was "trying to get some identity emphasizing Regional's strengths but it can be conceived very narrowly . . . as a sort of subtle pressure on everything we teach and research"' (Karl, Professor, STEMM). At Go8, the focus clearly was and always had been on university-wide structural realignment internationally, to extend research reach and move up world rankings.

Vignettes of Change: Middle Managers Storying Down

In turn, in a distributed model of responsibility and risk, Deans and Heads of School had to develop storylines that both appealed to their superiors in order to win resources and protect their unit, as well as convince those within their responsibility to become actors in the plot (Brewer and Walker 2011). Managing in the middle meant constantly plotting. The strategy at Go8 was to appoint new Deans, many of them external, as change agents and more willing to act as without prior affiliations. Gary (Dean) took on a restructure of a Faculty (HASS) at Go8 in phases because it was positioned as in a 'crisis structural deficit and a whole lot of denial particularly some traditional elements'. The Faculty 'got rid of' ninety academic and professional staff and had a timeline of three years to embed the new structure. Gary positioned himself as 'not to blame' by informing staff: 'I have been asked by the VC to sort this problem . . . I didn't invent the problem and so I didn't really attach much to the history', treating it as a problem to be fixed, thereby distancing himself psychologically from its affective effects (Skorobohacz 2016). He first addressed the budget and reduced costs by increasing teaching loads which was not 'a punishing strategy . . . just the reality of no money'. Three years later, out of deficit, the second phase was to use funds to build a graduate school and grow. He felt he had won back a few staff 'who were cheesed off' and made new (largely external) appointments so that 'a new history was being created'. Renewing leadership at faculty executive, school and programme levels took three years. Phase three meant more devolved leadership to run the operating side of the faculty. Gary therefore focused on a coaching mode with a focus on specific projects, for example international programmes. 'It's felt like three different kinds of deanships.'

In each phase, Gary developed a new plot with different actors relevant to the situation. One plot was to build leadership capacity by establishing a committee of thirty-five academics outside the organizational structures, therefore widening the sense of ownership of decision-making. 'It was still part of the general committee structure. . . . People have a certain number of committee assignments that they need to tick boxes on their annual review.' He considered committees consumed time and being a good academic citizen often did not gain formal credit. The committee represented the disciplines as school structures no longer did with 'the risk that they obliterate disciplinary identity'. Gary clearly understood the academic habitus (as ERA) was closely tied to their 'disciplinary world' and there was a need for 'republican self-governance'. Meeting monthly, this committee was more 'a high-level advisory think tank' which he used for 'talent spotting and talent developing. We consider the hot issue of the day and some policy . . . but working creatively, contributing and then going back and talking to colleagues'. Gary looked to this group for future Associate Deans and Heads. The committee served a key symbolic purpose by providing a sense of agency through participation among those academics generally sidelined, but strategically bypassed the professoriate, who retained strong institutional memories of how it was previously.

Jay, another Dean at Go8, focused on communicating what was happening and argued that people are more accepting if they know why decisions are made. A consultant (Frank) observed this Dean's practice: 'He had You Tube videos of him talking to the PVC with graphic drawings as outputs of workshops, put them on the web, sent emails to everyone, talked to each program group, and said this is what we've done and why. Textbook management, but most people don't do it.' This Dean was acting out his plot to colleagues to make it meaningful. Similarly, Andree, a Director of Research Institute (STEMM) at Go8, described himself as 'an agent for cultural change' to explain 'why it needs to be done' when seeking to encourage partnerships and diversify research funding sources. After being questioned in the annual review by senior management why they were not 'punching higher', he 'set the bar higher and many of them rose to the occasion'. In Go8, academics' interests lay with the Institute's survival requiring high-level performance, a more coercive mechanism of targets to incentivize with many staff in precarious employment positions but disadvantaging those, particularly women, who did not have the additional home time required.

At Regional Adam (Head, HASS) was confronted with 'a thousand students . . . trying to build a research program, a hundred staff and new physical site'. He adopted a distributed management model' because he 'loved the job once he got the right people into place and a structure that worked'. He set up a cabinet based on portfolios (directors of students, education, integration, etc.) not disciplines with a rural and remote geographic mix supported by a very good senior school manager, a flat distributed structure, devolving as much as he could but not the budget. Adam's position was 'that we (managers) need to get out of academics' way and provide supports . . . while achieving broad consistency . . . enabling people to create a culture and structures but also take a lot of pressure off in terms of the vertical shit coming down', a view most professors also advocated.

Sara (Dean, HASS), at Regional, took a more assertive role after twenty-two months during which she reviewed and restructured the faculty and sought to realign services, requiring a university-wide initiative. This Dean established a business and improvement review team with the DVC administration and created another team to look at services for academics and students, formed a cross-university working party 'to validate' the plan, then presented a paper to the VC's Advisory Committee. She argued that such working party should continue with a Dean as line manager as 'the DVCs are out of it and the Dean is where the rubber hits the road'. Deans are the 'people, that want to make it work but have enough feelers down that they know what doesn't work. The bullshit detectors'. At that time, she argued that having a consultancy firm would speed up the working party process and ended up partnering with EY in the review.

These vignettes indicate how the vertical management structures were no longer capable of undertaking the work of meaningful organizational change. Senior and middle managers focused on providing a sense of ownership and agency by recognizing disciplinary identity and sense of shared purpose, although their actions were not without professional and emotional damage to those who did not 'fit' of 'follow'. Just as often, academics formed informal groups to resolve a problem in their everyday practice, or to propose an alternative proposition to management, drawing from their practical mastery, trust and shared purpose (Tinning and Sirna 2011). O'Reilly and Reed (2010: 961) argue leaderism is when individuals use particular 'moral, intellectual, interpersonal, cognitive, material, or politico-cultural resources in order to achieve social co-ordination'. But 'to perform this role leaders must be empowered by giving them sufficient room to manoeuvre – the 'right', or authority, to lead; and those who lead require effort and commitment from others. As exemplified earlier, middle managers recognized the impediments to change: often worked outside formal structures to capture the interest of particular audiences, appealed to the academic disposition of collegiality, created supportive conditions within budgetary constraints, always working around resistant or recalcitrant players.

Storying Up the Line

At the same time, Deans and Heads of school had to develop a strong and clear storyline up to the executive when developing a strategic plan and budget, a positive story about how to resolve any issue, and not just to 'cry poor'. If student numbers could not be filled by one faculty or school, in this competitive environment, they would be quickly snatched up because student numbers were capped. Faculties with high student numbers, particularly business schools with a high percentage of international students, often felt positioned as cash cows. Lauren (Dean, Utech, HASS) saw external factors leading to a reduced size of her faculty, a dangerous position in a possible restructure of an amalgamation and appealed to university strategic goals. She relied on 'the strength of numbers, data and messaging. Don't go and try to influence unless you've got something to influence with'. Lauren also knew the gender politics and had spent considerable time educating key personnel in finance and administration (predominantly men in senior positions) who could impact on the Faculty because of their view of the discipline's 'perceived relevance' and their capacity to develop unfavourable budgetary measures. Administrative staff had the resources and knew how financial systems worked but lacked knowledge of specific fields. She realized that 'we do have an extraordinarily collegial and supportive culture. Sometimes influence isn't necessary because there is an understanding. But our faculty is grappling for numbers, so you meet with recruitment and finance. Success was when the resource planning guy sends me an article of interest to me. I am encouraging them to learn about our field.' The VC, Laren felt, realized her Faculty's research strengths as she had been strategically developing a storyline about the faculty over time as she knew his disposition:

> He thinks in terms of his university. He likes to sprout how good his university is at these things, and about our faculty and tells me what he hears from outside, my main interactions with the VC being around government influence and policy. I've been telling him for years about why numbers are shrinking, and I think he's got it.

But the message down was clear if you couldn't tell a good story. Telling a good story up was apparent at Go8 for Brett, PVC responsible for student equity:

> The VC really respects me . . . because I give him a narrative. I deliberately do it. He needs a narrative as it is bloody hard to understand a complex university. When given the narrative, he is word perfect. But despite his formidable skill set, he doesn't understand student equity, because he's obsessed with achievement and excellence it's hard to marry that with equity. My contribution is an insightful clear narrative and you can see the clogs ticking over in his mind.

Equity is inevitably a major disruptor to the corporate logic (Chapter 8), often requiring counterintuitive practices, and challenges academic norms such as what constitutes merit (Thornton. 2013, Riley 2017).

Another Dean at Go8, Jay (HASS) argued storying was critical in the highly competitive environment among Deans. He was appointed because 'the faculty was considered a basket case, a poor research performer, a drag on the university'. Despite the faculty bringing in huge sums of money, 'the other faculties didn't care'. So Jay sought to establish relations based on the 'usual thing, trust, respect . . . but it's not about being intimidated and therefore cowering, showing that you are part of a university community and demonstrating this faculty actually had value'. He reflected on how the change process worked in his faculty: 'A long process which looked at scenario planning that allowed staff to initially engage in discussions. . . . This led to a discussion of what sort of structures might best suit that strategic intent also taking on board a lot changes occurring externally in terms of regulatory agencies, financial implications as well as government decisions and future government positions.'

As Dean, Jay still felt they did not get it right as 'sometimes individual staff don't want to know . . . staff referred to the discipline rather than the institution'. His academic habitus had been informed by disciplinary training from STEMM, business and community, and consequently he was not 'precious' about any specific field. Now Jay's interests lay with the Faculty. He argued: 'you have to decide whether you want to be part of the institution and where it's going, or whether you want to be part of the discipline and go somewhere else'. This was not how academics tended to view the world, but his message was clear – institutional loyalty first.

At Regional, Monica (Dean, HASS) commented: 'We've earned a place at table with the VC. She likes that we've tried to fit the strategic intent.' This Dean made her faculty visible at the senior management committee by using a faculty review to 'talk about our position in the wider university context and coming out from the shadow of the sciences into a more privileged position'. Being at 'the table' was a signal of being included and gained access to the VC, while reminding the other Deans that HASS was a competitive player in the game and not always talking about difficulties. Monica invited the VC to a book launch to celebrate: 'People in this faculty are fiction writers and novelists.' This success story illustrated to the VC how research metrics fail to recognize the cultural work of HASS and was an anecdotal 'good story' for use by the VC when considering priorities.

For the PVCs, often part-time professors seconded from faculties as at Go8 and without the same institutional investment, power was not felt despite appearances. The PVC's role was to collect university-wide data as to their specific issues, work with stakeholders externally and internally, develop policy and then use the 'soft power' of gentle persuasion, etc., to implement change within the hierarchy of committees. Carla (PVC, Go8) noted:

> Persuasion only, even if you sit in the central leadership role, because the dean employs the academic and professional staff. I'm still an academic in a school, reporting to the Dean through the Head. . . . If the deans want to do something it can usually happen. If the deans don't want to do something, it's much, much harder . . . that's where the soft power comes in.

Soft power meant mobilizing specific policy discourses to gain legitimacy for action in their portfolio, 'talking and testing initiatives' with Associate Deans and Heads of School. Changing a university policy required going through Academic Board and its subcommittees. For Carla on the Teaching and Learning sub-committee: 'I ask for advice . . . they either say okay or that's rubbish.' Each layer offers input as to the impact of any change in policy or procedure on their unit. While time-consuming, this practice often avoided significant unexpected detrimental effects on students or staff, reviewed finally in Academic Board. Yet any decisions could be overturned in terms of funding and strategic planning by the executive.

Consultation, Consensus, Compliance and Conflict

Each university was constantly managing an entangled environment of unpredictable external pressures: policy shifts, stakeholder expectations, changing workplace rules, financial and other crises. Strategic plans or blueprints sought to provide certainty and direction internally for up to five years and formed the basis of the corporate storyline. But the purpose, process and effect of reform was understood differently by multiple stakeholders with an array of perspectives, interests and strategies at play. For executives, the practice of producing and disseminating the storyline meant they had ownership and personal investment that was not necessarily shared widely outside the senior corporate bubble. The strategic plan emerged out of an imperative for developing a consensus. The extended time it took to develop a blueprint, consult and then implement a new blueprint over years had unsettling affective effects because the process signalled a major restructure for Regional, as it had been for Go8. Consensual change is more likely to come out of collegial practices rather than driven top-down or through 'subtle' but coercive accountability mechanisms (Shore and Wright 2000). Both approaches imply to academics a lack of trust, make academics agents of their own reform in which they reluctantly comply while often disagreeing with the reforms' assumptions and objectives.

Stories are important as they tap into existing organizational practices and norms and develop justifications for change. The most powerful stories which tapped into the affective domain of academics were the fear of not surviving; the desire to excel, the passion for social justice. Less successful narratives were not grounded in what academics experienced and valued and led to cynicism and resistance. Poor leadership is when 'communications between leaders and followers in higher education are less than positive, "academic distancing" can occur . . . especially when interactions are transactional rather than relational' (Skorobohacz 2016: 1055). Kezar and Eckel (2002) argue that practitioners need to become cultural outsiders able to observe institutional patterns and therefore capable of changing them. But this requires the political will of executives to listen, and structural capacity of universities to establish processes of meaningful feedback, which facilitate mutual engagement and reciprocity upon which to build mutual trust. Leadership is a practice of doing, being, relating and saying, situated in interactive spaces of people and ideas, socio-material contexts, constantly in tension due to differing perceptions and understanding.

Chapter 6

THE PROFESSORIATE

AN INTERESTING BEAST OR LEADERSHIP IN CRISIS?

While leadership is the mantra in entrepreneurial universities, ironically, with the corporatization of higher education, the positioning of professors as leaders has been undermined and is increasingly ambiguous and ill-defined (Evans 2018, Macfarlane 2012a, Parke 2012). The troubled relationship between academic managers, professional staff and the professoriate evident in the United Kingdom, the United States and Australia arises in part from executive power or leaderism being mobilized, shifting power away from intellectual capital based on disciplinary expertise and authority earned through intellectual pursuits towards managerial capital gained through appointment (Bacon 2014, Bourdieu 1988a, Evans 2014, 2017, MacFarlane 2011, 2014, Morley 2013, Wright and Shore 2017). The professoriate not in management positions in three Australian universities – Go8, Utech and Regional – considered they had been marginalized and were no longer positioned as integral to key university decision-making, a pattern evident internationally (Ekma et al. 2017, Macfarlane 2014, Parke et al. 2012, Rowlands 2017, Shattock 2017, Wright and Ørberg 2008). Furthermore, the professoriate's perceptions and experiences of managing and managerialism have resulted in many professors either not seeking or exiting academic-management positions, creating a succession planning and workforce problem across the sector (McWilliam and Hatcher 2007, O'Connor 2015).

Magnifying these concerns, the leadership research in higher education has focused more on academic managers than professors (Macfarlane 2011), although there is increasing interest regarding the transformation of academic work and careers (e.g. Evans 2017, Strachan et al. 2012). Overall, research on leadership development suffers from an 'attention deficit' (Evans 2014) and its impact goes unexamined (Lumby 2012). Professorial leadership research has largely focused on individual life trajectories, building research capacity and academic professional development (Dopson et al. 2016, MacFarlane 2012b), recognizing the professoriate's capacity to influence others either intentionally (mentoring) or accidentally (Ball 2007, Evans 2014). Other than this, the professoriate's role in the corporate university is unclear.

'A Different Beast'? The Changing Profile of the Professoriate

When asked about the role of the professoriate not in formal positions, many senior and executive academic managers responded: 'that's an interesting question' that they had to 'think about'. Most professors not in academic management just laughed. These edifying responses signal the ambiguous role of the professoriate in the contemporary university. In her early career, Tanya (DVC, Go8, STEMM) recalled becoming a professor was the height of academic achievement: 'There was no promotion to professor, and personal chairs were an elite group. A lot of the university thought that Rome was burning once promotion to professor was allowed. . . . There's a great sense of it as a crowning achievement and personal satisfaction in becoming professor.' Prior to the 1990s restructuring of higher education in the UK and Australia, Academic Boards or Senates comprised largely of professors acting as a community of scholars (Rowlands 2011: 5–6), promoting a discourse of collegiality (Kligyte and Barrie 2014, Macfarlane 2014, 2017). Until the end of the 1970s academic habitus was, therefore, constituted around the language of collegiality and internal hierarchies of professorial leadership that produced a particular discourse of the role and function of the university but also ensured an uneven distribution of the intellectual capital. This resulted in the marginalization of those staff (such as women) who were 'not part of the favoured group', and also meant key decisions were 'typically arrived at by a small cadre of decision-makers' (Ramsden 1998: 23).

Without a promotion pathway to professor, the appointment to a personal chair (held for life not linked to a job) was judged through international peer review, a process dominated by 'boy's clubs' (Mertz 2009) that acted as gatekeepers of the field and who tended to appoint those like themselves (Fisher and Kingsley 2014, Grummell et al. 2009b), thus penalizing both women and new fields of research such as gender studies (Gray 2013, Hark 2016). Before the sector was unified in 1992, elected professors rotated through Heads of School or Dean roles for a specified time, enacting the Humboldian tradition of the 'virtue of service' in academic life, based on an implicit contract of reciprocity; an ongoing practice in some European and Nordic universities (Macfarlane 2007, Paradeise et al. 2009).

The shift from intellectual to managerial capital marked a move from patrimonial (based on rule-bound legacies) contractualism to appointment by VCs appointing Deans and Heads of School or market contractualism: 'Heads of School and Deans are on contract. Pro Vice Chancellors are on a short-term contract as they're development roles and they go back to faculties. But Deans going back to being a full professor are far less common' (Lance, Professor, Go8, STEMM). Corporate governance comprised an executive (usually VC and DVCs) and senior management group or Vice Chancellor's policy and planning committee comprising VC, DVCs, Deans and administrative heads responsible for all policy, strategic and financial planning (Coates et al. 2010, Rowlands 2011, Shattock 2017). While most of the Deans were formerly involved in teaching and/or research, few continued to do so (Clift et al. 2015). Consequently, being a formally designated manager was a significant career change and it was increasingly viewed as a 'vocation rather than an act of academic citizenship' (Macfarlane 2014: 2). While research and tenure were gone, academic managers gained or retained the professorial title.

Mobility also became a promotion strategy during the 1990s in the context of increased commercialization and internationalization. In developing fields such Business and Law competing with external labour markets, selection criteria became looser (e.g. no PhD required in Law) and incentives were offered (rapid promotion, bonuses), increasing salary differentiation among academics above the industrial award. Mid-sized Australian universities were considered to be stepping stones to a Go8 university to gain a chair or become a VC, or as an outreach testing ground for predominantly UK aspirational VCs. Most often, professorial aspirants had to move to gain a position in another university, often internationally because of the harder road to gain a personal chair until a career pathway to professorship was developed by the 2000s (Evans and Nixon 2015). The need to be mobile to get promoted to the professoriate penalized many but not all women who tended to have greater familial obligations than their male counterparts (Jos 2011). At the senior management level, mobility is a 'taken for granted gendered transnational hierarchy, a major aspect of men's leadership in large multinational organisations' (Hearn 2010: 243) such as universities, now sites of transnational masculinities (Connell 2016).

Importantly, despite the discourse of universities being ivory towers and not real-world workplaces, the life trajectory of most early and mid-career academics in this study was one of working in various occupations (professions, government and industry) prior to entering universities and developing research careers, many then becoming professors. But increasingly, recruits are being parachuted to become professors from industry, NGOs, government and the professions, many without PhDs or research experience. These recruits now fill strategic senior management positions (DVC and Dean) and, in 2021, two are Vice Chancellors, one without a PhD. These moves have cross-field effects, devaluing intellectual capital and foregrounding managerial capital informed by an entrepreneurial disposition and habitus and impact on decision-making.

The professoriate age profile has also become younger as career paths are more transparent and differentiated with increases in research-only and recruitment of star researchers. As a Dean (STEMM, man) noted at Regional, 'people are moving through the system faster to higher levels so that they get to professorial level at a younger age.' In his faculty, the eldest professor was sixty-five and the youngest in their early forties. Becoming a professor was now considered to be just the next step in promotion in a career path due to the development of transparent promotion pathways, an increase in the size of the professoriate also due to equal opportunity policies, but with women largely located at associate professor level (Bell 2010). Yet on promotion committees, what constitutes merit, methodological rigor, 'value' and 'impact' continue to be contested, particularly around professorship (Belfiore 2015). Those working with post-humanist, constructivist, Indigenous or feminist epistemologies fight to claim intellectual legitimacy in the context of institutionalized mindsets and administrative practices that privilege quantitative methodologies (Thornton 2013, Blackmore 2020c).

Addressing unequal opportunities for women, interrupted careers are now recognized in grant applications by the Australian Research Council and in promotion. Larger teams in grant applications have seen women increasing from 26 to 30 per cent of teams on ARC projects, 27–34 per cent becoming team leaders and a higher average success rate of 20 per cent greater than men (Australian Research Council 2021). But this recognition coincided with and has been countered for many women by an audit culture ratcheting up expectations (Currie 2008, Curtis 2016, Rowlands and Wright 2020) and narrowing what counts as success (Symonds et al. 2006). After decades of EEO policy, the professoriate continues to be male-dominated, with women still constituting by 2016 only 30 per cent of full professors in Australia, the United Kingdom and the United States (Eddy et al. 2016, Grove 2017, Mellors-Bourne and Metcalfe 2013) and significantly, both professors and senior academic managers are predominantly Anglo-European (Arday and Mirza 2018, Oishi 2017, Solanke 2017, Squire 2017). Over thirty years, therefore the composition and size of the professoriate has altered, with multiple pathways to 'becoming' a professor, although cultural and gender diversity still lags (Oishi 2017).

Line Dancing with Management

The scope and scale of academic practice had also increased (Evans 2017) due to the 'multidirectional relationship between habitus and practice within and between fields' of industry, government and universities in the context of heightened competition (Rowlands and Gale 2019: 144). Academic managers at all three universities were clear that the professoriate should play a significant role as intellectual leaders and in academic development to maintain high-quality research, build research capacity, develop collaborative research partnerships and participate in Academic Board committees (Macfarlane 2012b). The life trajectories of early and mid-career academics, doctoral students and post-doctoral fellows were increasingly reliant on professors building research teams, training in research management (ethics, HR and finance), workshopping writing grants and getting published, offering theoretical and methodological seminars, advising about career priorities, curriculum development and introducing colleagues to national and international networks (Leberman et al. 2016). Ultimately, professors as intellectual leaders have become for aspirational academics 'quality yardsticks' (Evans 2014: 54) acting as role model, mentor, advocate, guardian, acquisitor and ambassador (Macfarlane 2011), which in this culture of interdependency, many professors without institutional and research experience are unable to provide.

Professors were also expected to display a commitment to both faculty and the university strategic objectives (Sheik and Agaz 2018). Dennis (Head, Utech, STEMM) saw the professor's role was to mentor junior staff but 'not make them clones of you or your servants, but to grow groups . . . we build new labs but they're not professor Jones' lab. They are facilities'. Lauren (Dean, HASS) at Utech agreed that while 'professors have a great mentoring role and an informal leadership role . . . they need to understand university directions and work towards that . . . I try and keep all the system stuff away from them and the budget side . . . but they have to step up to the plate'. The discourse among senior management was how professors had to 'toe the line'. Utech's senior management agreed with Veronica (Head, HASS) that 'our VC has been very focused. When people are promoted to professor, he wants to see their foot on the accelerator rather than relaxing on their former achievements'. Vanessa, a DVC (Utech, HASS), stated that professors were expected to

> get with the program. Now in some places those people are prima donnas' which means they can do anything . . . we don't quite do that. We have our great professors, and we'll support, promote and acknowledge them, but it doesn't mean they can do anything or treat people any way they like. . . . So there has been a little bit of culture to change.

She recognized this created a dilemma with regard to recruiting star professors and getting the balance right: 'We do want to have the influence of what they've got to offer in the culture but we don't want a lose our fundamentals in the culture, so that's tricky'. Vanessa also acknowledged that for those who did not fit, 'better to part company rather than try and force problems that might exist', although this was not common practice.

At Go8, with six hundred plus professors dominating the winning of research grants internally and nationally, the refrain of research excellence was articulated by a PVC (Brett, HASS):

> Professors are supposed to lead the research agenda of the university. . . . If you want to improve research income you appoint a level E because they'll bring in the grants. A professor teaches a little bit and researches a lot. Most are passionate researchers. A few are passionate teachers and researchers. Rarely are they mainly teachers and they usually run departments.

While research was foregrounded, an ever-present tension for professors was how academic managers viewed the professors' role in teaching. At Utech, the teaching–research nexus discourse was strong. The VC Eric happily cited a new Dean asking the professoriate: 'Why is it that you people aren't connected to the undergraduate teaching program, isn't this your bread and butter . . . there was a lot of anxiety because that's the professor bit'. This Dean argued that senior staff should teach undergraduates to attract students. The research/teaching demarcation in the status hierarchy of the professoriate at Go8 was clear: a professor excelling in research and managing research institutes differed from a professor who teaches or manages. A research institute director in STEMM at Go8, Oliver, argued his role was to identify and build the next leadership pool in research. While a professor-as-mentor was built into workloads, performance management countered this:

I have all this knowledge, but I no longer want to go into the classroom . . . even though I know how to do it really well. The passion at my stage in career is to convey my research knowledge to fellow staff and the new generation. But there's nothing in our system that takes that really seriously. My Head asks how many discovery grants did you help other people get rather than how many did you get which keeps my reputation up *and* gets someone else into the game (Oliver).

In recruitment and promotion there was agreement among most professors with the Head in STEMM (Dennis) at Utech stating that 'while teaching is still absolutely critical, if there's no strong research track, applicants are just not looked at. Research is number one. Teaching is a very close number two. If it's a prof we're looking for leadership potential.'

Such practices discriminated against women who despite their increased research productivity tend to be judged on prior record not potential (Bell 2010, Diezmann and Greisheber 2009, Eddy et al. 2016). The escalating expectations regarding research and the metric tide, particularly in the material and medical sciences implicitly structured on career continuity, raised new barriers for women with caring responsibilities getting to be professors. Hyper-performativity becoming the norm after ERA resulted in many women deciding the price for themselves and family was too high (Huppartz et al. 2019). Star researchers were rapidly recruited and promoted, leapfrogging over those bearing the load of teaching (Saltmarsh et al. 2011). The 'hyperperformative' women who are seen to 'do it all' were often positioned in the university media and leadership development courses as role models, but their exceptionalism often discouraged those who felt the demands were too great, and those who valued a home/work balance. They often inspired some to compulsively strive too hard, which could impact on their health and well-being (Gornall and Salisbury 2012).

Picking Winners, Recruiting Talent in the Academic Celebrity Culture

This trend for multiple life trajectories into the professoriate was fuelled by the pressure for increased research output with productivity extracted through triennial enterprise bargaining agreements and research assessment as well as annual university and discipline rankings. Heightened expectations of research performance exacerbated discourses of excellence and external quality measures of global rankings, citations (h-index) and research income. This privileged a particular research professor norm in promotion and recruitment and, by default, devalued outstanding achievement in teaching, particularly in research-intensive institutions (Burrows 2012). Furthermore, the Go8 universities could afford to recruit star research professors, many on high salaries, bringing with them teams of graduate students and research fellows, often to take up named professorships funded by alumni, industry and philanthropists. Less wealthy universities, with fewer benefactors, weaker alumni networks, recruited stars at a cost to other faculties. To build intellectual capital, the three case universities were externally recruiting high-performing young academics through strategically targeted programmes or scholarships, tracking them into continuing positions with time out for research.

Recruitment of professors, because it was so strategic, was increasingly determined at the level of Dean and senior management and always linked to university research priorities rather than the needs of a discipline or school, unless they coincided. The key recruiters of professors – DVC Research, Deans and Heads of School and head-hunters if involved – were looking externally for a particular academic habitus. Dennis (Head, Utech (STEMM)) stated: 'It's always future potential . . . we're very proactive in looking for the high flying international reputable prof with already really strong track record behind them. It is an academic role but there's a real leadership dimension to the professoriate. We often won't promote an associate professor unless there's real leadership capability there.' Of course, possessing intellectual or managerial capital did not necessarily mean good leadership. But the picking of winners shifted where research investment was made and certainly reduced funds that could have been dedicated to early career researchers not included in programmes who also had heavy teaching and sessional loads, many of them women (Broadbent and Strachan 2016, Murgia and Poggio 2018, Saltmarsh et al. 2011).

Being strategic in recruitment meant aligning with institutional objectives. Larry, a Head at Utech (STEMM) said: 'we are trying not to spread our research foci too wide so we want them to fit into certain areas . . . very targeted so that we'll often not go to an open market. Rather we search for particular individuals and negotiate.' Not putting out jobs to the open market exacerbated any tendency to draw only on existing networks, which in some fields can be male-dominated. On interview panels, people often choose people like themselves because they feel more comfortable to work with them or recognize themselves in the applicant (Grummell et al. 2009a) or argue that they will 'fit' the disciplinary or organizational culture or position best, often resulting in less gender, race and epistemic diversity (Blackmore 2020).

Diversity was understood variously by the interviewees – most often as first-order differences such as gender, ethnicity or race, other times considered to be second-order differences such as leadership 'style' or disciplinarity (Ahmed 2004). One professor (Aaron, Regional, HASS) with a more entrepreneurial disposition argued diversity of industry background was important in senior academic leadership with 'people who are not only scholarly . . . but who have a sense of building a contemporary corporate university'. All mentioned the under-representation of women in leadership given that every academic manager's KPI quantified gender diversity. The fields of engineering, technology and the built environment were highly problematic yet areas of greatest expansion and future demand (Chief Scientist 2016) whereas other expanding fields of the health sciences and HASS were more 'gender balanced numerically' at all levels (Brad, Dean, Utech, STEMM). While the strategy of recruiting stars or restructuring aimed to strengthen targeted fields of research, this had implications for Heads responsible for staffing and budget. At Utech, a radical restructure of the Science

Faculty resulted in a school dominated by men at all levels and the dissolution of the HASS Faculty to create a new faculty resulted in a professoriate without women. Furthermore, star research professors only taught post-graduate students or were not in areas of high student demand because there is often little alignment between student demand and research priorities. Bryan as a Head (Go8, HASS) complained: 'Recruiting research capacity building professors . . . still go on and at my level but sometimes I'm not involved. Often at the whim of DVC Research . . . and that saddles me with the debt . . . it's not that I dislike the people, it's the mechanism.'

Across all three universities, directors of research institutes who are held responsible for research output in their KPIs could not understand why they were not on selection panels particularly at professorial level. Many had to rely on personal connections with the DVC Research, Deans and Heads of School to influence decisions. At Regional, a Director of a Research Centre (Jim) commented:

> I don't sit on the selection committees . . . I try to influence. I had a good relationship with the previous head. In the US I chaired search committees as well as department chair could shape, hiring, and tenure decisions to. Here I'm not on promotion committees ... because the research centre sits outside any of the departments, so we have little involvement in line management except informally. There's no line structure, it's through our own relationships.

The formal exclusion of the professoriate and even Research Directors or Heads in recruitment of either key researchers or academic managers meant research and strategic initiatives were being directed from above rather than those held responsible for building collaborations, research capacity building and outcomes.

Similarly, the strategy to establish strategic research institutes in response to ERA and ranking moved away from the longer-term building of research capacity and skewed towards faster quantifiable outcomes such as attracting research income and high-status researcher portfolios. On the one hand, most academic teaching and researching in the faculties had little knowledge or understanding of research institutes' role other than seeing them as inaccessible, elitist and outwardly focused. On the other hand, institute directors as research leaders often knew little of the research capacity of their disciplinary base being separate from mainstream teaching and research activities. A research director (Jim) at Regional commented: 'I don't even attend Faculty meetings unless there's something on research. I only go to annual planning days for the school and have an active role in that.' An A/Dean of Research (Roy, Regional) agreed, 'I don't know where all the researchers are.'

Finally, recruiting talent into research centres consolidated the trend towards research-only tracks for individual post-doctoral and fellowship scholars who in turn, if their contract ended, found it difficult to transfer into continuing research and teaching positions without teaching experience as career trajectories became more differentiated. Forced to live off 'soft money' on serial three-year contracts, many post-doctoral fellows interviewed considered leaving academia to go into private sector in order to 'live a life, get a house and have kids' (Judd, Go8, STEMM). Effectively, due to the low-cost institutional investment approach and high-cost individual investment, academic expertise built over the years was being lost, with long-term implications for the academic workforce (Petersen 2011).

Being Anointed: The Professorial Prestige Factor

The life trajectories of the academic managers and professors interviewed into the academy were wide-ranging across occupations (self-employed consultants, government, business, industry, teaching, welfare, medicine), countries and universities. Many had been research fellows and sessional teachers or contract researchers before gaining tenure, usually as Senior Lecturer. Nearly all had developed strong research records. Many who had remained at one university for twenty years or more provided a longitudinal lens of organizational change in one site.

Most professors, not academic managers, commented disparagingly about how the title of 'professor' has been bestowed on the rapidly expanding coterie of senior academic managers, many externally appointed and without teaching or research experience. Executives justified the title of professor as going with the job because it imparted senior academic managers with the credibility necessary to lead academics and to represent the university externally. The title also made management positions more attractive to external recruits, compensation for being on contract, although on significantly higher wages with bonuses for achieving KPIs. Martin (Pofessor, Go8, HASS) commented: 'People from outside would see this as an attractive place to be and like the status.' He pointed out this tension between academic and non-academics was 'evident in Academic Board'. In seeking this highest achievement for academics, some academics changed universities. A Dean, Dana (Regional, HASS), moved because she was unable to meet the academic criteria for full professorship at her previous university, despite arguing that 'every single executive dean right across the country was a professor some of them even from industry with no PhD. I could not convince the VC to go outside the policy'. Her condition on coming to Regional was being given the professorial title as 'I want to move up and I'm ambitious, and this is what I expect from Regional if I take on this role and fix your faculty for you'. Entrepreneurial capital required the professorial title for her sense of identity and legitimacy as Dean.

For most research and teaching professors who had climbed over an ever-increasing number of higher hurdles, the freer bestowing of the title anointed on those in positional roles had diluted the status of being a professor. Jeanette, a professor (Go8, HASS), laughed: 'The title and role of professor has been radically devalued. My day-to-day experience bares no relation to the idea of a professor and those professors not in management have the administrative burden. It is just a mess.' Furthermore, multiple trajectories into the professoriate and senior management meant some professors had highly specialist research-only careers and others had only government or industry backgrounds. Without having participated in the breadth of committee activities, teaching or research meant that the 'traditional' academic habitus of knowing, being and relating across and through all aspects of the university was changing as professors' institutional knowledge became more specialized or was non-existent creating a knowledge management issue (Barnett 2011).

External recruitments into senior management also altered internal career trajectories. '40 years ago you could go from being a very good researcher straight into a senior management role. Now senior management is more promotion through professional development to become professional administrators. . . . Currently, a lot of senior managers now just do stuff that they know is going to work' (Arthur, Professor, Go8, STEMM). The path from Dean or Academic Board Chair into executive leadership was closed, with many in senior management not 'having run anything' (Gary, Dean, HASS, Go8). Bryan (Head Go8, HASS) expressed his frustration 'because you have larger numbers of people in management positions who have not gone through that route. The VC, Provost and DVCs haven't been Head of School. No-one understands what a head of school actually does.'

In turn, the multiplicity of career pathways into the professorship changed the professor's sense of their role and responsibility to the university and academic service, impacting on shared understandings of what constituted 'being a professor'. 'There are more professors and you're not a Chair. . . . There's not the same sense necessarily of responsibility. There's a strong sense of responsibility for nurturing and mentoring in your discipline . . . but less a sense of now I'll take on a leadership (management) role' (Nicole, DVC, Go8, HASS). Many professors stated they did not like what managerial values stood for, others lacked the institutional experience and most did not want to relinquish their research.

To add to the complexity of who is a professor, institutional partnerships arising from engaging with industry and NGOs in research have produced a new class of associate or adjunct professors, particularly in medicine and health, with training hospitals and material science innovation sites built on or near universities. This trend was energized by the push towards clinical practice, internships and work-integrated learning in the professional fields. As explained by Rob (Dean, Regional, STEMM):

> I've got the head of the clinical school of the hospital, an oncologist. . . . We don't employ him, and yet half of his salary is paid for out of these funds. He has formal accountabilities for teaching, for management, for leadership. . . . Does the university only care if it's engaged with people with a pay slip? We anoint them with a title . . . a blurring of the lines where people are fractionally employed or not at all employed by us, but are ostensibly our agents and as real as any academic.

Doctors, engineers, journalists and bureaucrats have been strategically recruited as adjuncts to their discipline, usually part-time, but some as full professors to build engagement with external stakeholders. As outsiders they were often unaware of the escalating expectations of a professorship or felt they deserved it as they were bringing in different but equivalent expertise. Senior academic managers who knew the effort required expressed concern about acquiring the title of professor knowing that their internal credibility was linked to research status. Brett (PVC, Go8, HASS) cited a new executive academic manager's discomfort over her title. 'This is an old fashion way of thinking. The contribution she's making to the university is in her management capabilities and her leadership capabilities. Now if you don't recognize that with your professorial appointments then you're not recognizing the real way in which the place functions.' But as managerial and entrepreneurial capital claim equivalence to intellectual capital, becoming a professor has become easier for some to achieve, on the one hand, and harder for others; academic citizenship is losing ground. The title is losing meaning and status, a concern in post-truth times as a 'professor' may claim intellectual authority publically, taking ideological positions that are not research-based (Macfarlane 2007).

Recalcitrant, Rebellious and Responsive Professors

Various tropes were articulated among academic managers and administrators about the professoriate: their recalcitrance about becoming entrepreneurial, their rebellion against corporate management, some just 'cruising' and others 'never present in their offices and always travelling'. A dominant view was that the professoriate had autonomy and flexibility not offered in other professions (or administration), that the corporate world is tougher and therefore professors should be satisfied. Overall, the professoriate had to be 'managed' (Rhoades 2014). Comparisons were made of professors 'teaching in England and this informs their research. They're reading each other's work and talking to their colleagues in the university across the road and making certain curriculum is being discussed . . . it's very easy for that to slide here' (Nancy, Head, Go8, HASS). Another Head (Michelle Go8, HASS) considered the 'flattening of salaries at Level E' gave professors little incentive. Such caricatures of professors as being other-worldly, self-absorbed, self-aggrandizing or living in an ivory tower and therefore not good leaders (Macfarlane 2012a) ignored the transformation of the conditions of academic labour in the UK (e.g. Times Higher Education 2018) and the industrial conditions and funding arrangements peculiar to Australian universities (Bexley et al. 2011, Coates et al. 2010).

Furthermore, the professoriate was positioned differently within each university's corporate logic and articulated variously at the faculty or school level according to the KPIs of each Dean or Head. At Utech, building research capacity in STEMM was the focus as one Head (Dennis) stated. 'We have professors who are just blinkered and just write papers, produce grad students and teach. We can tolerate this if high performing in other areas but the expectation is that you'll take some junior staff under your wing, get them grant active, co-author the first few papers, bring them into the system.' Conversely, Dana, another Head at Utech (STEMM), was pressured to improve her discipline's publication and impact measures for ERA. She was finding it difficult to persuade some professors to publish, even though they were productive in research capacity building. Professors, she said, 'have to be able to bring funding plus write publications, provide evidence of output and impact, as well as mentor new people, provide feedback to graduate writing, partner up with people on projects and bring the next generation along'.

In a disciplinary area characterized by less research and more teaching due to escalating international student numbers, Veronica (Head, Utech, HASS) said all her professors ended up in formal leadership roles – Associate Deans, programme directors, research centre directors – 'because they have good management skills'. She was reliant on Associate Professors to undertake more informal than formal mentoring across various groups and projects, which she managed through a governance group which involved all committee chairs (research, teaching and learning). Her aim was to develop leadership capacity by delegating 'to let them do what they want to do and keep my mouth shut just to give them that responsibility. Then we come together as a group'. At Utech, Kirsten (Head, HASS) argued that the professoriate was disconnected from management because they did not fully understand the wider context:

> They have a key leadership role but . . . sometimes they don't fully understand the environment the university has to operate. It's not like it used to be, there's fear of the future. . . . They don't like budget restrictions. Sometimes they feel undervalued from a societal perspective, that government should fund universities more. That's lovely philosophically. Most academics always want to see data, studies and evidence and then they'll pick that apart and debate it.

This desire to have evidence for decisions in a university should be no surprise. Kirsten had moved out of research because of her evident practical mastery of management, and her disposition enabling her to accommodate corporate logics, assuming an altered habitus informed by managerial imperative. 'I guess I'm more pragmatic. If this is what we have and this is what we've got to work for, we need to get done. Have the debate, now make a decision.'

At the research-intensive Go8, the discourse of research excellence dominated but also required recalibrating the role of the professor in ways that addressed the new student 'clientele'. A Dean (Ken, STEMM) stated: 'The most essential role of the professoriate is developing new talent. It is not about defining the discipline, which is what the old professors think it is, or making the character of the department so that the department can deliver an educational experience. The students really don't care what that old fart thinks anymore.' Any sense of academic identity derived from engaging with and enhancing their own intellectual field was now gone, as if disciplinary identity did not impact on the student experience. The professor was now detached from the discipline, putting student engagement central while decontextualizing what was taught and why: 'it's not their team, it's not their department, it's the people they interact with whoever they are. They have to be agile in their thinking about the future of their knowledge, the future of their disciplines and the professions are changing. They must think about what a client needs' (Ken, Dean, Go8, STEMM). Curriculum in this context was now referred to by managers as 'content' (Colet 2017) and many considered content was secondary to student 'satisfaction' in evaluations (Blackmore 2009a).

Others at Go8 saw some older professors impeding rather than enhancing the careers of early or mid-career researchers. A Head (Jessica, HASS) when identifying potential of ECERs and strategically creating research incubators with funding for small collaborative projects found she 'helped a lot of people get promoted that have been kept back, often by professors. Yet the younger academics CV, sometimes were better than the professor', a defensive practice she saw produced by hyper-performativity in a research-intensive university. A new professor at Go8 (Meghan) noticed self-promoting professors in her faculty (HASS) and argued for performance reviews to have formal expectations regarding mentoring: 'It's a failure of leadership both in succession planning and the generation where it's all me, me, me.' One strategy undertaken by Heads of School and Deans was to circle around the professors and involve the 'hungrier' Associate Professors and Senior Lecturers: 'To open up different agendas in the school I tapped into people at level C and D, getting them to feel there was a space for them' (Justine, Head, Regional, HASS).

Expectations and the practices of professors were therefore varied, university- and disciplinary-specific. But academic management interviews identified an overarching sense that professors were disconnected from 'the university' in terms of what management wanted them to do. At Utech, a DVC (Martha) held the professoriate responsible for disengaging with the university and teaching in particular:

> The professoriate has disconnected itself from the business of the university. They don't really want to know about it. That's managerialism, it's negative, and they don't need to know about it and they're quite happy in their own space doing their own thing. Now if the core business of a faculty is teaching, and the professoriate is missing from it, what are they doing, where are they adding value because it's this core that's paying for them.

Management saw this disconnect from teaching a consequence of a resistant academic habitus to necessary reforms, whereas the professoriate considered the disconnect arose from rapidly changing work conditions, unrealistic and escalating demands in terms of the scope and scale of intellectual leadership, a lack of voice, managerialism and destructive leadership (Chapter 7).

The Management/Academic Disconnect

Across all three universities, non-management professors identified an academic/ managerial divide despite most academic managers having been academics, a pattern replicated in the United Kingdom and the United States (Shattock 2017, Rowlands 2017). In the parallel systems of decision-making and line management from VCs down to Heads, a techno-administrative infrastructure responsible to a DVC (Administrative); and Academic Board and its committees in Faculties and Schools, men dominated senior management positions across all three decision-making domains and women dominated the domestic labour of professional services and Academic Board committees (Rowlands 2019). Furthermore, the Academic Board now comprised ex-officio attendees (Deans, DVCs, PVCs), some without academic experience, outnumbering elected academics or students. Some Boards were chaired by the VC or Provost and not an elected academic, as at Utech (Rowlands 2017). University Councils are now dominated (average of 70 per cent) by non-academics, a lack of expertise not typical of governance in industry (Pelizzon et al. 2021). A Dean (Gary, HASS) referred to the more traditional Board at Go8 which largely comprised professors:

> I don't think the professoriate are a meaningful category and an old technology. We have an Academic Board structure that's still privileges the professoriate and nobody really knows what that is. There's hundreds of them and they don't have a shared status anymore or constitute a sort of qualified elite. They're just people who've been for all sorts of various reasons promoted to a certain rank or appointed.

Most of the professors interviewed felt they had little input into developing university research priorities and policies or recruitment. Selection panels for senior academic managers did not include professors and only the Academic Board Chair was included on selection panels for VC. There were no longer public presentations by applicants for senior management or professorial positions or meetings with the professoriate enabling input. The repositioning of the professoriate was summed up by Dennis (Head, Utech, STEMM): 'The professoriate used to be where the thinking of the university used to happen. It doesn't happen here so much anymore. It happens in the faculty executives and that's usually deans, heads of school, assistant deans, and any other people that they might pull in.'

While the role of the professoriate had both expanded in terms of the scope and scale of their activities (internationalization, engagement, research collaborations, research capacity building, policy service, scholarly output and media presence), the professoriate had reduced capacity to influence the university's direction (Colley and White 2019). This intensification of academic labour and reconfigured priorities created ethical issues. The pressure for income generation and winning highly competitive ARC grants with less than one in five success rates refocused professorial attention towards sourcing research income through industry partnerships, often just to keep contract staff employed. But multiple projects reduced their time to achieve measurable output. Partnerships with business or government took time and raised key issues for many professors over ownership of research, academic freedom and ethics and whether the funding was partner and not research directed (Chubb and Watermeyer 2017, Hancock 2020). In HASS, academics were more likely to seek philanthropic funding, which shared similar aims, but philanthropists have specific agendas for what they fund, do not welcome uninvited approaches, do not fund what can be funded by government and often require strong personal involvement of a sponsor. The relationship between institutionalized academic and public intellectual work had become complex, and some fields, such as cultural studies, are forever in tension, as is the humanities and social sciences generally (Andrews 2015).

For research professors, ERA and rankings had significant impact on how and who they worked with in projects and therefore their capacity to mentor. An entangled web of audit technologies such as research assessment, metrics, performance reviews, national and university priorities led to gaming about with whom, how and what research was undertaken, incrementally changing academic practice. Academics sought to second guess, drawing on 'the product of internalized knowledge – expressed as inclinations, tendencies and propensities – and which enable agents to make sense of not only what is taking place but what might take place, so as to realize a particular aim or objective' (Rowlands and Gale 2017: 140, Chubb et al. 2017, Hughes and Bennett 2013, Leathwood and Reid 2013, Lipton 2017).

Market contractualism had become embedded in the transactional mode of research partnerships and institutional mechanisms such as workload formulae, in promotions or applications where individuals are compared to each other on the basis of quantifiable outcomes such as student evaluations and metrics ('living with the H-Index') (Burrows 2012), practices converting collegial or pedagogical relationships into transactional ones. Such measures often have 'perverse effects' when individuals are 'incentivized to compete and perform according to the new norms of accounting' (Shore and Wright 2000: 422) rather than identifying what is significant in their field, practices that value the entrepreneurial disposition and can produce a compliance-habitus (Rowlands and Gale 2019), changing the product, process and value of intellectual capital. Macfarlane (2017) identifies a moral continuum ranging from the self-serving academic to the collaborative and collegial academic citizen. The entrepreneurial university encourages a more instrumentalist individualist approach to collaboration and less so a collective and generous disposition of practice that nurtures relational contractualism (Yeatman 2002). Macfarlane (2017: 472) argues 'forms of collaboration [which] are essentially self-regarding illustrating the pressures of performativity via increased research output (collaboration-as-performativity), through practices that reinforce the power of established networks (collaboration-as-cronyism) and the exploitation of junior researchers by those in positions of power and seniority (collaboration-as-parasitism)'.

Most professors in this study were critical of the performative demands which they considered undermined their passion for research (Bansel and Davies 2010). But there was a range of personal dispositions, attitudes and responses according to an individual's positioning and personal interests. For example, 'where personal, moral and disciplinary identities align with the impact agenda, the emotional response is positive and productive. For many academics, however, misalignment gives rise to emotional dissonance' (Chubb et al. 2017: 555). Senior academics expressed this dissonance, were positioned as advantaged and yet felt disempowered, unable to change how things were done. They experienced or were complicit in the exploitative aspects of universities being quasi-employers of sessional/contract staff. Many but not all recognized how

> bibliometric evidence of co-authorship has become a proxy for collaboration despite the multiple people involved in the socio-political and emotional and often gendered dynamics of the processes of its production of collaborative outputs – hierarchies between junior /senior academics, casually employed research fellows not included as authors on 'a continuum of moral permissibility based on the distinction between self-regarding and other-regarding behaviour'. (Macfarlane 2017: 475)

Most sought, where possible, 'collaboration-as-intellectual generosity in undertaking research as inquiry, collaboration-as-mentoring of colleagues and students, and collaboration-as-communication with the dissemination of their research', while adhering to professional ethics (Macfarlane 2017: 472). Collegial modes of collaboration meant sharing knowledge and practices in a mutually beneficial way for all stakeholders based on reciprocity and recognition of what is required to do this work: an implicit moral and ethics of care or relational contractualism (Hey and Leathwood 2009).

Such collaborations, while emotionally demanding and time-consuming, were rarely recognized or rewarded because there is no measurable outcome (Acker 2012), just as there was little recognition of the emotional damage done with audit technologies such as ERA (Chubb and Watermeyer 2017). Not counted in the pseudo-contractual arrangements of academic work but central to collegiality was academics being good academic citizens and feeling obligated to undertake public service. Most professors elaborated on their numerous roles: they were members of panels on national research councils; disseminated their accumulated 'grantsmanship' knowledge to build research capacity cross-nationally; led professional associations; lobbied for their disciplinary fields; wrote submissions to government inquiries; presented evidence in courts; organized conferences; were members of learned academies, doctoral panels, external committees, advisory boards, statutory authorities and university reviews; and wrote multiple references for graduates and colleagues. This doing of public service and saying of expertise was recognized externally, accrued individual and institutional reputational value, but was not 'counted' internally (Chubb et al. 2017). It was a gifting of academic labour done as unpaid 'structural overtime' in personal time, as Eriksen (2006) argued.

> A gift economy, which preceded the monetary based economy, is where individuals work collaboratively or share knowledge, ideas and goods without the assumption of reciprocity because it is the ethical/professional thing to do

and may contribute to the wider public good. . . . The gift economy is based on trust and the gift is unconditional. . . . The focus is on the gift and not monetary value. It is about gifting something or time freely and for free.

But the implicit psychological contract that underpinned academics gifting their labour in return for relative professional autonomy has been broken with market contractualism which explicitly defines the conditions and limits of the exchange and its monetary value, simultaneously appropriating and denying the relational labour (collegiality, care) upon which it relies (Adkins 2012).

Destructive Leadership

There is now recognition as to the emotional labour of teaching, researching and leading and the significance of the affective economy of an institute, faculty or school that is reliant on relationships. For example, Institute Directors relied heavily on their capacity to both mount a strong storyline and nurture a personal relationship with Deans and the DVC Research. These relationships were easily marred by interpersonal friction, the unequal social relations of gender and race, the assumed value of a field of research, and the Institute's success at meeting KPIs of winning grants, earning external income and doctoral completions. The professoriate and course leaders relied on the capacity of the Dean to relay the story up the line to senior management, requiring persuasive stories and compelling leadership. A professor (Karl, STEMM) at Regional bluntly stated: 'our dean is not that bright and the worst listener. A terrifying combination'. A course restructuring imposed by the Dean was 'a backdoor way to rationalize teaching offerings' and had the unintended consequence of creating increased work for academics and students with large class numbers with Masters' students in classes of 150 undergraduates saying: 'why am I spending all this money'? This professor argued that 'there's a difference between consultation and power . . . this was power' whereas 'consultation meant asking colleagues 'to help me come up with a way of achieving those objectives, then I think the spirit in the faculty would be very different'. Kurt's primary concern was that young talent would leave and the 'word would get out that this was not a good place to work'. Another professor, Roy (Regional, STEMM), concurred that there was lack of a clear story projected by the Dean who he liked 'very much personally but he's actually very weak at articulating and communicating and so people have just walked out of those meetings shaking their heads'. This dysfunctional culture required the intervention of the DVC Research. Generic management incompetence is one aspect of destructive leadership – 'when decisions are not informed by evidence nor negotiated, imposed without appropriate consultation, short term rather than long-term perspective, with an inability to realize the consequences, poor communication and lack of to understanding how change works' (Klaus and Steele 2020: 4).

Many professors in the three universities spoke of how a weak academic manager, a bullying or a narcissist manager or professor, could damage the work ethos. Narcissist management is when an individual filters every judgement through the self, does not accept feedback and often resorts to vindictive micro-management (Samier and Atkins 2009). Toxic managerialism is when individuals exert their power overtly through verbal abuse or covertly through proceduralism based on seemingly neutral procedures, which had the potential to become a form of institutional bullying (e.g. individuals negotiating workloads, using statistically invalid student evaluations to argue teaching incompetence) (Skinner et al. 2015). Some academic managers were seen to use discursive and institutional tools to punish even senior academics by blocking (or not supporting) promotion or appointments, not providing resources, closing courses or circulating negative discourses about individual professors. Universities were, because of this complexity, open to this form of destructive leadership with some in positions of power 'predisposed to destructive leadership behaviours' due to the 'unique nature of leading academic followers and their lack of preparation for the role of a leader' (Pawlowska et al. 2010: 482). Klaus and Steele (2020: 2) define destructive leadership as

> the systematic and repeated behavior by a leader, supervisor, or manager that violates the legitimate interest of the organization by undermining and/or sabotaging the organization's goals, tasks, resources and effectiveness and/or the motivation, well-being or job satisfaction of subordinates. . . . Destructive leadership behavior can be physical or verbal, as well as active or passive. . . . It does not require there be an intent to harm; therefore, it is possible a leader can act destructively without being consciously aware of it.

Bullying, as the professors at Regional in this instance feared, readily cascades down to influence daily interactions (Zabrodska et al. 2011). The emotionally corrosive effect is to produce a toxic environment which detracts from everyday work, diverts emotional and intellectual energy and time, creates divisions and reduces trust in management, thereby creating a level of cynicism towards what academic managers (or colleagues) say when knowing what they do.

Paradoxical Positioning of the Professoriate

The role of the professor is therefore situated ambiguously according to their discipline and university, complex in terms of contradicting perceptions and expectations, and as a cohort undergoing intergenerational change, experiencing an altered academic habitus as the ideal of academic citizenship has been eroded with the changing profile and repositioning of the professoriate. Despite decades of equal opportunity policy, positional and research leadership remains male-dominated. There was evidence in the data of 'traditional hegemonic white heterosexual able-bodied male-dominated status-driven hierarchies' of the 'god professor'; of bureaucratic micro-managerial masculinities; of corporate self-serving careerists; as well as entrepreneurial masculinities (Hearn 2010: 22). There were also examples of caring masculinities: 'masculine identities that . . . embrace values of care such as positive emotion, interdependence, and relationality' (Elliott 2016: 240). For feminist scholars, the issue was regardless of their leadership practices was whether these men recognized that their position of privilege was most likely based on their partner undertaking the greater load of familial labour of care and how that recognition changed their attitudes and practices both at work and in the household (Angervall et al. 2015). Similarly, there were examples of outspoken feminists, entrepreneurial femininities, micro-managing leadership and careerist women leaders. The feminist question was whether they had the disposition and will to advocate for women, or whether they appropriated feminism as part of a neoliberal rhetoric of individual success of being a woman (Colley and White 2019). While some professors identified as feminist, and overtly acted to improve gender equity, such identification was not made by any of the academic managers.

Overall, many interviewees considered that the competitive culture of the entrepreneurial university was producing a more aspirational and individualized career-driven, self-promoting performative academic habitus, one who was strategically astute and less inclined to be a good academic citizen unless with benefits. As summed up by Nancy (Professor, HASS) at Go8:

> The role of the professoriate? It's an interesting question. In any other organization they would be seen as the most senior respected colleagues and members of the university community. At one level they are, but only to a certain point. Ten years ago they were the most senior body that really had the interests of the university at heart. Now it is more individual interests for some at heart.

The pressure to perform led many academics to put self-interest first, being unwilling to undertake peer review for the journals in which they published while relying on collegial goodwill of others. Hyper-performativity, many professors believed, meant early and mid-career academics were beginning to instrumentally judge every new project or collegial relationship for its strategic advantage for them as individuals, as a transactional arrangement not collegiality, always looking towards the end game, therefore producing a 'compliance-habitus effect' with 'implications of this for sustained academic engagement and voice in academic fields' (Rowlands and Gale 2019: 156). The question is how much the academic habitus has accommodated to the new rules of the game of a market-driven sector. As the corporate logic has become naturalized, the academic habitus has become more differentiated, in a constant state of improvisation and 'pragmatic accommodation to contingent events' and external controls, thereby governing the self (Nixon 2015: 10).

Rarely articulated in the interviews with line managers about the role of the professoriate was the idea of the professoriate informing university policy or being public intellectuals. Only one Dean (Rosalind, Utech, HASS) considered the professoriate should inform thinking about the role of the university and how it relates to society: 'They are the academic leaders. They are part of what should be helping to keep us thinking about us being as a public good because they should be being reflective.' The notion of 'professing' was an anathema to many in executive management. They wanted loyalty to the institution (under market contractualism) and not a professor who as an academic citizen prioritizes the production and dissemination of knowledge for its own sake, has loyalty to the academic profession and who takes up responsibility out of a sense of service to community and the public to profess. This may 'add value' to the institution but does not have monetary value.

Underpinning this limited and limiting managerial view of the role of the professor as a public intellectual is a wider re-conceptualization of professionalism generally. In the twentieth-century welfare state the professions (education, health, welfare, law, journalism) were advocates for their fields and a critical conscience of the state and public policy. In the twenty-first century, professional expertise is increasingly treated as technical knowledge to be contracted as required by government or even universities who ironically contract expertise externally not internally. Market contractualism is premised upon individualized relations of privatized provision and not based on trust or commitment to the public good (Brint 2001).

Evetts (2009: 246) distinguishes between organizational and occupational professionalism. Organizational professionalism is based on 'rational-legal forms of authority and hierarchical structures of responsibility and decision-making. It involves increasingly standardized work procedures and practices, consistent with managerialist controls . . . and on external forms of regulation and accountability measures, such as target-setting and performance review', implying a lack of trust. Occupational professionalism relies on collegial authority and 'involves relations where employers and clients trust practitioners. Thus, authority – not control – is based on practitioner autonomy, discretionary judgment, assessment, particularly in complex cases' and any controls of self-regulation are based on 'codes of professional ethics monitored by professional institutes and associations' (Evetts 2009: 246).

This crisis in trust accordingly changes the relationship of professionals, including academics, with the state, their publics and students on the assumption that external accountabilities are equated to 'the public'. It is dangerous when the role of professors as public intellectuals is increasingly contested in a post-truth context where opinion is equated as equivalent to expertise. Bourdieu (1989) sees the intellectual as a bi-dimensional being who both belongs to a field of study and identifies with it, but also uses their authority and expertise to be a public advocate of that field, speaking on behalf of the disenfranchised and marginalized as that is often where their research leads them as there is increased social and economic inequality. And this is where public intellectuals may stray 'beyond their immediate academic expertise' (Macfarlane 2012a: 15), one which executive managers seek to control in fear of reputational damage.

Other cultural producers who provide an expert voice for their field are also losing ground against multiple sources of information, with many voices propagating misinformation and conspiracy theories, challenging the university as a key site of knowledge production and legitimation. This should be a major concern for university managers as academics are the producers and legitimators of knowledge based on their practices of peer review, collegiality and collaboration. The university therefore ironically cannot be characterized as a learning organization where there is co-production of knowledge and collegial expertise. Over the past decades 'academic (managerial) leadership, formal authority and power worked in ways which localized organizational capital trumped international scientific capital' (Fumasoli 2019: 401). By default more than intent, this devalues the 'critical being' of intellectual capital and the 'cognitive, affective and social dimensions of criticality' that are the core of academic work (Jameson 2019: xxvi). Certainly 'critical leadership, particularly of the high quality, other-serving deep-thinking kind, can be found to exist within positional management and indeed in governance, often linked with excellent academic research' (Jameson 2019: xxiv). But the trends charted here indicate a disturbing disconnect between intellectual leadership and positional leadership and a value dissonance as to the role of the university.

Chapter 7

ACADEMIC DISCONTENT, DISENCHANTMENT, DISENGAGEMENT AND DISTRUST

A CASE OF DESTRUCTIVE LEADERSHIP?

After two decades of higher education restructuring, there was an emerging problem in Australia, the United Kingdom, the United States and Europe for executive management in universities. All levels of academics expressed growing discontent with their work conditions and disenchantment with university management (Bexley et al. 2011, Blackmore and Sachs 2007, Brown 2015, Coates et al. 2010, Deem et al. 2007, Nussbaum 2010, Olssen et al. 2004, Waitere et al. 2011, Wright and Ørberg 2008). They expressed concern over the future of the university, as in, for example, Hil's (2012) *Whackademia*; Collini's (2012) *What Are Universities For?*; and Furedi's (2017) *What's Happened to the University?* Academic disenchantment with university management arose in part, as argued earlier (Chapter 6), from edu-capitalism's penetration into the field; from academics disputing the direction governments and executives were taking the university; due to their disenfranchisement from key decision-making; from a perceived disconnect of managers with core academic practices of teaching and research; and from job precarity and work intensification.

Academic discontent has been palpable in the plethora of texts, manifestos, blogs (e.g. *Shit#Academics Anonymous*) and conferences on universities in crisis, summed up by Peseta et al. (2017: 237):

> we wrestle with our location in the measured university: endless cycles of organizational restructure promising liberation from past inefficiencies; our capacities being counted in ways that exclude our participation from the process and the final outcome; and the constant accounting for the worth of our thinking and the quality of our judgements . . . academic life is a peculiar kind of difficult work. It is tough for an outsider to see past the privilege, and even harder for them to empathize.

Alternative perspectives about how to address this discontent are offered, in *The Good University* (Connell 2019), in the 'slow professor' movement (Berg and Seeber 2016, Enders and de Weert 2015) and *#WomenEd* (Fuller and Berry 2019).

More collective activity includes the establishment of the Australian Association of University Professors in 2019 and Dutch academics striking over structural overtime (Jongsma et al. 2020). Organizational theorists Alvesson and Spicer (2016: xi) argued in *The Stupidity Paradox:* 'for universities there were too many kinds of stupidity to mention; pointless branding exercises, ritualistic box ticking, misguided attempts at visionary leadership, thoughtless pursuit of rankings; which distracted from educating students and doing research.' They concluded: 'by avoiding careful thinking, people are able to get on with the job. Not thinking frees you up to fit in and get along.' While universities promote 'thought professors', Noonan (2014) argues 'thought time' has become 'money time'. All feared in 2021 for the future of the university after decades of managerialization, marketization, commercialization and privatization. A decade earlier, Bexley et al. (2011 x–xi) warned: 'There is a general disquiet with the leadership and management of institutions, although the extent varies greatly across institutions. . . . On the national [Australian] policy front, few academic staff believe the higher education sector is heading in the right direction or that there is strong government support for the university sector.'

Easy to reject as privileged professors complaining, but if taken seriously, for professors in whom the university's intellectual capital is invested to feel marginalized should be a key concern for executive managers and considered to be a major workforce issue (Coates et al. 2010, Bothwell 2018). The sentiments echoed by the academics at all levels in this study of three Australian case study universities (Go8, Utech and Regional) were of satisfaction with, if not pleasure in, their work (Bentley et al. 2013, Blackmore and Sachs 2007) but of being 'pulled in too many different directions' (Dugas et al. 2018). Academics also felt the workload was unmanageable (Ryan et al 2013), that administrative overload detracted from the core work of teaching and research and that job insecurity (NTEU 2018a) meant many were considering leaving the sector or going overseas (Bexley 2011: x–xi).

Careless Management: The Psychological Contract Is Broken

Underpinning this disenchantment was growing distrust in the university as an employer. Academic employment insecurity was endemic with 70 per cent of academics on contract or casual in 2018 and a shrinking group of continuing teaching and researching positions, all facing redundancy with any restructure (NTEU 2018a, Ryan et al. 2013). Academic managers, on contract and 'on call 7/24', were well compensated by high salaries and bonuses. Ewen, an academic manager, noted that Go8's strategic plan 'says we have to be available 24/7 to the students' requiring an addictiveness to work. The insecurities of market contractualism produced risk aversion behaviours and adherence to managerial imperatives or 'habitus compliance' (Rowlands and Gale 2017, 2019). Academic work has been reconfigured; stamped by auditing, standardization, financialization, overwork and unpaid overtime (NTEU 2018b, THE 2018); and scaled up through incremental creep as academics now teach off-campus, build national and international research collaborations and networks and internationalize at home to promote rankings. The scope of what academics do has widened – earning external income, developing industry partnerships, informing professional practice, working with local communities, offering policy advice, undertaking consultancies and producing measurable outputs to boost the 'metric tide' (Wilsdon et al. 2015). Escalating expectations have made academics into 'superheros', as indicated on position descriptions (Pitt and Mewburn 2016) that assume a 'hyper-professionalism' premised on long hours of unpaid labour (Gornall and Salisbury 2012, Gornall et al. 2015, Sang et al. 2015).

The speed with which academic work is done has accelerated due to digitalization of all aspects of administration, teaching and research (Hassan 2017). Response times have reduced, and space/time has collapsed. Work invades home-time and space where the familial physical and emotional labour is often greater for women than men (Sellar and Cole 2017, Wajcman 2010, Wajcman and Todd 2016). The normalization of such work practices is now endemic, and lack of thought time has reduced academic time to resist debilitating practices (Noonan 2014, Ryan 2012). The new modalities of digital governance afford academic management a new mechanism of steering from a distance (Williamson 2016a), digital systems which 'regulate individual freedom and personalization in terms of time, social relations, communication and the form and notation, management and control and shape what it is to "work"' (Selwyn 2014: 110). Digital technologies, built over decades, are resistant to change and often find an easy 'fit' with the 'tacit' grammar of higher education that is based increasingly on '"managerialist" techniques of measurement, monitoring, comparison and evaluation' (Selwyn 2014: 110), while developing its own techno-administrative logic and pace without regard for academic practice. Digitalization has reduced academic input over professional decisions regarding content and pedagogy because of the mediating role of digital and instructional designers, who control what goes onto the website and how it looks, standardizing more often than innovating (Neary and Saunder 2011). Academics' relations with government, industry, HDR students, partnerships and research grants are now managed by 'third space professionals': research administrators or 'audit market intermediaries' (Enders and Naidoo 2019, McClure 2016, Veles and Carter 2016).

Importantly, being institutionally nimble meant casualization of labour as well as 'intensification, exhaustion, and no spots for the people with energy and enthusiasm' (Kellie, NTEU). In the context of job insecurity, university productivity relied heavily on academic's professional, emotional and time investment in research, teaching and service (Bristow et al. 2017, Randall-Moon et al. 2013). Many academics felt exploited as they undertook significant unpaid 'structural overtime', driven both by a passion for their work, often a sense of moral purpose and professionalism, and by fear of not surviving in their job (Hughes and Bennett 2013, Ryan 2012). Flexibility meant more not less work for academics (Chung 2016). Research on academic identities indicates 'a collective anxiety about the deteriorating conditions of the accelerated academy . . . the occurrence of role overload . . . academic stress attributed to perceptions of job insecurity . . .

and mental health issues' (Macfarlane 2016: 1083), The Times Higher Education Survey (Bothwell 2018) put academic stress second only to health workers' stress (Shin and Jung 2014). Bourdieu (1988: 82), in *Acts of Resistance*, refers to how job insecurity impacts institutionally:

> Casualization profoundly effects the person who suffers it. ... Added to these effects of precariousness on those directly touched by it there are effects on all the others who are apparently spared. The awareness of it never goes away, it is present in every moment in everyone's mind ... it pervades both the conscious and unconscious mind.

The choice for academics has been between management having 'total discretion to allocate workloads and therefore implicitly agree to any work intensification this might involve; or concede some form of regulation of their workloads is necessary' (Lyons and Ingersoll 2010: 139). The latter would require management and policymakers to look for alternative means to fund additional staff. But 'the remoteness of academic managers from students and direct teaching roles ... generates ignorance of the consequences of their workload policy and other decisions' (Lyons and Ingersoll 2010: 139). The unspoken 'psychological contract' not written into an employment contract but which academics could expect for their commitment was reciprocation and a duty of care by universities, managers and HR: 'a collegial environment, informal mentorship, teaching load, support, office and working space, laboratory equipment and time to develop and grow as a researcher' (Peirce et al. 2012: 108). But all were being eroded.

Despite this careless approach to academic health and well-being, academics were expected to care for students, personalize their teaching, be sensitive to their specific needs to produce student 'satisfaction' (Blackmore 2009a). To boost student satisfaction, academics were told to be less critical and be more positive, as if criticality is not the core of academic work (Priess 2012, Jameson 2019) and pedagogical discomfort not necessary for professional learning (Boler 1999). 'Entrepreneurial subjectivity, such as having a positive attitude, is depoliticizing. When positive attitudes are valued at the expense of anger or despair, critique and the impetus to change, something other than the self have little use-value' (Scharff 2016: 113). While academics accumulated emotional capital in the form of achievement and loyalty through nurturing relationships with students, colleagues and disciplinary networks, they felt emotionally disconnected from university management.

Disenfranchisement

The articulation of this disenchantment with university management was particularly evident among the professoriate still undertaking research and teaching or directing research institutes, the producers of significant intellectual capital. While expressing differing personal, political, philosophical and epistemological positions, professorial concerns centred around the changing nature and role of the university and their incapacity as core workers to impact on change (Krejsler 2007). The professoriate saw the university had become too corporatized, with a value shift towards money not people. For example, 'I think the notion of the professoriate and its seniority has been marginalized quite significantly in this managerial structure. What's replaced them are the managers now because they're the ones who talk about the bottom dollar, finances and the budgets, and strategic directions. . . . But the core business is research and teaching which is weirdly peripheral to that' (Janice, Professor, Go8, HASS).

Such sentiments were widespread in Europe, the United States and the United Kingdom, with examples of academic resistance (Waitere et al. 2011, Anderson 2008, Lucas 2014). Overseas academics were still shocked at the level of managerialism and lack of academic voice in decision-making in Australia. Rob (Professor, Regional, STEMM) stated:

> I don't think managerialization is unique to Australia, but I was astounded to discover there was no such thing as a faculty council as in the US. Academics don't have a representative body in the functioning of the university. . . . They are elected onto the Academic Board and to the University Council but their role is not to represent staff.

Sean (Head, HASS) at Regional stated: 'Academic Board was losing power pretty rapidly. The faculties were gaining power at a huge rate, the Deans with a huge amount of power and the vice chancellors incredibly powerful.' This centralization of power encouraged managerial hubris which was evident within the regulated enterprise bargaining process. The NTEU representative at Go8 (Debra) argued that

> unions generally are representing staff and just making sure that enterprise agreements that we fought so hard for are actually enforced. There are examples of organizational change when we have battles with management, who believe they have the right to 'manage' and staff believe that they actually do know a bit of what's going on the university. On occasions change has gone through without our consultative committee.

Such practices induced a sense of distrust in executive management across all academic levels (Jameson 2012, Kosonen and Ikonen 2019).

When questioned about the capacity of professors to be heard and inform policy, a Head at Utech (Dennis, STEMM) reflected that while they had sought to ensure 'a good connection between the senior leadership at the faculty . . . and the professoriate where possible in at least the consensus forming part of the decision-making process', he agreed that 'the profs in the faculty, anywhere, they would say there's a barrier. They don't listen to us above. Mind you above would say they don't listen to us below. . . . Of our 150 odd profs, there's cohort of about fifty that we use regularly as a ginger group and they're good at filtering messages'.

The discourse of collaboration expected of academics did not extend to managers collaborating with academics regarding their practice despite their institutional and disciplinary knowledge. Within faculties, consultation with professors was minimal and occasional, reduced to reviewing promotion applications and grants but not key research appointments even in their field. At Utech, a Dean may call the professoriate together to 'discuss some ways of doing things differently' (Dennis, Head, STEMM), but 'for the most part, the professors are out of the story' (Veronica, Head, HASS). Vanessa wanted her professors to actively promote the School and 'be strong, comparative with other faculties' rather than include them in decision-making. The effect was as summed up by Roy (Professor Regional, STEMM): 'We do lots of very good things but a sense of purpose has gone missing. I think in the past a lot of people would do something simply because they felt it was the right thing to do . . . I think increasingly consultation has just become another task in the workforce plan.' Academic leadership even for Heads was being denuded of its moral and ethical purpose.

Recognizing this, some academic managers attempted to re-engage the professoriate. At Regional, a former chair of Academic Board recalled the VC having tokenistic 'wine and nibbles' to cajole the professors 'you are a special group, our leaders, what have you got to say about the issues'. The current VC, Adrienne, at Regional argued the professors had 'every opportunity to engage' at the annual senior staff conference mandated for the senior managers but voluntary for the professoriate 'if they're not too busy doing field work . . . It's very important that they're there and contributing'. Many professors saw these ad hoc or yearly discussions as a time to catch up with other professors but agreed that such sessions often reduced to executives disseminating information to gain professorial cooperation and did not impact on policy significantly. The multiplicity of opinions put forward left the executive to pick and choose what they wanted. Such meetings were considered tokenistic attempts to 'engage' professors because they were called at the whim of management.

The professorial sense of disenfranchisement was most evident with regard to the reduced role of Academic Board as a 'rubber stamp' without an alternative organizational mechanism of input. Executive and academic managers brought predetermined agendas and the Board's time was absorbed procedurally in the domestic labour of passing sub-committee recommendations. Debates were largely restricted to internal matters unless a proactive Chair created opportunities (Rowlands 2019). Eric, the VC at Utech (who chaired the Board), confirmed this perception as he regarded the executive as

> the driver and academic spaces for collective debate are relics in our system . . . staff clubs, professoriate boards and academic board. The board can only be oversight as too big and the serious work goes on in the committees. You've got to have your policy settings at the university [executive] level and hope that . . . faculties and institutes work underneath that.

In the process of restructuring at Regional, the Academic Board was under review. Because no one wished to be chair, as an inducement, the Chair was included into the Vice Chancellors Advisory Committee (VCAC) as a full-time position, a practice also at Go8. Adrienne (VC) said the Chair should be 'independent . . . a professor. I like this separate scrutiny and I know that's not the fashion'. The Chair, Jeremy, found this repositioning seductive and 'quite exciting' to be 'involved in where the university is going, actually see how the university operates and to do something quite useful and powerful', enabling him to 'leverage change'. While seemingly empowering the academic voice, the Chair and Deputy of Academic Board were appointed by Council based on expressions of interest and not elected, but the Chair felt that they 'would not appoint someone not acceptable to the Board'. The Chair was therefore positioned ambiguously: 'I'm a representative on the executive, but I'm not an executive', requiring 'trust on all sides', but also co-opted into the 'corporate bubble'. This positioning seemingly resolved for management academic complaints about having no input (Rowlands 2015a). But being on VCAC required the Board Chair not be a dissenting voice outside VCAC and inside the Chair whose role was not to 'represent' academics relied on his individual intellectual capital while the Deans, DVCs and Division Heads possessed positional authority and economic capital.

At Go8, Gary (Dean, HASS) also considered the Academic Board structure was problematic and out-of-date due to its composition: 'I think we've got a bit of a disjuncture between the speed and accuracy of the executive class and the capacity of the academic community to stay in touch with it and that's the world outside driving that. . . . We're using the board as though it were the representatives of the academy community, and it's not.' The Board comprising the professoriate plus ex-officio members was 'older and more likely to be male than the average academic . . . more science oriented as proportionally science had more professors than non-science . . . and they're not representative'. Discussions at Go8 included creating a special distinctive rank of super professors as 'the notion of professor has expanded' (Gary, Dean, HASS).

Paradoxically, therefore, at the moment that the role and function of universities as legitimators of valued knowledge is under attack externally in the media, by politicians and conservatives, the university was itself failing to recognize academic expertise through its organizational structures, decision-making processes and leadership practices. These findings confirm the Times Higher Education (Bothwell 2018) *Staff Survey of Academics* in the UK, which stated 'around four in ten university employees feel unable to make their voices heard within their institutions' and stress factors identified were due to 'reduced autonomy, lack of role clarity, lack of support, work relationships and lack of say in decision-making, for example, job control + job insecurity' (see also Schulz 2013).

Many of the professors and mid-career academics interviewed expressed concern that senior managers were not aware of the transformed nature and conditions of academic work. Romaine (Go8), a former chair of Academic Board, cites meetings with management and professional staff about research. 'The gap between management and academics has just widened so significantly in terms of commonality of interest and purpose, workplace understandings and the gulf that management have to day-to-day workings of academic life, even if nice people or good scholars.' The occasional campus meetings were not enabling conditions to address academic and administrative staff concerns but were more likely to quieten dissent due to academic politics of niceness or reduce to an informative/ performative exercise and where attendance is dependent on availability and individual willingness to speak out. Such fora were not considered by academics to substitute for institutionalized process-driven and representative decision-making with at least nominal representation of a range of different interests.

Have University Executives Lost Their Heads?

Surprisingly, this sense of disconnect with senior management was articulated by many if not most of the Heads of School in the three universities, for whom the problem was managing academic discontent. Gerald (Head, Regional, STEMM) puts it succinctly:

> At the school level there is a remarkable homogeneity with the level of frustration that we feel in terms of management coming from above . . . the centralization which we don't feel really benefits the school very much. As schools we feel isolated from the service the university provides. We are the business units that make the money and are being taxed heavily but we don't receive the service that we really need to be able to do this at the best possible way. Deans have the purse-strings, they need to negotiate with the schools.

Adrienne (VC, Regional) agreed: 'head of school roles are probably the toughest roles in the university . . . a thankless job', mediating the tensions between different worlds – the disciplinary functions of teaching, multiple management systems and institutional strategic goals. This meant that 'on the one hand, they (Heads) could be seen as a shield protecting academics from impositions of the managerialist culture and associated bureaucracies. On the other hand, the Head can be seen as a "corporate lackey", serving the purposes of the institution and running the risk of alienating colleagues in so doing' (Gentle 2014: 16). Tanya (DVC, Go8) also saw the Head of School's position as the most difficult in the university because 'you are constantly struggling with how to balance your budget and 95 percent of your budget is salaries and you've got no levers. One enormous structural problem is that the people responsible for actually delivering on the university's corporate goals are not the people who have the money or who have the power.'

Academics interviewed agreed they did not apply for academic-management positions because they witnessed the demands of the job, would be on contract and unable to continue with research, concerns articulated by Arthur, a Research Director (STEMM):

> One of the wisest decisions I made was not to become Head as this is the worst job in the university. You've got all the responsibility and all the risk and tell your staff 'Oh, we need to do really well in our quality of teaching surveys'. But

you've got no power. There's a huge disconnect between what the university says is important and what the promotion panel takes as important. If you're a good corporate citizen and you do your teaching well it counts for naught without research. . . . As Head, what advice do you give to people?

For Heads, managing up and down as well as their own desire to make a difference led to frustration. One professor Colin (STEMM) at Regional liked being Head because 'it was not too close to the Vice Chancellor'. Brent (Professor, Utech, HASS) saw the Dean's role was 'the meat in the sandwich between Vice-chancellor and Heads, caught in the middle' because 'they sit on the VC committee, they are the messengers from the vice-chancellor's gun and they are the harbingers of bad news'.

Underpinning this disconnect between Heads and senior academic managers were different perspectives about organizing academic work. Rob (Head, Regional, STEMM) argued that senior managers see it from 'a top-down type of approach of things. Many of us at lower levels view this as a bottom-up type approach. . . . If we don't like it, we protest, which we can't do here, or at least we thought we can't do here'. All Heads in the three universities expressed a sense of dis-empowerment because of their exclusion from decision-making within the corporate logic, which defined their role as gaining alignment of staff with the strategic plan within budget. Hence Sean, an experienced Head (Regional, STEMM), was frustrated when arriving from overseas and began to develop a strategic development plan for his school. He was told categorically there is 'only one Strategic Development Plan generated by the VC that then gets distributed down to the faculties, the faculties do the strategic plans, the schools are not supposed to be doing strategic plans: we just implement'. Another Head at Regional, Colin, agreed that 'Heads of School are like many places, the last to hear about stuff that happens. . . . Even though they are going to be impacting upon those in their school'. Bryan (Head, Go8, HASS) spoke about the uncertainty due to funding and changing government policies: 'I've never had an occasion where I come to work and think well "what am I going to do today" because we're waiting on the federal budget.' Most of the Heads agreed with Tom (Head, Regional, STEMM): 'Heads have no financial discretion to the extent that we used to have, and we don't have a say in matters anymore.'

While many Heads loved the job, those who had been in it for some time commented on their reduced discretionary power, limited budgets and incapacity to influence policy, exacerbated by the executive leadership lacking academic experience or even displaying practical mastery of management. 'The top-class universities are more likely to have a scholar in charge, as at, for example, Harvard . . . Australian universities concentrate on people who are valued for various management skills and activities . . . very good at managing but not very good academics' argued Ken (Head, Go8, STEMM). A colleague, Bryan (Head, Go8, HASS), stated that 'I increasingly think that my job is a dead-end job. The Head used to be two things. One, you had more involvement in strategy. Two, the setting of fees. Now, absolutely no involvement at all. Why not ask the HoS, they might know something, they actually talk to students.' This lament was repeated with another Head (Trevor) at Go8:

> the role of a head of school is being reduced day by day, hour by hour. I've been HoS at four different universities in UK and here the university sector is very hierarchical. The very small amount of time I have with senior management has reduced to nothing. There's no connection at all. I talk to the dean, the dean talks to the senior managers, but they don't do it.

Power rested with the Dean, who negotiated funding with the executive and then between competing Schools. Bryan (Head, Go8, HASS) considered 'the restructuring process ironically enough is meant to be reducing the power of the professional staff, but it's actually increasing centralized power over the faculties'. Those familiar with the system and with the desired intellectual or personal capital could mobilize their advantage. One Head commented that Go8 was 'run like a fiefdom, a hierarchy rather than a flatter structure' because 'we now have had a VC who's been around forever so he's lost touch very much with what's happening on a day to day level – so its run like a court', reducing to 'collaboration as cronyism' (Macfarlane 2017: 472). Often, as Czarniawska (2014: 99) comments, 'reform that sets out to change a system and that if is undertaken within the parameters of the system, reproduces the system'.

Dominating the Heads' concerns across the three universities was a dysfunctional funding model which 'reduced discretionary capacity to innovate at the lower levels' (Jim, Professor, Regional, HASS). There was the structural mismatch between where funds were earned and spent, a key source of tension between and within faculties, because research concentrations did not coincide with student concentrations. This is a sector-wide pattern noted by Eric, the VC at Utech: 'Australian universities have a vulnerability that our excellent research is mostly located in the biological and medical sciences and physical sciences. And is not really spread and is rather weaker in the social sciences and economics.' A Head (Ken, Go8, STEMM) referred to the 'distortion in the Australian system because the way the university earns money is not congruent with the way the university wishes to do research'. Ken continued:

> Having a good Faculty of Science is a great way to move up the rankings but we don't have the greatest earning capacity, it's the Faculty of Business. We struggle to appropriately remunerate faculties like science that are research-intensive teach a lot but with few fee-paying international undergraduates that bring in the money. We have a gap across all our externally funded staff of a million dollars a year which we have to find other sources just to pay their salaries. Schools of commerce who do significant teaching of internationals feel undervalued and under pressure to do more research.

This funding issue had implications for academics as to workloads, for students as to quality and for Heads of School for managing this misalignment. Jessica (Head,

Go8, HASS) stated: 'CSP is around $11,000, barely changed since I was a student. It costs double that to provide a high quality, tough, engaging, rigorous education, which you can't do by shoving 200 people in lecture theatre, but that's how they're paying for it.' While some universities required a redistribution of funds, at Go8, the faculties earning the money had the 'right to spend the money' after they pay tax back to the centre' (Martin, Professor, HASS). The NPM principle of subsidiarity that devolved financial responsibility down to local units to compete for resources created dysfunctional behaviours. Rick (Head, Regional, STEMM) referred to the incredible competition between two schools in his faculty, which together 'carried' the research reputation of the university: 'We're fighting with each other, duplicating courses, trying to snatch each other's post-graduate and foreign students. The splitting up into business entities that are not big enough to be self-supporting and setting higher targets leads to larger student numbers and bigger staff workloads within units not sufficiently supported centrally'. This was exacerbated by the practice of accrual (cruel?) accounting, which required all budgets to be expended annually, with any surfeit being clawed back to the centre, also led to short-term planning and wasted expenditure. Furthermore, sudden federal policy changes immediately impacted on academic staff. An efficiency dividend on research infrastructure imposed by the Coalition government reduced funding over three years and for Go8 was 'just a body blow on top of other body blows' (Tanya, DVC, STEM) and led to greater reliance on international student income.

The convergence of funding allocations and accounting practices had flow on effects at the faculty and school level. Michelle (Head, HASS) argued that the more successful a school or research centre was the more difficult it became to maintain quality or retain staff. 'The flawed funding model means that the more successful we are, the more perilous our financial situation becomes because our research income has gone through the roof but our income from the university has flatlined. We have to fund professional staff to service all the business activity from grants and external resources.' Soft money failed to account for salary increases which are built into research projects and government policy changes after budgets are set by universities, with a ripple effect on staff retention. Regional's VC, Adrienne, saw the issue was 'encouraging the next generation of academics into joining us and in terms of the sort of research that can be funded and how that's done'.

Disengagement: Ac/counting, Auditing and Compliance

Rapid change, multiple tensions and contradictory expectations accumulated to make the professoriate feel disengaged. Vanessa (DVC, Utech) saw disengagement as an issue because we 'need their thought and academic leadership. Some professors are fantastic, very engaged, know what's going on, well connected to their fields and to partners, their stakeholders. They've got great influence. Others are not . . . typical of large organizations'. Contributing to academic frustration was the paradox of federal funding based on income earned, graduate completions and satisfaction, and impact (monetization), and but less on publications just when ERA was increasing pressure to improve citations (which fed rankings). This tension was evident in individual workloads (Kenny 2018, Lyons and Ingersoll 2010). Furthermore, quantification and digitalization were driving accounting and audit mechanisms but multiple databases in universities did not talk to each other because each was developed for a different purpose. Yet workload models assumed coordinated up-to-date data. The lack of synchronization and flaws in the design of 'ac/counting' systems increased academic frustration, exacerbated by decisions about what counted often being made by administrative and not academic staff. Rick (Professor, Regional, STEMM) bitterly recalled:

> administrators do compliance on our research productivity. I was lead author on a article in *Nature* with 215 co-authors. I got nothing. My boss is saying you should not be so collaborative. I said do you know what it's like shepherding a 215 co-author paper in *Nature*, just the impact? Internationally people say wow you led that effort. And the audit chucked out non-refereed papers. A little annoying cause I do a lot of popular writing in *New Scientist, Australian Geographic*.

This highly awarded researcher was producing Gold Standard research, communicating science to the public and working collaboratively as expected. Such misrecognition of important academic work echoed throughout professoriate interviews. Keith (Head, Regional STEMM) described it this way:

> I think academics are as a whole a very clever group of people. If you want to assess them, they can play the games. . . . The majority just love their profession and the research. If you put performance measures, they would just perform to that level. . . . But is the reporting the government spend on it worth it? Academics just conform, spend as little time on it as possible and hate it.

Many resorted to 'being seen to do something' or 'ticking a box' for the performative effect then changing as little in their practice where possible, as professors could, but this led to a sense of alienation from their institution (Blackmore and Sachs 2007).

While some Heads felt constrained, others felt they could exercise some agency. Rob (Head, Regional, STEMM) declared he 'loves the job because it is grounded' and saw his role as acting 'as a buffer against top-down pressures'. He did not seek promotion because he would 'lose contact with my discipline. Schools are where the battle is fought and where I can stall things and make things move'. Others focused on the doable in mediating conflicting expectations and on building supportive relationships with colleagues. 'If you're a good HoS you've got your staff onside, know every individual in your school, their strengths and help them build that strength' (Roy, Head, Regional, STEMM). Some experienced academic managers did not seek to stay in management because it was 'killing me softly', many of them women (Acker 2014, O'Connor 2015). Miranda (A/Professor, Go8,

HASS) had worked in multiple academic and administrative positions in Australia, the United States and NZ but considered similar roles or higher at Go8 'would suck the life out of you' as they were no longer 'doable' (See also Chesterman et al. 2008). Miranda felt she had paid her 'penance and done some leadership as a good citizen'. Romaine (Professor Go8, HASS) believed that 'there aren't that many people who are willing and able to take up management roles' as there was not the same structure or opportunities to be 'a good academic citizen anymore'. When I was Dean 'it was different to how this university runs now'. They now employ external people as deans who 'do not have loyalty to existing practices' (Romaine).

Many professors and Heads confirmed they did not like the top-down approach or the values that were on display where money and managerialism trumped all. Karl (Head, Regional, STEMM) stated that 'I complain a lot about the way universities are run. The current DVC probably wants to do the right thing . . . but it is very top down. I favour a consultative strategy for driving change, possibly not possible for senior managers'. George, also a Head (STEMM, Regional), considered there was a lack of strategic thinking at executive level: 'We deal with the financial constraints, and the practicalities of making sure that everything runs and spend relatively little time thinking about strategy'. Moving into academic management roles was perceived to be just that – management by strategic plan. Yet, many professors argued, it is at the higher levels where the purposes of change and strategic direction had to be debated. Some considered that attempts to inform debate were rejected unless they fitted with executive view. Oliver (Institute Director, Go8, STEMM) argued that 'there is a reticence to let people to actually expand into spaces that they wish to. When people put up their hands and want to do things, they're often poo poo'd and told to go back into their little box'. The command–control mode of the corporate logic provided little opportunity to exercise agency. Over time, worn down and worn out, many disengaged from seeking to inform senior academic managers or becoming one.

Further evidence of disengagement with academic management was that despite the rapidly increasing size and younger professoriate, Australian universities paradoxically faced a shortage of applicants for academic-management positions. Brad (Dean, Utech, STEMM) complained: 'I've got seven schools and two headed by associate professors but multiple professors, supposedly academic leaders, none of them want to put up their hand to actually lead.' Also a Dean at Utech in HASS, Rod argued for coherent succession planning but the changing professoriate profile was complex. Previously 'someone fifty-five to sixty-five years old would formally succeed him, now they are forty-two or forty-five – do they want the job that long?'. The paradoxical relations producing disengagement were articulated by Ryan (Professor, Go8, STEMM):

> The disengagement is because the universities strategic plan and the priorities of academics are a disconnect. You get rewarded for doing your research, but the VC tells us what he wants us to do, this grand vision. But why should people play to that grand vision. They're not being rewarded or recognized for it. Why get involved in doing that unless you're paid to do that job . . . a big

disincentive. Academics do not engage with the grander policy of the university. They're not empowered or part of the formation of the strategic plan. They're not encouraged to think strategically. So they go to survival mode or where they're most comfortable and disconnect because no one ever asks them 'what do we need to do in order for you to do your job better'? Sometimes it's impossible, sometimes it's straight forward.

Ryan pointed to this as a 'recipe for trouble' because the KPIs of the Dean are not the KPIs of the staff that the Dean is supposed to lead. Academics therefore felt less of an obligation to a university which they felt was careless about the academic voice, their commitment and work–life balance (Lynch 2010). Most professors did not want to sacrifice their research, tenure and then adhere to corporate values with which they disagreed (Connell 2019).

Managing Discontent

Among executives there was some awareness of professorial disengagement. Vanessa (DVC, Utech) attributed it to the different composition of the professoriate, many of whom did not understand their role as did older generations. Therefore, she sought to develop, a 'collective sense of a professoriate': writing a professor's job description, organizing university-wide gatherings addressing 'what it is to be an academic leader' and creating a committee of professors, Deans and Heads of School with no clear role. An increasingly common practice, as at Utech, was to make professors responsible for each academic's performance planning and review 'because they've got to have a reason to get together'. Repositioning professors as supervisors, an HR term with which many academics were uncomfortable, subtly appropriated discourses of collegiality and mentoring. In performance reviews, supervisors are often expected to rank colleagues, with significant legal implications for all parties in cases of an employment or professional dispute. This practice meant managerial labour was being delegated and adding to the workload of professors who had no resources or decision-making power to alter the conditions for their colleague.

The critical literature on distributed leadership argues that devolving responsibility without authority or resources to change anything creates further frustration and sense of disjuncture between the rhetoric of collegiality and experience (Jones et al. 2012, Lumby 2013). The supervisory role changes the relationship from being collegial and mentoring based on advocacy to one with more managerial and legalistic overtones, thus confusing performance-based outcomes with collegial support, factors not raised when inducting professors in performance appraisal roles. Such 'bandaid' solutions misrecognize the problem.

Many academic managers were acutely aware that 'some academics seriously dislike the shaping of the university in a particular direction' (Keith, Dean, Regional, STEMM). At Utech, Erica, the VC, indicated she was aware that 'in any organization there'll be hotspots at any time . . . and we monitor that. The overwhelming data is that people stay and sometimes too long.' But retention does not necessarily signal agreement. People stay because of loyalty to research centres, disciplines, colleagues, students as well as a lack of opportunities in their field elsewhere, familial circumstances and regional location (Skinner et al. 2015). More astute academic managers realized a widespread sense of disengagement was an issue. At Utech, Vanessa (DVC) responded to say that 'we've done a number of things more bottom-up than top down because we've had some faculty restructures. We are trying to distribute leadership and make the best of the professoriate but sometimes top-down dominates.' This was work in progress.

An unusual response from middle managers (Deans and Heads) was to develop an alternative structure which enabled a collective voice, such as a university-wide forum comprising all stakeholders in which to have substantive discussions to feedback to the executive. At Regional, Karl Head, STEMM) was lobbying 'to get a senate that has all senior academics, directors, the union, VCAC, PVCs, student representation, coming together monthly to debate academic issues from research to outreach, to teaching and learning, to keep everybody informed and keep a common vision, and from an academic perspective of collegiality, understanding the academic position'. Karl accepted that executives were nervous about open-ended forums because 'you'd see an avalanche of complaints if we really let the barriers go. And that may be counterproductive. But deep inside a lot of people are so frustrated. We need to move on. I think people feel disenfranchised from the decision-making process'.

Some Deans organized the professoriate to meet and respond to university policies. Few senior managers mobilized intellectual capital to persuade academics other than at Go8 where the VC, in response to resistance in one faculty to the blueprint and developing a different degree structure, downloaded information on reforms in the field and at other universities, thought up some ideas and went to the Dean with his suggestions. 'A leader who can do that is pretty useful' (Brett, Professor, HASS). The VC's personal intervention changed the discussion and led to his desired outcome.

Paradoxically, organizational structures and practices of universities have become more monolithic, about compliance rather than creativity, centralized rather than dispersed leadership, standardized rather than encouraging diversity. Instructional and administrative technologies have imposed templates, set criteria, determined timelines and created boundaries that restrict rather than enable academic teaching and research. The various managerial remedies to address rising discontent and disengagement failed to address the core issue of academic disenfranchisement arising from top-down decision-making and technologies of compliance which implied a lack of trust in academics who were becoming disillusioned and despairing about the future of the university.

Dissension and Distrust: Affective Effects

For every successful management story or strong corporate storyline, there was usually multiple counter-narratives circulating among academics of failure or dysfunctional change. 'When competing narratives are uncovered and "voiced" they shed light on and expose the limitations, prejudice and socio-political process through which stories are constructed and particular positions and versions of events corroborated' (Dawson and Buchanan 2005: 846). It is too simplistic to argue that resistance occurs because 'everyone who is against change is either self-interested or doesn't under-stand the "real world"' (Parker 2014: 281).

Academics and academic managers negotiated daily competing role expectations and values within paradoxical relations of autonomy and control, accommodating tensions, contradictions and ambiguities, feeling ambivalent until expectations were in overt conflict with their values and priorities in ways that impacted on their academic integrity and professionalism (Winter 2017). We need to view

> control and resistance as co-productive, interdependent, multidirectional, and constitutive of identities and relationships . . . [and] resistance (to organizational strategies and policies) and resistants (those who resist such strategies and policies) co-emerge, within and through complex intra-actions of entangled discourses, materialities, affect and space/time [and] moment-to-moment co-constitutive moves that may be invoked when identity or self is put in jeopardy. Resistance, we suggest, is the power (residing with resistants) to say 'no' to organizational requirements that would otherwise threaten to render the self abject. (Harding et al. 2017: 1209–10)

Professors were on the one hand hypercritical of command–control centralization when it impeded and devalued their work but on the other hand still responded to managerial discourses of collegiality, care and collaboration while realizing they would be judged as individuals under competitive conditions. 'People are not fools; they are much less bizarre or deluded than we would spontaneously believe precisely because they have internalized, through a protracted and multisided process of conditioning, the objective choices they face' (Bourdieu and Wacquant 1992: 130). It is not that academics don't resist or lack agency, it is just that many of these changes have been incremental, subtly altering the habitus, exploiting their desires and guilt, while appealing to academic dispositions of competitiveness and perfectionism, a tendency to work alone in their heads, and a desire to excel (Lorenz 2012). Competition, Evans (2014: 20) argues, is 'hardwired into the DNA of academics . . . the very structures that oppress us are . . . the very structures that we cling to most often' (e.g. merit, excellence and impact).

Professors interviewed recognized the contradictory relations in which they worked and that there is no innocent position as 'the logic of domination means that submission and resistance are interlinked in an apparently paradoxical relation' (Lawler 2004: 123). For academic managers to disingenuously argue that they only used persuasion not coercion meant neglecting to mention the complex web of institutionalized arrangements and dispersed mechanisms of power that governed academic lives. They were not stressing 'a compulsion to act as those who hold power wish but the creation of a context in which people will choose to do so', or put another way, 'leaders create a culture within which it is perceived to be acceptable to speak and act in only certain ways' (Lumby 2019: 1620). Therefore, 'although some people may be discontented with aspects of a power-holder's actions, they nevertheless hesitate to challenge them, as questioning is seen as transgressive' (Lumby 2019: 1620). Hence the 'paradoxical resilience of collegiality' in academic leadership where 'collegiality is a subliminal fantasy that represents an important interface between "leaders" and those who are "led"' (Kligyte and Barrie 2014: 157).

Drawing on discourses of collegiality and collaboration, universities were effectively harnessing academic passion for their research, teaching and performative anxieties though multiple mechanisms of managerialism – audit, performance review, workloads, research assessment, student evaluations – which had affective effects (Iqbal 2013). Professors expressed feelings of guilt for surviving restructuring or not being able to employ casual staff in ongoing positions. Feminist academics in management positions referred to their sense of a 'colluded self' (Acker 2012, Ozga and Deem 2000). In being complicit they therefore 'contribute to their own domination by tacitly accepting, in advance, the limits imposed on them, which often takes the form of bodily emotion (shame, timidity, anxiety, guilt)' (Bourdieu 2000: 169).

Adding to the affective economy of survivalism was the 'exhaustion effect' of continual reform and work overload, the creep of the audit culture, datafication, digitalization and the ratcheting up of productivity expectations – all reduced time for dissent (Woeler and Yates 2015). Additionally, academics no longer comprise the majority of the university workforce. There was greater differentiation among academics, with a new techno-professional class accruing capital within the field by mediating relationships between academics and their stakeholders, and a diverse professoriate lacking a collective identity. Individual academics also benefitted as their interests lay with audit regimes, celebrity culture and rapid promotion (Shore and Taitz 2012). Evans (2014: 20) argues that 'academics have been forced into so many different contexts of competition with so many sanctions against resisting the accompanying pressures that their collective will has been weakened'. 'Resistance can be alienating and submission liberating . . . such is the paradox of the dominated and there is no way out of it' (Bourdieu 1994: 155 cited in Wilson et al. 2021: 33).

Emotional expressions of frustration, anger and disillusionment of the professoriate were indicative of a wider malaise within the affective economy of the academy in Australia, which can both paralyse the individual and be disruptive of the norm if understood as a collective practice. The stress experienced more widely across the academic workforce produced increasing distrust of executive management due to its 'carelessness' (Lynch 2010, Jameson 2019). This stress was experienced differently with many women academics in the study experiencing greater work–life conflict, lack of time and being more susceptible to work precarity. The psychological contract of universities providing safe and caring workplaces no longer existed as market contractualism dominated (Lam and de Campos 2015). Even for women moving into management, compliance was expected because '[O]pportunities for leadership by non-traditional powerbrokers, such as women or minority scholars, are viewed through the prism of command and control in the sales-driven hierarchies of prestige, credentials and power' (Oleksiyenko and Ruan 2019: 407).

The disposition of the academic habitus under circumstances out of their control was for academics to focus on shared interests with their colleagues and intellectual community within and outside the university whereas the interests of academic managers and professional staff who worked closely together lay with the university. The collegial enterprise focused on the service needs of students and stakeholders and all the complexities of those relationships whereas a corporate bureaucracy as a system driver sought to reduce risk with a 'culture of consistency, centralization, compliance and control' (McNay 2005: 162–3). Martin, a professor (Go8, HASS), sums it up thus:

> Academics want to focus on their own work and disciplines and their colleagues rather than the institution . . . the institutional loyalists are nearly all on the professional staff . . . who carry the personality and the identity of the institution . . . . Academics are also mobile. We can walk away. And professional staff walk away to but while on site they're loyal. Whereas the academics are mobile and not necessarily loyal and that's a virtue . . . academics work to disciplines and are more than just corporate employees.

The affective and moral as well as intellectual dimensions of academic work informed everyday casual discussions cementing localized relationships. 'Corridor stories' created a sense of shared experience. Furthermore, Jameson (2018: 378) refers to the 'almost hidden commentary, arguably a form of serious gossip within institutional talk' and the 'sharing of survival stories'. Resistance stories increase loyalty to colleagues and feed mistrust of management' (2018: 379), echo chambers of the dissonance between the managerial storyline and how organizational life was experienced. Such 'struggles over meaning' lead to the 'deployment of resistant identity work . . . including cynicism, irony, and humor, which become an important part of the repertoire of resistance practices' (Mumby et al. 2017: 1159). A more collegial ethos allowed individuals to express dissent, positive and negative emotions, failures and successes and display frustration. In contrast, a more individualistic culture created more stress, allowing only positive display while maintaining the illusion of coping.

The discord and fraught relationships between the professoriate and management arose from the structural and cultural reforms characterized by what many considered to be the de-professionalization of academic work. At the same time there was a re-professionalization of administrative work, an unbundling of academic work to be re-bundled as techno-professional work and the pincer movement between managerial and market accountability. The intensified control over academics without reciprocity in terms of security and care produced a sense of a crisis of trust in academic management. At the same time it altered pedagogical relations between academics and their students, with health and well-being effects (Schulz 2013).

Criticality: The DNA of the Academic Habitus

In this context, dissension and debate were often mistaken for criticism and negativity by managers who positioned many professors as being recalcitrant or resistant to change. For some academic managers, criticism challenged their self-efficacy and inability to control.

> Disputation, the essence of disciplinary development, is seen as dissent when policy is presented for delivery, and scant allowance is made for diversity. More emphasis is put on blame for mistakes than on the lessons from them. Little attention is given to low paid staff who are at crucial access points to students and the public, their attitudes and opinions. (McNay 2005: 167)

Reissner et al. (2011: 426) concluded that academic questioning of managerial decisions are responses to be expected in a complex process of organizational change in the context of political, social and economic uncertainty. As with all good change management, 'critical questioning of organizational change and its management is an important function in the change process to test the drivers and potential merits of a change initiative and to allow for modifications at an early stage' (Jameson 2019: 11, Meyer 2012). The academic habitus is one formed through interactions of those disposed to critical inquiry.

> Since universities are organized around knowledge, the knowledge basis for reform ideas tends to be questioned and discussed in the same way as other knowledge domains. Hence, reform ideas concerning 'quality', 'autonomy' or 'internationalization' will often be confronted with a critical attitude by those affected, questioning the logic and arguments provided in favour of reform. In other words, changing mindsets and values of individuals is not a straightforward task. (Stensaker et al. 2012: 6)

Academics also expected similar criticality to be evident among academic managers. Jameson (2019: 5) refers to how criticality underpinning leadership practices in higher education would involve first, individual critical thinking skills as argumentation and judgements including interpretation, analysis inference, explanation, evaluation and metacognition; second, leadership as a critical being in relation to 'knowledge, self and the world' (critical reflection, ethical awareness, action and creativity); and third, the social-cultural aspects of criticality (e.g. critical pedagogy, critical inquiry and critical management theory). Feminists would argue that the focus of critical leadership practice should also be to utilize these dispositions, capabilities and resources to redress unequal power relations with a focus on social justice (Blackmore 2019).

Yet academic discourses identified an absence of critical leadership practice. University executives, many professors argued, were not using their intellectual capital and institutional position to address global issues of climate change, mass migration, poverty and inequality, or valuing the public service role of academic citizen with regard to a good society. Furthermore, the academic-management discourse rarely referred to the professor's role as being a critic or a public intellectual. Nor were academic concerns over professional autonomy considered as indicative of deeper concerns about the role of the university, the nature of knowledge production, professional ethics and academic freedom. Rick, a professor at Regional in STEMM, was shocked, returning from South Africa stating: 'There is no academic freedom other within your own little subject area . . . but very little resistance to broader societal trends. I don't know why we've lost it, with our students as well, the students are sheep, seeing education as something they pay for as a service.' This Head's observations were symptomatic of professorial concerns as to whether the vocationalization of universities was producing the neoliberal self-interested student and academic, reflected in the lack of academic and student activism, the former due to overwork and the latter a consequence of working twenty hours a week to pay fees. Many professors feared that the next generation of scholars formed as neoliberal subjects would not realize alternative ways of organizing, being and doing as academics because they had been taught and learnt to play the game so well and adhered to performative demands and wasteful managerial practices rather than talking back to destructive leadership (Ryan et al 2019).

The last line of defense for many but not all academics was to protect their intellectual labour and to teach and research with democratic intent. Academic freedom in Australia is guaranteed in the Higher Education Support Act (2003) to be a 'critic and conscience', but enterprise agreements explicitly stated that academics only speak publicly on their field of expertise. Collective action is only legal when negotiating a new EB in Australia, some of the most restrictive in Anglophone nations (Bailey et al. 2011). Codes of conduct monitor academic practice, and evidence of misconduct can lead to dismissal or disciplining of 'academics who make controversial or embarrassing public statements' (Norton 2012: 16). Increasingly professors are expected to sign individual contracts which require loyalty to the university, thereby trumping academic freedom. Activism as a public intellectual was seen to be a form of dissensus by management with involvement in social movements or being advocates for marginalized groups as either a distraction or creating political tensions with potential partners (Gray 2013).

There is a 'moral economy implicit in industrial agreements about expectations about how a democratic society should function' (Bailey et al. 2011: 432). Most of the professors interviewed argued that universities had unique organizational characteristics and positioning as well as a civic purpose within democratic societies. Universities required a values-based leadership that could resolve the paradox of management: 'maintaining control, while allowing autonomy' (Klaus and Steele 2020: 1). The strong adherence to collegial values expressed by professors interviewed was not seen to be replicated among managers where relationships were often more transactional. Trust as a positive form of relational capital and central to leadership was more likely to be achieved through deliberative and inclusive decision-making processes which recognized multiple knowledges and experiences or epistemic justice (Kosonen and Ikonen 2019). The professors interviewed were critical that university managers had not protected academic and professional staff from deluges of reform which diverted attention away from the core work of the university nor undertaken risk management given their awareness of potential crises regarding international students and their financial investments. 'Arguably, if leaders are able to focus, listen, act with discretion and skillfully contain negative emotions arising from uncertainties, rather than rush to implement imprudently deterministic solutions, they are more likely to inspire trust within their institutions' (Jameson 2012: 395). Leadership under conditions of uncertainty and austerity requires 'negative capability', a capacity to 'sustain reflective inaction' rather than action, a capacity to create conditions to gain further insight given the 'imaginative plasticity' of alternative ideas while displaying integrity and honesty.

Part III

LEADERSHIP DISRUPTORS

Chapter 8

DIVERSIFYING TO DISRUPT LEADERSHIP

Despite the policy mantra that diversity in leadership is good, the lack of gender and cultural diversity in managerial and research leadership in universities internationally is enduring, and academic women, particularly of colour, continue to experience marginalization (Eddy et al. 2016, Showunmi et al. 2016, Jarboe 2017, Johnson 2017). As change agents, diversity practitioners in universities sought to disrupt the managerial logics of practice sustaining unequal relations of power and disabling conditions of work and address the enduring pattern, as this study shows, that men continue to dominate both academic management and professorial positions and few women or men in these positions were of colour other than white. While ambiguously positioned within Human Relations (HR) units, diversity practitioners enacted purposeful leadership to implement diversity policy and monitor its effects.

Misrepresenting 'the Problem': Women's Under-representation in Leadership

Feminist critical policy analysts (Bacchi 2000) ask: What is the policy problem here, how has it been conceptualized and why in this context? Academic managers and professors in the three case study universities expressed concern about the lack of women in senior academic management and research leadership. Despite equal employment opportunity (EEO) policies premised on merit (and not affirmative action) implemented over thirty years and the presence of EEO practitioners in universities, women's progress has stalled with women constituting only 30 per cent of the professoriate but the majority of the academic workforce (WGEA 2020).

   Policies have moved from using concepts of equal opportunity and equity in the 1980s focusing on changing women to changing masculinist cultures and then diversity in the 2000s, diversity incorporating multiple intersecting forms of difference (gender, sexuality, race, ethnicity, ableness, socio-economic background). Diversity is a much used and abused term in the lexicon of policy, management and leadership (Ahmed 2004, Blackmore 2006, Squire 2017). Within a social justice frame premised upon principles of equal access to resources, recognition of difference and participation in decision-making (Fraser 2013), diversity policy would mean equal opportunity for all individuals as an ethical and political right in a democratic society (Kezar and Posselt 2020). Gender and cultural diversity in political and organizational leadership signifies representational justice (Fraser 2013) and is considered more likely to improve decision-making and create more inclusive organizations and greater social cohesion (Catalyst 2013). The neoliberal framing of diversity makes the business case that workforce diversity in decision-making increases productivity to gain the 'diversity dividend' (Deloitte 2017), that social cohesion is conducive to economic development (Hunt et al. 2018) and that innovation (often equated to STEMM) emerging from diverse workgroups stimulates economic growth (Boston Consulting 2018). Any investments in women's participation therefore benefits families by 'boosting corporate profitability and national competitiveness' (Roberts 2015: 209), thereby co-opting talent of 'the Other' as a resource to be mined.

In universities, epistemic diversity brings multiple knowledge positions, with interdisciplinarity providing innovative responses to wicked problems and 'supporting creativity' (Hunt et al. 2018: 1). Diversity policies in universities therefore symbolize an inclusive place to learn and work. These moral, political and economic approaches to diversity, while interconnected, ignore how diversity policies are enacted under contemporary conditions of academic work. Furthermore, feminists consider diversity as a policy concept is weaker than equal opportunity, arguing that it individualizes issues of difference and ignores historical systemic inequality of particular social groups (Ahmed 2004, Blackmore 2006, Arday and Mirza 2018).

Diversity practitioners, previously located in autonomous units directly informing the executive, had been incorporated into HR with restructuring in the 1990s. This uncomfortable positioning meant diversity practitioners were responsible for both auditing and redressing equity issues, were possibly domesticated, with little positional authority and few resources. Tracy, the diversity manager at Utech commented: 'everyone was over hearing about equal opportunity and the diversity discourse was more acceptable (and perhaps less challenging).' Certainly, diversity policy provided a vocabulary and rationale for action. Diversity practitioners relied on this warrant to 'meddle wherever and whenever they like across the university' (Alison, Diversity manager, Go8) and intervened on multiple issues such as recruitment, promotion and leadership development. At Utech, Tracy had reviewed and reformed the internal promotions scheme, analysed the data and helped write criteria. Having achieved her KPI of 40 per cent of academic and professional senior staff being women, progress had plateaued. Diversity practitioners worked through university and faculty committees, with Deans and Heads, and developed, with HR leadership, programmes on mentoring and shadowing, workshops on getting grants and publication, many focusing on women. They simultaneously questioned, and were complicit in, the performative exercises of ramping up productivity in the name of improving opportunities for women.

Concern over 'wasted talent' due to the lack of women in STEMM had led to the establishment of the UK Athena Swan Programme in 2005 and its sister programme, Science in Australia Gender Equity (SAGE), in Australia in 2015.

The Athena Swan/SAGE accreditation approach relies on universities auditing structures and processes to identify discrimination including a new focus on unconscious bias in selection, promotion and review panels. Again, feminists argue such programmes are 'moderate feminism' informed by neoliberal practices relying on data and proceduralism which are not gender or race neutral. The corporate tools of 'accountability, metrics and the performative work of "doing" equality work require minimalist cultural shifts without real commitment' (Tzanakou and Pearce 2019: 1191). These fail to address the subtlety of everyday sexism and racism.

Significantly in policy the 'problem' of female or minority group under-representation in leadership is now recognized as not being due to their lack of aspiration for leadership or of talent, but rather a structural and cultural issue in universities. But the rules of the game of academic work have been constantly changing, repositioning academics and women particularly as marginal casualized workers in the context of the intensification and speeding-up of academic labour (Wajcman and Dodd 2016, Lopes and Dewan 2014/2015). At Go8, Alison (Diversity Manager) cited the paradox evident in a staff survey on engagement with, and perceptions of, leadership that indicated an overall 'commitment, job satisfaction, and intention to stay' but no satisfaction with workload, administration or senior management, with women most impacted as in international studies (e.g. Bothwell 2018). The VC at Go8 had included improving gender representation into the strategic plan, but women were not applying for line-management positions. Alison explained that women and those with caring responsibilities looked at the workload expectation at that level and said: 'I simply don't want to put myself out there.' Research also inevitably took a back seat (Lipton 2017). Furthermore, Alison's aim at Go8 was to break the trope that women are more caring of students, as if they are invested in mobilizing the emotional capital they had 'naturally' accumulated due to their familial responsibilities (Reay 2004). Alison was 'particularly alert to stereotypical assumptions that might underpin that distribution of workload' and that performance plans are 'mindful to distribute opportunities to achieve expectations equitably . . . but we're not there yet by a long shot'.

Overloaded, Overtime and Overwhelmed: Work/Life Conflict

Work/life conflict was a key factor across all universities, for those with caring responsibilities and in a science career pathway in particular because it requires continuity (Ylijoki 2020). Tina (Head, Utech, STEMM) argued that 'women have to make decisions and family often comes first . . . there's no question that for working mothers this is tough environment . . . I look at that more favourably when I review grants and promotions of female staff . . . paternity leave has to be on the table'. In Australia, the data show that women continue to work part-time significantly more than men and do most of the domestic and caring labour in Australia, with labour shared more equitably between same-sex couples (Baxter 2021). In heterosexual relationships, women's unequal investment in family provides men with a competitive advantage, with few taking paternity leave (Pillay et al. 2013). Furthermore, Gary (Dean, HASS, Go8) argued, 'tax policy doesn't make paid childcare a very attractive proposition for junior academics or part-time work. While the academy is a flexible working place, flexibility can be a trap for younger women . . . doing a lot of caring because "oh I'll fit that around work". Time stress was a key factor for many women (Macfarlane and Burg 2019). Ken (Professor, Go8, STEMM) explained. 'Women's career structure is impeded by having families and the biggest single thing that needs to be done is proper childcare facilities on campus.'

Added to this were escalating expectations or normalized hyper-performativity to continuously improve the quality teaching and research, generate income and increase research output due to ERA and ranking (Lipton 2020, Lane 2012), creating conditions which led many women early in their career to 'choose' teaching-only positions or work part-time, thus limiting their career pathways. Alison (Diversity Manager, Go8)

> used evidence to counter the 'loose talk about the impact of work/life balance issues as if women aren't pulling their weight by being part-time. They are as productive as men when you take fraction into account, and more productive in terms of measures like outputs, publications, grant applications, supervision than men . . . despite them juggling and balancing and working their butts off.'

Working part-time often meant working more hours than required (Saltmarsh and Randall-Moon 2015). Furthermore, the promotion process was not only daunting but time-consuming with inconsistent outcomes. Jeanette (A/Dean Research, Regional, STEMM) commented: 'I try to tap people on the shoulder . . . too busy. I'll do that next year. It's a very onerous process and then it depends on the promotion committee. They're reasonably fair but you've got to have good people who speak up for their disciplines.' Recognition by the Australian Research Council of career interruptions provided leverage for diversity practitioners to embed similar criteria in promotions and appointments and assisted deans to 'calibrate quantity and quality' (Gary, Dean, Go8, HASS). Martin (Professor, Go8, HASS) was less optimistic:

> It's easier to get promoted on merit, but you've got to get into the promotable tenurable stream. Gender ratios haven't changed much. Women have done better on the professional side and executive leadership than in academic leadership. For all the talk about enabling child-bearing years taken into account it never works in research grant formulae so you don't go to professor or associate professor quickly. Men just don't carry the major responsibility for children, accumulate big points between 30 and 45 and get promoted.

National grant schemes focus on STEMM and continue to favour men in Laureate and NHMRC programmes.

Women faced an additional career hurdle, Aaron (Dean, Regional, STEMM) believed, because they were 'often appointed at a lower level when entering a field'. Academic women are discouraged, therefore, not due to lack of aspiration for leadership (Menzies and Newsom 2008) or because of their assumed natural disposition for care, but because they lack the resources (time, energy, money, conditions of work), are positioned lower down the organization, teach more and bear the brunt of familial responsibilities. The policy problem is not one of 'fixing women' but more about' fixing national priorities', 'fixing universities' and 'fixing men' (Burkinshaw and White 2017) while also recognizing in policy the complexity of gender diversity.

Furthermore, the focus of government and institutional policies on celebrity and early career researchers to improve ERA rankings created a workforce issue of mid-career academics being left behind, with many women remaining senior lecturers. At Utech, Tracy (Diversity Manager) had 'geared our leadership to mid-career as the next wave to skill up'. At Go8, in contrast to Utech's 'grow their own talent' approach, recruiting externally offered rapid promotion to higher positions where salaries could be re-negotiated favouring high-achieving researchers, predominantly men in science. At Go8 Gary (Dean, HASS) commented: 'you've got to move out to move up' with 'another wave of incidental discrimination creeping in'. He admitted head-hunters for senior recruitment referred to 'a gender issue with women with families being less able to tow their family behind them than men'. Tracy (Diversity Manager, Utech) cynically reflected on how head-hunters 'just round up the usual suspects . . . despite instructions around gender and indigeneity. Search firms have their own predispositions and unconscious bias'. Often female applicants are invited to apply just to 'get the numbers of women' regardless of their chance of getting the position, raising false hopes and wasting their time. Deans and Heads more often used their networks and key professorial gatekeepers within the field who 'have their hands on a lot of appointments in different institutions just 'cause they're regarded as trustworthy . . . informal head-hunters in a way' (Tracy, Utech, Diversity Manager) (Loomes et al. 2019). 'Being known' by these 'field gatekeepers' required significant self-promotion online and academic networking, leading to exclusions based on gender politics and institutionalized epistemic injustice, with feminist, post-colonial or Indigenous scholars often not included in malestream networks (Thornton 2015).

A key sectoral priority was the 'wasted talent' of women in STEMM informed by the business discourse that diversity brings innovation (Blackmore 2014). This mantra focused on the lack of eligible applicants in the pipeline for leadership positions due to few women in environment engineering, molecular sciences, chemistry, biochemistry and IT resulting from the hyper-masculinist cultures of STEMM, the gendered occupational divide in the professions and school subject choices (Johnson et al. 2017). Dennis (Head, Utech, STEMM) felt little had changed even though he told selection panels for chemistry 'everything being equal I would prefer appointing a woman' but it was harder for women in STEMM to get to the position of 'being promotable into the professoriate' because the masculinist culture was off-putting (Zeb, Professor, Go8, STEMM) (Leathwood and Read 2013). Zeb continued: 'any improved position of women overall in HE is partly due to the growth of the feminized fields, which has now halted. But in engineering and

IT no improvement at all . . . IT is very weird and strange, not really a profession, more an enclave in a darkened room.' Precarity of jobs in STEMM was also a major deterrent. Ken (Professor, Go8, STEMM,) recalled a really good post-doc going to work in the public service because 'she needed a life because sick of being on contract for ten years. That's a science issue' (Petersen 2011).

The lack of women in research leadership has also been exacerbated with research assessment, ranking and enterprise bargaining squeezing greater productivity out of academics while narrowing what counts as success to the 'measured sciences' (Burrows 2012, Rowlands and Gale 2019, Oancea 2019). The introduction of ERA in 2010 saw the numbers of women in STEMM in the Go8 group reduced (Lane 2012) and HASS fields where women are concentrated continue to be under threat (see Chapter 3) (Rowlands and Wright 2020). Paradoxically, the practices of evaluation and assessment of reputation that stem from ranking and ERA may, in fact, detract from other university goals such as interdisciplinary work or student-centred teaching. Women's professional self-efficacy in teaching, often the majority of sessional academics, also challenged staff because of perceived lack of credibility, even though many had PhDs (Read and Leathwood 2020). Women, queer and academics of colour are most subject to student abuse (sexism, racism) in student evaluations and in online rating scales (e.g. *RateMyProfessors*) (Rosen et al. 2018, MacNell et al. 2015, Heffernan 2021b), all factors discouraging them from seeking promotion as well as having damaging emotional effects (Burford 2017).

With regard to academic management, the data indicated that women were more likely to take up acting positions, to test out whether they liked the job (Eddy et al. 2016, White et al. 2012). Many took up the job out of a sense of service or when it was suggested to them by others, continuing a pattern of accidental leadership for women (Gornall et al. 2015, Blackmore and Sachs 2007). June, a Research Director at Regional, recalled it was a leadership course that had provoked her to apply and that 'I was asked by several people. It's recognition and not self-promotion'. June also felt that 'being a good academic citizen has given way to "what can I get out of each new position of leadership I take up" for myself'. Other women left academic management psychologically damaged (O'Connor 2015). The reality at Go8, Martin (Professor, HASS) warned, was that

> no amount of slippery promotion application about service and leadership will cover up a lack of a research record. The opportunities women are being given to move into management, they would be better advised to stay away from them. . . . At level C get your research done. But that wouldn't help the faculty so it's a double-edged thing because the school says it's helping you but actually you're serving the school above yourself.

Paradoxically, competitive individualism and the default devaluing of teaching ingrained in competitive university cultures encouraged any disposition towards self-interest. Individual aspiration trumped institutional needs leading to academic reluctance to take up management.

Conditions of im/possibility therefore affected many academics and women in particular in this study. Neoliberal policies of commodification and quantification, escalating demands for excellence in teaching, research and engagement, together with time-consuming datafication, the accelerated pace of work (Wajcman and Dodd 2016, Gibbs et al. 2015), and employment precarity (Vicary and Jones 2017, Broadbent and Strachan 2016), led to endemic work/life conflict (Ylijoki 2013). Moving into positional leadership whether in research or management for women was more, not less, difficult to achieve. Many also had to contend with organizational subtexts discriminating against 'the other'.

Subtexts of Sexism, Racism and Class

Within these structural and cultural systems of inequality and power, the intersection of gender, race, ethnicity and class produced differential subject positions (Collins and Bilge 2016). Rarely mentioned in interviews other than by women and those of minority group background was the undercurrent of everyday sexism and racism. Carla (Professor, HASS) expressed shock when she 'felt like a stranger' in the masculinist university culture of Go8 after her previously experiencing a 'galvanizing feminist model' of a non-Go8 university. Carla was the only woman at a research directors meeting at 8.30 am.

> They're all in suits. I've just put my two daughters in creche. The DVC says good morning, looks at me and says: 'I was going to say gentlemen but I suppose I can't'. And they all laugh . . . I go ha, ha. What can I say, I've been there six months . . . and they go yes, yes, yes, we must do something about this gender issue but let's move on to business.

Interviews with women at Go8 indicated a particular 'socio-cultural dimension about what constitutes hegemonic masculinity, socialization, habitus and identity formation' (Connell 2016, 305). Such comments, Carla felt, were normalized interactions at Go8 that women collectively endured (and were expected to feel grateful for being there) but which she felt positioned her as lesser. Carla argued: 'It was "not just the numbers", it's the culture, the masculinist way of operating within the professoriate' (Ahmed 2012). Connell (2016: 306) argues hegemonic masculinity should be viewed as 'a collective project for realizing gender hierarchy', one which is 'historically constituted and reconstituted under different conditions, in different universities and disciplines'. The internal gender politics of Go8, Romaine (Professor, HASS) argued, meant that the only opportunities for women getting 'up the ranks was through taking on extremely onerous unglamorous high-level coordination jobs of large teaching programs with the promise that would help their career', but 'they are stressed out of their tree'. This strategy impacted their research and therefore promotion possibilities. Bourdieu (1984: 26) concurs: 'the educational institution succeeds in imposing cultural practices that it does not teach and does not even explicitly demand, but which belong to the attributes attached by status to the position it assigns, the qualifications it awards and the social positions to which the latter give access.'

Again at G08, Carla was the only academic woman of nine academics and two managers (women) on the Faculty Executive (HASS) which met every Monday recalled:

> The committee was a rubber stamp . . . no disagreeing. When the Faculty equity person spoke about new programs for women one male Prof said 'I think we're pretty good here. We're encouraging, there's no barriers. It's a good program but we don't need it'. I said: 'Actually I think across the university we have a pretty bad image'. Shock and horror. Then the faculty manager said 'Yes, we have a real problem: there's too many women level B'. That's the mentality.

Many references in the three case study universities were made to how traditional masculinities were resistant to evidence that women were systematically disadvantaged (Crimmins 2019, Thompson and Langendoerfer 2016), but with signs that 'younger male attitudes were changing' (Phillip, Head, Utech, STEMM). Yet powerful traditional masculinities flourished. Bruce (Research Director, STEMM) referred to his family of seven children and his 'wife who juggles their lives . . . I do a lot at her direction . . . It's not me that has the feelings'. Bruce believed 'that when women put up their hands for a leadership position, they do get preference', but then said:

> We start off at equal entry points. At associate professor it falls off partly because many women are not willing to put the effort and hours in and they don't have the competitive spirit. No it's true, women do not have the same fire in the belly. The ones that do, do just as well as the men. . . . What makes a successful academic is a single-minded ambition and it's more common in the male.

Blaming women for lack of ambition excused recognizing how women were disadvantaged by the sociocultural ethos and temporal organizing of the academy.

Diversity managers considered that such lack of reflexivity and gender bias were prevalent. While white masculine privilege was never named, its dominance created an institutional inertia and lack of will to address sexism and racism. On the one hand, a discourse of excellence enabled unconscious bias by defining what constitutes merit advantaging male academics (Thornton 2013). Rob (Dean, Regional, STEMM) referred to 'those subliminal things . . . I've been saying "go for promotion" to one woman but other people will often say to me "oh she's not that good". But she's as good as some of the blokes they appoint . . . unconscious stuff about gender and race.' On the other hand, the idealization of celebrity female academic researchers as role models produces the perception that women 'to be counted' had to be exceptional in 'managing it all', be care-free and childless (Grummell et al. 2009b), display a 'fire in the belly' and have a competitive spirit (McManus 2018). A performative culture (Blackmore and Sachs 2007: 108) encourages a forgetfulness about the multitude of 'invisible others' – partners, families, research fellows, colleagues, professional staff and students – who have enabled this performance, which in turn enhances the institutional performance for which already privileged individuals get rewarded (Angervall et al. 2015).

The Whiteness of Leadership

The lack of cultural representation in leadership is not foregrounded in diversity policies in Australian universities as it is in the UK and NZ, and the dominant whiteness of leadership was only mentioned by Indigenous or non-Anglo/European interviewees. 'Whiteness tends to be visible to those who do not inhabit it' (Ahmed 2006: 3). There was a notable absence in 150 interviews of non-Anglo-European professors and senior managers other than one DVC, two professors and three Heads of School (in STEMM), a pattern of whiteness confirmed by a scan of university websites, despite the cultural diversity of students and staff. In 2015 only 3.4 per cent of DVCs were Asian-Australian whereas 33 per cent of DVCs and 25 per cent of VCs were born overseas in Europe or North America (Oishi 2017: 6).

Sociocultural as well as structural issues impeded accessing leadership for Asian and Indigenous academics as they are 'positioned in a liminal space of alterity' (Rollock 2012: 65), experiencing a kind of belonging and not belonging, a 'both/and' orientation as the 'outsider' or 'stranger' within (Holvino 2008: 2, Moreton-Robinson 2004, 2013). White privilege advantages some individuals as it is built on systematic practices of embedded racism and sexism in institutional life that impart power (which knowledges are valued more) and that have become a given 'because they are not the object of perception' (Ahmed 2012: 21, Earick 2018). Difference informs interpersonal relationships in contradictory ways because privilege and marginalization occur simultaneously: the privilege of a white female professor marginalized in a male-dominated faculty or with a Black female professor treated tokenistically in a white female-dominated faculty (Fuller 2021, Showunmi et al. 2022).

Arguably, diversity policies have created only a tempered disruption of these givens (Manfredi 2017). Diversity practitioners sought to get those on recruitment and promotion committees to consider gender and cultural diversity as well as merit with 'recognition of non-traditional career paths and how you sort of globally and holistically assess a person's capacity across a range of criteria, not necessarily either selecting in your own image or people like us' (Tracy, Diversity Manager, Utech). A constant phrase used by academic managers, professors and diversity practitioners was whether individuals 'fit' – into cultures, teams or roles. Liera and Ching (2019: 119) refer to how in their evaluation of 'fit', 'search committees evaluate, often uncritically, a candidate's body language and social interactions to identify and distinguish those whose behaviours aligned with unspoken workplace norms'. 'Best fit' can often be the proxy for selecting 'people like us' or homosociability, because people like to be with others or recognize in others similarities which make us feel comfortable (Grummell et al. 2009a). Notions of best fit, as that of merit, are constructs informed by 'local logics', which can mean selecting 'safe' candidates according to known and familiar qualities, thereby 'normalizing particular leadership qualities' (Blackmore et al. 2006) and ensuring the reproduction of socially homogenous organizations in gendered and racialized ways (Blackmore and Rahimi 2019).

Thus, unconscious bias informing decision-making goes unchallenged. 'Best fit' assumes organizations or disciplines are mono-cultural into which people must 'fit', allowing male-dominated fields to 'effectively "clone" themselves in their own image, guarding access to power and privilege to those who fit in, and those of their own kind' (Grummell et al. 2009b: 330). As Bourdieu (1984: 102) argues:

> The members of groups based on co-option (. . .) always have something else in common beyond the characteristics explicitly demanded . . . those secondary characteristics which are often the basis of their social value (. . .) and which, though absent from the official job description, function as tacit requirements, such as age, sex, social or ethnic origin.

Not fitting in implies marginality, which feminist and Indigenous standpoint theorists (Moreton-Robinson 2013) argue can be a privileged position of knowledge and sensemaking for women of colour, differently from men of colour, in a white masculinist context. Women have to mobilize strategies of 'learning to use anger appropriately; finding a voice in a balancing act between silence and outspokenness; gaining strength by with-drawing from men' (Holvino 2008: 5). Marginality facilitates understanding organizational practices differently. Bourdieu refers to a 'perspective advantage' as experiences and analyses from the margins offer 'a wider lens than the white majority located in the privileged spaces of the centre are able to deploy' (Rollock 2012: 65). Different perspectives from the margins follow.

Connected to Country and Knowledge Practices But Not Yet Belonging?

Over twenty years, Australian universities routinely commence meetings and conferences with a Welcome to Country by the local Indigenous elder or Acknowledgement of Country by a convenor (Davis 2020). The issue for Aboriginal scholars is more fundamental; about whose knowledge is valued and who speaks for Indigenous people against the background of the failure of Australia to address issues of reconciliation, constitutional recognition of sovereignty and long-term collective trauma created by dispossession of Aboriginal lands, deaths in custody and the lost generation of children, now adults, forcibly removed from their families (Moreton-Robinson 2004). 'Indigenous leadership has been further compromised by the historical-legal legacy of terra nullius, the decree of the Crown stating that Australia was free to those who found it because it was "no man's land"' (Evans and Sinclair 2016: 474). The practice of Acknowledgement ignores the structural and cultural discrimination that Indigenous people experience on a daily basis and how the Indigenous 'leadership problem' is defined (Davis 2020).

There has been a powerful claim for recognition of Indigenous knowledges, the result of social movements in Canada, NZ and the United States (Tuhiwa-Smith 1999, Moreton-Robinson 2004, 2013; Bullen and Flavell 2017). The role of universities in the mis/recognition of Indigenous knowledges and culture is fraught, due to their objectification of Indigenous people over centuries and complicity in the processes and effects of colonization exploitative of Indigenous peoples. An Indigenous scholar, Patricia (A/Professor, Regional) commented: 'Attending university is seen by many "blackfella" activists as a sell-out, not real life, but Indigenous scholarship has been crucial to fighting issues of recognition and reconciliation.' Indigenous scholars and leaders had created for her the possibility for 'activism in the academy and the requirement to reconfigure the imagined ideological spaces that imprison us, literally and figuratively' (Patricia). Such activism has seen national ethics protocols requiring recognition of Indigenous knowledges and co-ownership of research with Indigenous communities.

Yet the 'problem' of under-representation of Indigenous students, scholars and leaders after decades of structural inequality and cultural exclusion is often located at the feet of Indigenous people. As Patricia put it: 'Diversity is a problem to be managed. Women are the problem, blackfellas are the problem . . . whereas in fact whitefellas are the problem – token statements and superficial behaviour to create images of "helping" while removing funds.' The solution offered is Indigenous leadership, but the problem is that when Indigenous scholars speak up about racial inequality and institutionalized racism within an institutional and political context, hegemonic whiteness is not named.

Indigenous leadership is itself a problematic term, a 'White male' and Western idea (Evans and Sinclair 2016: 471). Without essentializing culture and values as fixed and unitary, Australian Indigenous people view decision-making (not leadership) as a collective practice based on the relationship between elders and their communities in a two-way dialogue. Individuals are called upon to 'lead' for their learned expertise dependent on situation. It is also purposeful, with Indigenous leaders' commitment to cultural authorization, identity and belonging, being the custodian of cultural values and expressing and containing trauma, while empowering and generating hope (Evans and Sinclair 2016: 475).

Indigenous leadership is also a gender issue. White (2010: 11) argues white invasion changed the social relations of gender from one of equal complementarity of Aboriginal men and women by repositioning Aboriginal women's status within European patriarchal frames of reference. Aboriginal women's roles in traditional society were, she argued, 'misinterpreted or distorted due to a male bias in early reporting' that 'rendered the Aboriginal woman invisible and subordinate'. White colonization produced new forms of oppression with persistent everyday gendered racism of white Australians and chauvinism as Black men adopted white modes of masculine dominance. The first Indigenous woman to be a magistrate and bureaucrat, stated: 'It is not easy being a black woman at the top of a white bureaucracy. The hardest part has been dealing with chauvinist males (mostly black) who are threatened by a woman having this much power' (Pat O'Shane cited in White 2010: 13). Indigenous women have resisted this positioning and been in the forefront of community capacity building, as scholars, policy activists, bureaucrats and advocates for reconciliation.

Australian universities have adopted an incremental and symbolic approach to Indigenous reconciliation, initially appointing Indigenous Australians as Chancellors. Indigenous professors heading dedicated institutes have been expected to communicate and integrate Indigenous perspectives across the university (Bunda et al. 2012). Indigenous students and academics are therefore expected to 'fit' the university which 'imposed its colonial, Western educative framework' (Perry and Holt 2018: 343). Such contradictory positioning means, Moreton-Robinson (2013: 340) argues: 'In our everyday existence we deploy a "tactical subjectivity". . . . For example, one can present a seminar paper and perform according to the protocols of the white patriarchal academy while simultaneously challenging its episteme.' As Indigenous scholars, their language is tempered, framed and informed not only by normalizing academic practices but also 'from the constraints of history, power (or lack of it) and context . . . sharing stories and suspending disbelief and cynicism to engage in imaginative possibilities' (Evans and Sinclair 2016: 485).

The Indigenous professors in this study spoke about 'having to negotiate complex tensions in their leadership, such as being both inside and outside of Aboriginal culture and practising leadership through storytelling, which honours the natural world, while also meeting performance accountabilities' (Evans and Sinclair 2013: 473). Indigenous leaders acted as outsiders-inside a culturally inscribed 'whiteness' of university leadership. Their leadership practices included 'conventional leadership work, such as formal representation and advocacy', working with elders and carrying on traditions and 'embodying their cultural identities just through being present' (Evans and Sinclair 2016: 485).

How Indigenous research institutes or professorial appointments were located relative to senior management, as with diversity practitioners, was critical in terms of proximity to power. At Utech, a DVC (Vanessa) had assumed responsibility for the Indigenous Unit, appointed an Associate Professor in Indigenous Knowledges and Indigenous HR staff to address specific difficulties in recruiting and retaining Indigenous staff. Utech had advertised for Indigenous applicants in the highly competitive early career scholarships (STEMM alone had 395 applications for 9 positions). Vanessa argued that 'there's that balance between the best and trying to give Indigenous applicants a real chance', only partially recognizing that notions of 'the best' are culturally biased while realizing we need to develop 'the capability with all staff around intercultural and indigenous knowledge'. What constitutes 'merit' is in contention.

The strategy most utilized across the university sector was to establish a dedicated Indigenous Unit (Bunda et al. 2012). At Regional, the Indigenous Unit head, Patricia, felt they lacked senior line managers or a senior academic dedicated to the job which meant there was no voice at the executive level, hence little progress. Liz, director of Teaching and Learning, was working with the designated Aboriginal women leaders to design a subject for transforming teaching practices for Aboriginal and Torres Strait Islander (ATSI) students. Liz acknowledged that it was 'really difficult territory for a non-Indigenous person to navigate but I'm really committed to the idea that you have to take some responsibility'. She was building on well-established programmes and practices at Regional for Indigenous students in education and health in remote communities, a strong history in Indigenous Studies and student support officers, two female Aboriginal professors as previous Heads of School and dedicated scholarships. All acknowledged that previous gains were at risk without Indigenous issues being integrated through all aspects of the strategic plan.

With restructuring underway, other equity areas were at risk, with no targeted programme for women or those of non-English-speaking background and in the blueprint there were no 'visible statements about indigenous leadership' (Hannah, Associate Head, Research, Regional). At the school level, attempts were made to mentor Indigenous academics in research and into leadership. Hannah considered cultural awareness was lacking among many academics, and this was exemplified when a federally funded project on Indigenous cultural competence in leadership was told by the funder: 'You can have the grant but you've got to have an Indigenous CI. The white CI said, why didn't I think of that?' To add to the sense that Regional's diversity story had 'lost the plot' was the widely expressed disappointment over a white man without experience being appointed as diversity manager.

Increasingly, most non-Indigenous academics in all three universities recognized that Indigenous units or senior academic positions placed the burden of responsibility for Indigenous practices, knowledge integration and culturally appropriate pedagogies onto the few Indigenous staff, thus allowing 'whitefellas to get away with ignoring learning about Indigenous stuff' (Patricia, A/Professor, Regional). Adam (Dean, Regional, HASS) agreed that

> we do lots of superficial things that white people do around cultural issues. We've got one Indigenous support person who's paid one eighteenth of the rest of us are paid. We give her two-hours notice to do a welcome to country, we send every aboriginal student over to her, and we ask her about any aboriginal issue that arises. It is absolutely problematic.

Universities were moving towards replicating the gender mainstreaming approach of the 1980s by embedding Indigenous issues into the corporate plan to produce cultural change. At Go8, Phil, an Indigenous Professor, was appointed into a dedicated PVC position. Phil had full authority to access the key committees and aimed for 'a fundamental re-conceptualization of Indigenous higher education' through recognition at the centre to 'position Aboriginal higher education as a key enabler rather than the boutique end of policy outcomes'. His strategies included 'developing a framework that will find success around participation', focusing on Indigenous under-representation in STEMM and the professions that meant a 'move away from conceptualizing the equity problem as a deficit' and to see 'Indigenous participation as an asset'. To achieve these aims, Phil sought to embed in strategic plans and KPIs of deans and service providers around Indigenous students and staff, strategies to 'work within the mission, the history, and the vision of the organization' because 'the leverage for Indigenous higher education space is weak and it gets weaker if you're moving against the flow'. His agenda was to intervene in academic and organizational development, student and staff recruitment through a 'centralized service' integrated into the university business plan. This approach to changing policies, processes, practices was to 'hook into those existing structures and as those structures change we will be developing new approaches'.

While Phil claimed there was a 'reservoir of goodwill ready to be mobilized', there was the danger of working within the corporate logic. Bullen and Flavell (2017: 583) argue that the 'application of Western "quality indicators" to learning and teaching for Indigenous content demonstrates an innate lack of institutional understanding of the complexities of teaching interculturally and the "unlearning" which needs to occur for students [and staff] to become critically self-reflexive and develop capacity for ontological pluralism (essential for graduate intercultural capability)'. For an Indigenous PVC to be close to the executive linked both the moral authority of Indigenous recognition and the traditional 'masculine' authority required within this particular university. The ambitious whole-of-university scope was legitimated by the executive, very different from the shakier claims of authority of Indigenous units distanced from executive power, usually run by women and positioned to service the faculties rather than demand action (Bunda et al. 2012). The danger is whether mainstreaming leads to domestication, reducing the disruptive energy of diverse leadership practices, knowledges and ontologies.

The Visible Invisibility of Ethno-Racial Difference

While Indigenous voices have been gaining recognition, silences enveloped issues of ethno-racial difference. When asked about cultural diversity, most academic managers and professors referred to recruiting academics from Western nations: the United States, the United Kingdom and Europe. The usual trope explaining the lack of cultural diversity in senior management and the professoriate was that there was a lack of eligible academics in the pipeline. Yet academic staff were culturally diverse and there was a growing cohort of international non-European post-doctoral fellows from China, India, Vietnam, Singapore, Indonesia, South America, Africa and the Middle East. Yet few were recruited even at lecturer level, with most international graduates returning to their home countries with few doctoral graduates staying to work because changes in visa and migration policies made appointments complicated (Blackmore et al. 2016). For those who stayed, Martin (Professor, Go8, HASS) commented: 'It's hard to break in especially if you're a woman and non-English speaking from Asia.' Martin could cite only one, an exceptional Vietnamese graduate who was a fluent English speaker and writer who gained a continuing position. He predicted: 'she'll go to positional leadership, she's really smart and knows how to lead, [produces] quality work that counts and so ticks every box. Very nice person, works hard and manages two kids. Her husband's an academic, smart, very nice and positive', and he knows the game and supports her. Exceptionalism was again required of 'the Other' to gain entrée.

The lack of ethno-racial diversity was an emerging issue for academic managers. Roy (Head, Regional, STEMM) named the paradox of seeking to position Regional as Asian oriented and the lack of Asia-Pacific diversity as 'around the room you see Anglo Saxons . . . Irish, Canadian, US, Aussies . . . one person who was not white'. He confronted the Western-centric colonial view of what constitutes quality and excellence when he was trying to recruit from China, India, Indonesia and Papua New Guinea. 'Someone said: 'I think it would be quite difficult to find the quality.' I took exception with that. 'There are tons that rise to the top. I have a female Indian student that's amazing.' Adam, a Dean (Regional, HASS), was seeking to change the profile: 'We've appointed staff that wouldn't have fitted the dominant culture in the past . . . deliberately mixing it up.'

When asked about why the many non-Anglo-European academics who study and work at the Go8 don't get jobs or selected into senior levels, a professor at Go8, Martin (Professor, HASS), commented: 'We allow them to compete on merit . . . then some people say on a selection committee they like people who look like them . . . really flawed. The classic NESB person is slightly better than everyone else in the field, they get short listed and not selected.' Ken (Head, Go8, HASS) agreed: 'We have bright doctoral students from Indonesia or China. There's no way they're getting even apprenticed into the university as academics here. Are none of them going to fit the mould? Is this something we need to talk about?' The non-Anglo-European outsider does not 'fit' the team, the culture or the job (based on criteria such as fluent English), which justifies implicit sexism and racism (Blackmore et al. 2006, Grummell et al. 2009b).

Ahmed (2004: 2) talks about how whiteness becomes a 'familial tie . . . a form of racial kindred that recognizes all non-white others as strangers'. Discrimination is based on arguments that difference causes discomfort for the dominant group, disrupting social interactions and relations, contrary to discourses about the value of diversity. These exclusions fail to challenge dominant gender, class or racial capitals nor the hegemonic whiteness of leadership and white, masculine and scientific dominance of knowledge hierarchies with all their Western epistemological and ontological assumptions (Blackmore 2020). Difference is positioned as problematic. White homogeneity of the corporate bubble of executive and senior management is about being and relating comfortably, thus discouraging non-Anglo leadership aspirants because they fear feeling unwelcome.

Trespassers and 'Bodies Out of Place'

Race and class matters were raised primarily in interviews with women at Go8. A Dean (Jay, Go8, HASS), having lived and taught in Denmark, the United States and Hong Kong, also found Australia was 'a far more aggressive society to the extent of bullying. . . . The misogyny is very explicit and I was quite horrified by the racism'. Alison (Diversity Manager, Go8) said while policies and procedures around issues of gender and race were the 'bedrock stuff' of discrimination and harassment, the issue now was 'how we're going to question, problematize the implicit, and previously unquestioned, and how we are going to say, to senior people on promotion committees, what's in their heads and get them to think differently'. Ahmed (2012) talks about institutional speech acts where issues such as racism and sexism are named (in policy), but they are non-performative as there is no action following. Saying is not doing but saying can produce symbolic violence if many women and ethnic minorities do not experience inclusion.

The following three vignettes illustrate how the specific institutional context of the performative culture of Go8 creates a duality of visibility/invisibility due to the intersectionality of gender, class and race difference. Black and post-colonial feminist standpoint theorists argue that storying 'does not valorise experience as an explanation or justification in itself but should be seen as an interpretation of the social world that needs explaining' (Mirza 2009: 5).

Ichika's Story

A female A/Prof, Ichika, had come to Go8 from Japan after the earthquakes. She and her husband, an expert in IT, had worked in the United States and the United Kingdom and left the 'autocratic and 'patriotic nationalistic education' in Japan to seek citizenship in Australia. 'Being Japanese was definitely a racial ethnic advantage' she felt in her appointment. Her disciplinary area was inclusive and welcoming, other than bullying by a senior male Japanese professor. Meeting with HR did not solve the problem, but she refused to resign: 'I'm going to keep fighting. He is Japanese and so it's a sexism and gender thing, it's not racism.'

Outside her discipline she felt her embodied difference when cultural tropes and everyday racism were articulated in meetings such as 'I don't want to supervise Asian students because there's too much work . . . the English problem.' She found 'being a 'body out of place' in white institutions had 'emotional and psychological costs to the bearer of difference' (Mirza 2009: 115) and was shocked at the deprecating way in which other cultures were talked about in meetings such as 'all American are deadbeats' and 'their PhD dissertations are not the same standard'. She was targeted by a male PVC because of her Harvard PhD: 'it's inbreeding, you guys don't have an external examiner system for your dissertation.' Another PVC intervened saying, 'that's too insulting'. Having worked in many universities and for the United Nations, she had never experienced humiliation like this. She said: 'I was serving the President of Finland and advising foreign ministers. Nobody in a higher-up position says that kind of thing to put other people down. If you're a leader you bring people up.' In other meetings she felt 'some people try to put me down probably because I'm an Asian, a woman, and try to position me as a second-class citizen'. At her first faculty meeting over two hours 'nobody said hello and just talked to each other' and when 'nobody looks in your eyes, you feel excluded psychologically'. Calling on Bourdieu, Puwar (2004: 51) talks about how 'over time, through processes of historical sedimentation, certain types of bodies are designated as being "natural" occupants of specific spaces . . . some bodies have a right to belong in certain locations, while others are marked out as trespassers'.

Black or Asian bodies are 'constructed as not representing the racial norm' in white institutions. As 'space invaders' their visibility is apparent merely by entering the room. This female Japanese professor referred to 'the double take as if you are not meant to be there' and a feeling articulated by Puwar (2004: 51).

> There is an infantilization, as if you lack authority to speak or are only expert in race and or gender according to your body and not the authority as universal white masculinity claims . . . you are both invisible but also under hyper-surveillance, and all speech and bodily acts are considered to represent the embodied other and yet you are misplaced with regard to your authority.

This professor's response was to speak up and dispute the cultural stereotype of Japanese women being submissive and passive. 'Yeah, I'm supposed to be quiet and I can be vocal, I say things that I think it is right and some people don't like it.' Emphasizing her proactive stance and how the academic habitus 'can also be controlled through the awakening of consciousness and socio-analysis' (Bourdieu 1990: 116), this Japanese professor researched the lack of cultural and gender diversity in leadership. She talked with the Chancellor, citing top-ranked international universities which monitored minority representation. Even top universities in Japan 'which is such a racist society, and Chinese universities have African Vice Chancellors. . . . But here they're all white males. If you talk about diversity inclusion while keeping leaders white males then it's not leadership.' She cited how top journals such as *Nature* 'feature articles on the importance of ethnic and cultural racial minority representation in the field'. In Australia, no statistics are collected on minority ethnic representation other than for Indigeneity by any university, the Commonwealth, ARC or Universities Australia, rendering the dominant whiteness in leadership as unproblematic.

Additionally, this gender and racial injustice were magnified by epistemic injustice as her expertise went unrecognized. Her deputy director was shocked when he found out she had been an advisor to a federal minister in Japan only when a TV company wanted to do a programme on her: 'I was quite big over there . . . I have some influence . . . don't talk about it unless I get asked. . . . Here, I'm totally excluded. I'm like a hermit.' She felt mentored at the UN more than at Go8 because here 'academia is very self-centred and our goal is to put ourselves up above anybody else. Like everybody is encouraged to be selfish . . . there is no collective goal'. A new appointment of a diversity inclusion director in the Chancellery and the SAGE programme gave her some optimism for women in STEMM but not her field. She had to counter stereotypes that 'Asians don't want to be leaders, arguing there were a lot who wanted to lead but can't'. Because of her experiences of exclusion and bullying, she preferred to mentor rather than take up a formal position 'because I have family and I want my personal life and to do research'. Ahmed (2004), when she names racism, is reminded by others that she is a professor, as if blackness of a woman professor means the whiteness of the organization recedes and based on the assumption that she has power to bring about wider change.

Chi's Story

At Go8, other women also felt like 'a body out of place'. A Vietnamese female migration scholar had a transient career as an international undergraduate then PhD student in the UK, Singapore and Europe. Now married with two children after seven years on contract and in a senior lectureship, she still struggled with being an Asian woman at Go8. Despite her self-proclaimed problematic accent, she had 'very high teaching scores'. While she initially mixed with her colleagues she felt that 'I didn't belong . . . it was so white' and 'very alienating not knowing the rules of the cultural game . . . I have to work hard to show that I fit in.' Chi confessed that 'I feel lost. Like I have an identity crisis. On the one hand you have to fit in and perform in a way that people don't question your credibility, your exceptionality. On the other hand, you don't feel that you belong here or to the homeland anymore.' Ahmed (2012) argues it is difficult to speak about race even when race is present in terms of who was sitting around the table.

As a mid-career academic, Chi's response after her second child was to withdraw from any form of leadership 'because it traumatized me, I didn't feel like I got the respect. . . . There's a lot of politics'. Exclusion also has health and well-being effects (Burford 2017). She felt that 'the biggest problem that I struggle with as an Asian person' was that promotion required taking on bigger leadership roles whereas in the United States or the United Kingdom, good research was enough. 'In this university if you don't get an ARC grant you can't be promoted to Associate Professor . . . I'm a qualitative person so it's very hard to collaborate in a niche area of one or two people . . . and this field was pushed around in the ERA game.' Again, epistemic injustice was produced and experienced personally as failure due to systemic policies and institutional practices. Despite publishing well, being mentored and advised to do a leadership course, she lacked the social and academic networks that many Australian international students had developed through their supervisors (Heffernan 2021a). For her, multiple factors (gender, race, discipline, career history) converged to produce a sense of isolation.

Anita's Story

Anita's story illustrates how the intersection of gender, class and discipline impacted on her as a feminist queer scholar in gender studies. Coming from a government school and single-parent family background, she lacked the intergenerational cultural and economic capital associated with the elite university but had accumulated sufficient intellectual capital by winning successive scholarships. Her early career fellowship contract at Go8 allocated her 40:40:20 research/teaching/service, but 'it's like 100, 100, 100. I teach three subjects a year, have to publish and do a lot of administration.' Anita felt 'out of place' at Go8 whereas her previous Go8 university had a 'more liberal middle-class atmosphere . . . not like this Go8 with old money, upper class, kind of thing and just physically a sandstone. And the way that people feel like it's a really important place just to work here, it's alienating. Even teaching, I feel really different from my students.'

Additionally, she came out as queer, the triple jeopardy of being female, queer and working class (Wilson et al. 2021). Despite finding it difficult to link to people of similar background and with a similar 'oppositional disposition' due to this sociocultural disjuncture (Keane 2011: 449), she felt privileged. But, as for her Japanese and Vietnamese colleagues, she did not have the emotional investment in, nor did she acquire, the same emotional capital that their colleagues accumulated from Go8's prestige, and she felt psychologically distanced from the institution, her colleagues and students.

In this context, for these three women, any display of agency was disrupting normalized relations and disconcerting as not 'fitting' due to assumed sociocultural stereotypes about 'Asian women' or working-class women. All three, at different stages of their careers, felt out of place, invisible yet highly visible, bearing the emotional costs (anger, anxiety) of alienation from their organizational context, unable to distance themselves emotionally, as could men who assumed that their bodies had power (Burford 2017). They were expected to represent and 'perform' diversity within the university (Thunig and Jones 2020) and also bore the burden of guilt and emotional labour of pastoral care for those students and colleagues who also felt marginalized or out of place (Wilson et al. 2021). The daily experiences of exclusion discouraged them from aspiring to formal leadership which they knew would make them even more open to surveillance and discomfort because they were in a 'structural position of being the guest or stranger, the one who receives hospitality, which keeps us in certain places, even when you move up' (Ahmed 2009: 43). They had become familiar with local academic practices but still felt out of place, belonging and not belonging, living with an 'hysterisis effect', in which one is constantly aware of and anxious about one's place in a social space or leadership position. As outsiders-inside, these women needed to both find out and mobilize the 'rules of the game' by 'strategizing' while never getting a full sense of the game, forever feeling like 'double strangers' (Atewologun et al. 2016). Regardless of their personal disposition, their gender, race and class positioning meant they felt they were unable to convert their intellectual capital into the same social and symbolic capital considered as prerequisite for leadership.

Universities are uncomfortable places for academics who are not Anglo-European. While Asian-Australian academics made up 15.4 per cent of academics and 16.8 per cent of PhD holders in 2016, they felt their contribution to knowledge production, international collaborations and output due to their cultural capital had gone unrecognized. Over 60 per cent felt they were under-represented and saw structural and cultural barriers for advancing into senior management with 40 per cent experiencing racism, ethnic stereotyping and/or marginalization', and female respondents reporting the double bind of gender and minority status (Oishi 2017: 7). Indigenous scholars similarly cite significant cultural and structural boundaries to them accessing leadership (White 2010, Aikman and King 2012, Anderson et al. 2008).

Academic women even in senior positions were astutely aware and self-conscious of how they were historically situated within the doxic structuring of gender, power and knowledge within the university. Indigenous feminist, Moreton-Robinson (2013) argues from an Indigenous standpoint, being marginalized provides an individual with a capacity to understand what the impediments are to being treated as equal within an organization both systemically and interpersonally. Bourdieu (1999: 511) came to a similar position later in life stating that '"occupants of precarious positions" within social spaces frequently become exceptional "practical analysts". (T)hese individuals are constrained, in order to live or to survive . . . to practice a kind of self-analysis, which often gives them access to the objective contradictions which have them in their grasp, and to the objective structures expressed in and by these contradictions' (Bourdieu 1999: 511, Murgia and Poggio 2018). Bourdieu depicts this insider/outsider perspective as the productive reflexive resource of a 'cleft' habitus. The same level of reflexivity appears to be lacking for many men living an untroubled coherent academic life of a white masculine scientific professorial habitus in an elite university. For universities, diversity discourses focusing on those who are different leads to misrecognition of masculine domination. At the same time, men as academics may be systematically advantaged, but as 'men can be caught up on the same form of imprisonment; that is, maintain an attachment to certain performances of masculinity which are no longer acceptable or functional, and this is counterproductive' (Webb et al. 2002: 25).

In this university context of dominant white masculinist leadership of Go8, there was a Western presumption about what constituted leadership. Research on university leaders in Vietnam illustrates how women leaders negotiated layers of gendered cultural, religious, ideological, colonial and anti-colonial impositions, negotiating strong public roles while maintaining strong familial obligations (Do and Brennan 2015). Decolonizing cultural stereotypes (East/West, masculine/female styles) of leadership requires recognizing the complexity of the hybrid identities of academic lives (Blackmore et al. 2015). But in the contemporary university, diversity is both a problem and a paradox for those who embody diversity, and ultimately as a discourse can be a 'cop-out or a cuddly term' for institutions (Ahmed 2009: 43).

Beyond Diversity Management

Multiple forms of injustice – gender, race, class and epistemic – continue to be mobilized through the structural/cultural dynamic relations of the academy. Universities are not exemplars of inclusion despite being badged as good EEO employers and representations of gender and cultural diversity on websites. These representations often constitute a form of symbolic violence as the

> model of diversity in our organizations which reifies difference as something that exists 'in' the bodies of others. Visual images of 'colourful' happy faces are

used to show how the university has embraced difference. In fact, just using the very word 'diversity' is seen to 'do things' for the institution. The very arrival of the black/othered body into white/normative organisations is used as evidence that spaces of whiteness and privilege no longer exists, and so to speak about racism is to introduce unwanted 'bad feelings'. (Mirza 2009: 5)

Diversity policy can be seen by academic women as a performative institutional act or asset and not what many women or non-Anglo academics experience. This domestication of diversity policy allows academic managers to assume a 'moderate feminism' by taking a softly softly approach. Missing from these moderate feminisms of many women in senior academic management is a focus upon collective action and the role that structural and cultural forces play in the cycle of erection, fortification and defence of gender-based inequality. Instead, these moderate feminisms venerate neoliberal ideals, with a discourse that focuses on the primacy of the individual and the language of the market (Tzanakou and Pearce 2019: 1192).

This assimilationist approach, which focuses on changing the other to 'fit' the organizational goals and dominant cultures and not recognition of and/or respect for difference, informs leadership development. Mirza (2009) points out that proceduralist approaches to EEO (e.g. Audits) are not race neutral and work–life policies fail to address cultural difference. Leadership development continues to use worn-out corporate tools of 360 Degrees or Myer-Briggs to raise self-awareness but do not name institutionalized racism and sexism. Nor do these programmes require as a starting point, self-recognition of whiteness and/or hegemonic masculinities (Blackmore 2010b), and never use the stickier words of racism, whiteness, systemic inequality or power (Ahmed 2012). Leadership development programmes focus on 'developing' leadership 'competencies', as if emotional intelligence is a skill and emotions are apolitical, under the general notion of 'relationship management' (e.g. conflict resolution) rather than addressing the core issues of how power and difference work through everyday relationships (Gentle 2014: 75–6). For Black women in particular, it means that the diversity discourse is vacuous (Squire 2017).

Diversity has therefore become an 'institutional thought structure', which now appears as a 'given or common-sense based on a belief-value system, strategy and organizational rationale as well as authority structure that it is assumed is shared' (Litvin 2002: 70). It's liberal democratic frame relies on flattening out into a system of differences that can be accommodated as varying degrees of sameness. Diversity therefore remains 'reframed in terms of what it can do to improve management, not what it can do to develop the conditions of social justice and democracy citizenship in Australian society' (Yeatman 1990: 16). Current approaches to diversity do not disrupt the dominant corporate logic of practice. Indeed, when 'the documents that document racism are used as a measure of good performance [and when] race inequality becomes a performance indicator you know you are in trouble' (Ahmed 2009: 42). For example, the aggregates of social statistics and data gathering facilitate wide generalizations and have a stabilizing function in a situation in denial of gender and ethno-racial hybridities, fluidities and identities (Czarniawska and Hopfl 2002: 3). Remedying racial and gender inequality requires a radical rethink. The 'traditional emphasis of EEO legislation on policies and procedures to bring about gender equity in academia needs to be accompanied by cultural change programs that make explicit and challenge behaviours that reproduce and reinforce male hegemony in academia' (Kjeldal et al. 2005: 431). Inclusivity requires engaging organizational members at all levels in questioning their assumptions, biases, values and preferences to consider how the way they work may advantage or disadvantage some and not others. It is about what values are dominant, how success is represented and enacted, what heroics are overvalued and what background work is undervalued. It requires an explicit equity narrative from executive leaders as a strategy to keep gender and cultural difference upfront in all planning and execution working both within/against corporate logics.

Chapter 9

CARELESS MANAGEMENT, THE VULNERABLE UNIVERSITY AND CRITICAL LEADERSHIP

The vulnerability of Australian universities due to careless leadership of politicians and university executives over thirty years was fully exposed by Covid-19 in 2020. Writing this conclusion in the liminal state of living/ working through the sixth lockdown in Melbourne in 2021, I tracked university restructuring yet again with over 40,000 redundancies that could be counted across thirty-nine universities (Guthrie 2021a). Before Covid-19, changing geopolitics in Asia and the Indo-Pacific region had already heightened risk for Australian universities vulnerable to rapid shifts of policy and student mobilities. The pandemic amplified the significance of leadership in all its forms – intellectual and populist, toxic and empathetic. Covid-19, the great disruptor, has had devastating consequences for academics, professional staff, students and communities. Recovery also offers possibilities, if the lessons are learnt, of a more caring, inclusive and purposeful leadership for socially just, sustainable and responsible universities and societies.

Significantly, Covid-19 also exposed the looming crisis in relations between knowledge, society and the state. International studies have charted the reconfiguration of higher education over thirty years due to long-term state disinvestment and privatization, regimes of competitiveness (rankings and research assessment), audit cultures, institutional capture by the administariat, entrepreneurialism and the monetization of academic practice (Wright and Shore 2017: 5–9). Higher education has shifted from being a public good to becoming a private investment. In Australia, serial organizational restructuring has achieved greater flexibility and productivity at the cost of work casualization and overload. Academic disenfranchisement has led to widespread disenchantment with and disengagement from management and with achieving leadership. Academic managers have been entrapped in the survival discourse of the 'neoliberal psychic prison' because universities are 'strapped for cash' (Eric, VC, Utech). Higher education is in a state of 'hysteresis' as the 'field undergoes a major crisis and its regularities (even its rules) are profoundly changed' (Bourdieu 2000: 160).

Game of Thrones: Winter Is Coming

In the late twentieth century, the 'Australian single idea' was of a university 'owned by the state but self-governing, meritocratic and secular, comprehensive rather than specialist', teaching professional courses (Davis 2017: 14). Three decades of serial restructuring responding to volatile contexts and policies means the Australian comprehensive university has become a specialized brand, the unified sector is now differentiated, stakeholder governance has become corporate governance, a state-funded model is now a user-funded model and the public university has become an entrepreneurial university. To achieve such substantive shifts, Australian higher education, as elsewhere (Gupta et al. 2016), has moved through phases of reform focusing on massification and internationalization in the 1990s secure in the geopolitics of a rule-bound order; quality teaching and research in the 2000s in an increasingly world-risk society post-9/11; research excellence and global ranking in the 2010s despite increasing social and economic inequality post-GFC; and now the 2020s, with digitalization and datafication dominating an era of geopolitical tension and pandemic anxiety in which international education and research collaboration are being weaponized and mobility thwarted (Hsieh 2020). The corporate practices of marketization, managerialism, internationalization and financialization have become embedded in university priorities and policies, reconstituting everyday academic practices of teaching, research and service.

Australia stands out as a striking 'case study' of higher education reform. Australian universities, products of colonial histories, geography and an instrumentalist cultural sensibility regarding education (Forsyth 2014) are positioned within competing national narratives: of racism and multiculturalism, of being built on migration but closing borders against 'the Other'; negotiating a Western-centric orientation within an Asian-emergent geopolitics. Politically, universities have been both actors and targets in national debates over recognition contested by, on the one hand, Indigenous people and marginalized minorities of a multicultural and a multi-faith society and, on the other hand, a white masculinist conservative Christian political elite supported by the populist Murdoch media driving social division and waging culture wars against progressive thinking. Externally, academic epistemic authority has been questioned by rising public distrust in democratic institutions due to disinformation fed by social media and conspiracy theorists regarding experts generally and science in particular (Byford 2011).

Internally, issues of cognitive injustice have been raised by feminist, post-colonial and Indigenous scholars (Moreton-Robinson 2004, Fricker 2007). The post-truth era challenges the authority of the university legitimating advanced knowledge when anyone's opinion is equated to expertise (Bell 2017). Rigorous processes of knowledge-making are attacked on websites such as *#RealPeerReview* and systematically disseminated misinformation. Populist politics globally display a rude and dangerous masculinist authoritarianism fuelling divisiveness, imprisoning dissidents, journalists and academics. The Australian Coalition has politicized research by intervening in the Australian Research Council recommendations for funding, specifically against the humanities, five times since 2013 (Jayasira and McCarthy 2021). Democracy and universities are under siege, experiencing increased risk associated with foreign powers and hackers influencing elections and appropriating IP (e.g. state-based hacking of the Australian National University in 2019).

Australian governments have been careless of universities, treating universities as a cost and not an investment, regulating them through strong accountabilities while shifting costs onto students (fees) and alternative fund sources (international students, industry). Since 2010, government funding of commonwealth supported places (CSP) reduced from $11,730 to $11,240 per student, while costs of educating an increasingly diverse student population have increased (Howard 2020: 9). Domestic HDR completions increased 61 per cent and international HDR completions quadrupled (Howard 2020: 63). Paradoxically, while STEMM dominates national priorities, government expenditure on science, research and innovation has increased marginally from a low base of $3 billion in 2000–01 to $3.5–4 billion by 2019 (Howard 2020: 56).

Facing declining funds and increased costs (e.g. research assessment, technology, campus upgrades and diverse student needs) to maintain rankings, university managers have sought to diversify funding, with non-government sources increasing by 158 per cent from 2000 to 2018 (international student fees, industry, philanthropy, etc.) (Howard 2020: 58). Overseas student revenue was 35 per cent for some universities by 2019, with Chinese international students making up 30 per cent Australia-wide (Howard 2020: 10). Australia was second to the United States and ahead of the United Kingdom, Canada, Germany and France in international student recruitment (Australian Government 2020). In 2016, Daniel (PVC, Go8) stated: 'we are deeply rooted if we lose our international student cohort.' International student priorities in choosing study destinations in 2019 were cost, safety and graduate employability, which favoured Australia (IDP 2019). But competition has increased with source countries (e.g. China, Singapore and Brazil) becoming providers for international students in the Indo-Pacific region (Mok 2016). Professional labour markets are more volatile, devaluing the institutionalized capital of the credential (Blackmore et al. 2018). In Australia, the period between graduating and gaining a job in a chosen specialism had stretched to three years from eighteen months (QILT 2019).

This situation fed the VC's fetish for rankings, restructuring and prioritizing with all universities following the money in STEMM, commercialization and international students. By default, the effect has been one of devaluing and downsizing the numerically feminized HASS fields, a pattern of 'dehumanizing' the academy replicated in the United States, the United Kingdom and Canada (Coleman and Kamboureli 2011, Belfiore 2015, Hazelkorn 2015, Morgan 2016, Nussbaum 2010, Small 2013). University rankings, strategic priorities and research assessment have skewed recruitment and promotion practices further towards research and away from teaching and cost-cutting by recruiting more academics at lower levels. Global rankings and research assessment using the quality proxy of metrics privilege older research-intensive universities happy to assert their historical muscularity, creating conditions of impossibility for less research-intensive universities to both teach and research (Rowlands and Wright 2020), resulting in greater differentiation between research-intensive, teaching and research and teaching-intensive universities. A professor (Jeanette, Go8, HASS) in 2018 stated: the system is 'not just two-tier but has a polarized residual sector' with 'policies trending towards a university not doing research but still able to offer PhDs', contrary to the long-held view that research informs teaching. A former DVC (Rosanne) commented: 'I don't know that Perth can sustain five universities or Adelaide three. The Gum Trees are not thriving, nor second-generation universities.' In 2017, six universities were in deficit compared to none in 2009 (Howard 2020).

Australian university executives expected no improvement in funding for teaching in 2018, predicting further casualization, industry partnerships and shorter degrees as improving funding required significant political will. But Australians have been convinced they live with a high taxing regime rather than one of the lowest in the OECD. Yet 'restraining taxation and the resource base available to public institutions compromises the capacity of institutions to prioritize and fulfil their public good role' (Hetherington 2015: 27; Guthrie 2021b). Eric (VC, Utech) commented: 'What's going to happen to use the "game of thrones" analogy . . . winter is coming, and I think it's going to be tougher and never sufficient to the task.' The university funding model was broken even before it was exposed with Covid-19 in 2020. Yet the constantly improving positioning of Australian universities in global rankings with twenty of thirty-nine Australian universities in the top four hundred in rankings and eight under one hundred in 2021, over 90 per cent of units in assessment at or above world standard ERA in 2019 and education services the third largest export (Universities Australia 2020), governments could ignore higher education's vulnerability because it was 'pumping above its weight', but at what cost?

Academics Squeezed Out and Squeezed: A Crisis in the Making

In summary, this text has shown that universities have been caught within the corporate managerialist bind of rampant global capitalism; the legacies of Humboldian imaginaries of a university; and the presentism of surviving in the context of global economic, social, political and environmental uncertainty. The 'triple helix' of university/public/private means universities have become less 'civic', confusing the core functions of teaching and research with economic, not social, impact, such as educating not training professionals for the public good (Walker and McLean 2013). Close relationships with big business driven by market contractualism have meant HASS fields cannot anticipate taking the same autonomous, critical, ethical and moral stance, a concern echoed in the EU, the United Kingdom and the United States (Campbell and Slaughter 1999, Hancock 2020, Lynch et al. 2012). The social contract has shifted from one of trust to 'a transactional arrangement based on agreed-upon strategic goals and tangible outcomes' (Sorensen et al. 2019: 17).

Academics in Australia and internationally have criticized university executives' lack of imagination and intellectual leadership (Besley 2010, Coates et al. 2010, Fredman and Doughney 2012) as they sought to manage the arbitrariness of government intervention in quasi-education markets 'distorted by ranking' (Jessop 2017, Baker 2020). Management's strategies such as branding, diversifying income sources, partnerships with multiple stakeholders and increasing student numbers, while addressing multiple governance accountabilities, have transformed the university workforce (Marini et al. 2019, Maycock 2017, Whitchurch 2018). Senior academic management has multiplied with a large administariat acquiring new forms of entrepreneurial and techno-administrative capital to address external accountabilities, audit internal research and grants and broker new income streams (Enders and Naidoo 2019, McClure 2016). Another non-academic workforce supports student welfare and campus life ad environment.

Furthermore, a digital architecture underpins such activities as universities move into a phase of digital governance characterized by standardization, financialization and datafication (Decuypere and Simons 2014, Selwyn 2014, Williamson 2016a & b). Educational technology experts, 'para-academics', design online learning management systems (Macfarlane 2011) and buildings have been transformed into student-focused purpose-built spaces. Instructional design has meant disaggregating the pedagogical process into curriculum, teaching and assessment to be 'delivered'. Academic practice is being digitally mediated and micro-managed through templated unit guides, assessment rubrics, graduate attributes, timelines and deadlines, even in doctoral supervision. Courses have been unbundled into consumable packages enabling the twenty-first-century learner-earner to negotiate multiple pathways from micro-modules to access higher degrees, a modularization that often renders content less coherent and fragmented while claiming user-friendliness (French 2015). Curriculum decisions are often made by those outside discipline areas.

Quality assurance and external accreditation have imposed regimes of 'tickbox' criteria. Reductive measures based on external citation indices determine what counts with ERA. Technology, therefore, has facilitated standardization while intensifying academic work by requiring constant upskilling, communication on multiple platforms, shorter response times, thus collapsing time/space and accelerating activity schedules (Sellar and Cole 2017, Decuypere and Simons 2014). Many academics felt deskilled in their core work and de-professionalized, while constantly being required to upskill on marginal activities, feeling like educational outworkers to serve the core work of management, their labour counting only when monetized. Many spoke about 'living with alienation' from their core work in a state of 'regulated autonomy' (Lyons and Ingersoll 2010).

While academic work is unbundled and repackaged, academic managers strove for 'the joined up organization as they recognize the importance of having good information and good data to make good decisions, identifying students at risk and then putting in interventions to support them' (Rosanne, former DVC).

For academics in this study, joining up required alignment of their teaching and research practices to institutional and national priorities, constantly reinventing themselves to meet each new priority while displaying evidence of leadership at every step (Enders and de Weert 2015, Ennals et al. 2016). Academic position descriptions and promotion applications expected academics to publish in high-status journals, produce employable graduates, use inclusive pedagogies in flipped classrooms, undertake blended learning, input data into multiple repositories, build industry partnerships, develop international research collaborations, engage with multiple stakeholders, impact on policy and practice and be media active while improving the quality of teaching and research as determined by student evaluations, research assessment and citation indexes: the 'academic superhero' (Pitt and Mewburn 2016). Despite such diversity of academic practice, the organizational structures and practices of universities have become more monolithic and heteronormative rather than heterotopic, about compliance rather than creativity, echoed in centralized rather than distributed leadership.

The Crisis of and for Leadership

University executives also worked under conditions of im/possibility but have become careless about their staff as charted in this text. Caught in the squeeze of underfunding and regulated autonomy themselves, living the 'psychic life of neoliberal subjectivity' (Scharff 2016), executive managers have not, while playing the game of being agile and nimble, ranking and reputation, protected academics from overwork and precarious employment. To be responsive to market and policy volatility, university management sought institutional flexibility by creating, intentionally or not, a 'permanent class of itinerant academics' (Bentley et al. 2013a, Jongsma 2020, Lopes and Dewan 2014, May et al. 2013, Whitchurch 2018). In 2019, academic staff expenditure in Australian universities had reduced since 2000 despite student numbers trebling (Howard 2020: 71). In 2018 over 65 per cent of all staff were on contract or casual, but only senior managers on contract were financially compensated for precarity (NTEU 2018). The Senate Committee on the Future of Work and Workers (2018: 3) stated: 'labour market deregulation . . . has really overshot the mark, and workers are bearing all the costs of flexibility.' The business model of universities has relied on academics gifting a significant number of unpaid overtime of over ten hours a week in order to complete core business, with significant detrimental health and well-being effects, particularly for women (Ribiero 2020, Strachan et al. 2012). This lack of corporate responsibility regarding structural overtime and precarity of work (Rafnsdóttir and Heijstra 2013), a pattern replicated in the UK (THE 2018, Lopes and Dewan 2014/5), Denmark (Opstrup and Pihl-Thingvad 2016), the Netherlands (Jongsma et al. 2020) and Finland (Kallio et al. 2016), showed that HR has protected management and not academic interests, creating further mistrust of management (Leišytė 2016, Lempiäinen 2015, Murgia and Poggio 2018, Read and Leathwood 2020, NTEU 2018a, Waring 2007).

Furthermore, dissatisfaction with management resulted from the squeezing out of academics from decision-making symbolized by the sidelining of Academic Boards/Senates (Rowlands 2017). Highly successful professors felt disenfranchised and disenchanted with corporate values, and therefore many did not aspire or apply to be managers (Chapter 6). Instead, heightened surveillance of the audit culture reduced their sense of being trusted or of trusting management (Schlesinger et al. 2017, Vidovich and Currie 2011, Woeler and Yates 2015). An NSW Legislative Council committee (Matchett 2021 np) concluded that if 'the role of universities is to create new knowledge and disseminate that knowledge to students then the people who do this critical work need to be valued and respected'. The report called on University Councils to act or 'show a failure of leadership' with Australian Vice Chancellors being paid up from $800,000 to $1.5 million (Boden and Rowlands 2020).

In particular, the intensification of labour has been a disincentive creating unsurmountable hurdles to attain research leadership for women in particular. Recruitment of star researchers in the ranking and research assessment frenzy has meant mid-career teachers and researchers, largely women, remain at 23 per cent, a shrinking of the pool of potential leaders. Because Excellence of Research in Australia (ERA) counts only 'research active' staff, universities increasingly recruit teaching-only (called teaching scholars) and research-only positions, thus limiting academic career opportunities and thereby reducing teaching and research positions (Howard 2020: 73). Martin (Professor, Go8, HASS) predicted this pattern would incrementally lead to greater differentiation among academics and universities: 'Academic work is going to be de-bundled. . . . Research won't find its way outside to industry or research organizations but certainly from teaching. And once you reduce teaching costs and administration and servicing costs become impossible, middle-level institutions just get pared right back.'

Consequently, the lack of diversity in senior academic and management continues. In 2019, the typical Vice Chancellor (UK/Australia) was a man aged sixty-two, a scientist, a domestic appointment (UK) or international in Australia, had five years tenure in UK (seven to ten in Australia) and was extremely well paid (in Australia seven or eight times a senior lecturer's salary) (Boden and Rowlands 2020). In both countries the numbers of women VCs stagnated at 20 per cent (Baker 2019). While Indigenous staff had increased 72.6 per cent since 2005, only one-third were academics with 3 per cent of them in senior roles and 70 per cent female, positioned in a service rather than in research capacity building roles (Howard 2020: 81). The Diversity Council of Australia indicates that ongoing lack of gender and cultural diversity statistics in government and Universities Australia data for senior roles make it difficult to track ratios of gender and cultural diversity progression. In general, Australia has dropped in the Global Gender Equity Index from 23rd in 2010 to 50th position in 2020 (World Economic Forum 2021: 11), a devastating result given Australia's leading role in developing gender equity policies internationally in the1980s.

Many academics in this study contemplated leaving the university or not trying for leadership positions due to job precarity. Many rejected the values and practices of corporate leadership and were penalized by the hyper-performativity of research leadership which assumed a continuous track record of publications, research grants and partnerships, lacking the time capacity to rapidly respond to research grant calls (do Mar Pereira 2015, Petersen 2011, Pells 2018). Australian women and same-sex couples with children continue to bear the triple burden of work, community and domestic labour, the lack of universal child care and a tax system penalizing part-time work (Hetherington 2015, Wajcman and Bell 2010). Furthermore, women continue to experience implicit biased understandings of merit and everyday sexism (Apter 2018, Inge 2018). While women have gained a sense of the game of the performative academy and corporate management and displayed a disposition for practical mastery of management or research, the rules and conditions of work are continually changing, impeding rather than facilitating their advancement. Many but not all women remain positioned within a masculine/neoliberal normative framing of disciplinary hierarchies and management, excluded from being in key sites of power in any critical mass that could allow significant cultural shifts.

Higher Education: A Risky Business?

Higher education as a field is shaped by a heightened sense of risk that arises from policy volatility, transformed workplaces, geopolitics, technological innovation, environmental unsustainability and now the global pandemic. A key leadership skill should be to understand and minimize institutional risk (Lumby and Foskett 2011: 30). This risk environment creates 'structures of feeling': 'a particular quality of social experience and relationship, historically distinct from other qualities, which gives a sense of a generation or period' (Williams 2015: 1) and which constitutes the unseen and unspoken affective infrastructure underlying the material and social infrastructure of everyday life within nation states and institutions. Higher education has also become a site of 'generalized anxiety' for aspirational middle-class families and traditional users seeking to maintain their advantage, anxieties which inform an individual's risk calculus (Blackmore 2009). Beck (2013: 10) argues that differences between subjective perceptions of risk (individual responses based on prejudices, fears or individual risk calculus) and cultural perceptions of risk (national politics and contexts) are disintegrating. Fuelled by the ubiquitous social media, risk is 'collectively visible' creating a sense of shared risk (Beck 2013: 8).

Perceptions of risk and the risk calculus of families have become increasingly important in the field of international education (particularly with the pandemic) as to which provider countries are considered safe, of economic value and promise graduate employability (IDP 2019). Furthermore, the value of the university credential, its last point of distinction for Global North providers, is being challenged by Asian-centric providers (China and Singapore) and multiple on/offline providers offering cheaper and shorter specialisms and micro-credentials. Workplace training and new forms of cultural capital (work experience, internships, localized knowledge) are being valued by employers (Tran et al. 2021). Australia has failed (other than the New Columbo Plan) to fully recognize the cultural benefits of migration and intercultural exchange resulting from international education as an investment to consolidate national power 'softly' within the shifting geopolitics of the region and rise of China.

Universities are also high-risk environments for academics. Significantly different by 2020 was the ubiquity of social media which has enabled the rise of democratic social movements and student activism and shifting debates around gender with the game-changing *#MeToo* movement in the United States in 2017 and *#EnoughisEnough* national march against sexual violence to Parliament House by women in Australia in 2020 (Mendes et al. 2018). These social movements have put all men in positional power and government on notice for the ongoing violence against women and the enduring gender pay gap. Social media is now changing practices within the higher education field. Bourdieu, before social media saturation, argued academics have to work with activists, and practise reflexivity as 'Our dream, as social scientists, might be part of our research to be useful to the social movements' (Bourdieu 1998: 58). The digital scholar can network and be a scholar activist linking the university to communities' and 'offer innovative routes to learning' (Daniels and Thistlethwaite 2016: 5). Social media also enables marketing a university's brand online (Hassan 2017), putting pressure on academics to develop an online profile, use social media in teaching and research dissemination and promote their university. Having a media presence is becoming a factor in recruitment and promotion (Lupton and Smith 2018).

But conspiracy theories and 'alternative facts' in a post-truth era challenge the legitimacy of university knowledge and academic expertise as well as the role of universities within the demos (Brown 2015). Social media is also a site of orchestrated trolling which disproportionately target women, people of colour and LGBQTI in universities (Ringrose 2018). A subculture of blogs and fora is 'centred around hatred, anger and resentment of feminism specifically, and women more broadly, 'spread by algorithms of ignorance spawning "online misogyny" or "e-bile", anonymized "mediated misogyny"' (Vickery and Everbach 2018). Furthermore, sexual harassment and toxic masculinity have been exposed as being particularly rampant in Australian elite university colleges (Human Rights Commission Australia 2017). University management have failed to protect their academics from sexist and racist attacks online and in student evaluations (Mitchell and Martin 2018, Rosen 2018) or addressed the psychic trauma that results (Ringrose 2018). This heightens academic mistrust of management.

Equally critical to academics was an apparent carelessness of executive management about the academic values which most considered central to being a university. The professorial discourse is one of educating citizens not just job-ready graduates (Jameson 2019), having the academic freedom to pursue critical inquiry in their research and to speak on matters of public interest (AAUP 2022, Hil et al. 2021). Academics expressed not just the ethical issues arising from business and government collaborations translating research into production or policy service, but how higher education field is being transformed not only by the intrusion of politics and the media but also by multinational edu-businesses such as Pearson (Hogan et al. 2015), edu-philanthropists (Ball 2012) and multinational consultancy firms (Rhoades 2014).

Furthermore academic freedom is also under threat. In 2019, Associate Professor Schroder-Turk, the elected staff representative on the Murdoch University Council, spoke publicly about the lowering standard of international student recruitment. He was dismissed from the University Council, threatened with losing his job and taken to court by Murdoch University to recoup lost revenue due to reduced numbers of international students. The case was thrown out of court as ludicrous and condemned internationally, with Schroder-Turk reappointed to Council (Knaus 2019). The Australian Association of University Professors, formed in 2019 to provide an alternative academic voice to Universities Australia, stated that the Murdoch executive's action demonstrated that university management views international students 'Not as future cultural ambassadors to our country, but as a revenue stream. Just as severe is the fact that *a university* takes it upon itself to limit public and academic debate' (www.professoriate.org.au). Other academic whistle-blowers have been penalized for raising issues publicly about being pressured to pass international students (Cook 2019).

Academic freedom has frequently been confused in public debates with freedom of speech by conservative commentators and radio shock jocks railing against 'political correctness' of universities, selectively forgetting that neoliberal economists, conservative commentators and politicians acquired their 'practical mastery' in student politics in the academy (e.g. Standing Committee 2008). The French Inquiry (2019) concluded that freedom of speech was not an issue. University management's contradictory position has been to defend student protests but less so academic's right to speak out as a public intellectual. In response, new sites of collective activism are emerging, such as blogs (#*ShitAcademicsSay*) and the international Scholars at Risk Network (https://www.scholarsatrisk.org/the-network/).

Academic freedom as a universal principle continues to be tested by university codes of conduct in enterprise agreements which seek to restrict academics to speak publically only in areas of their expertise. Many academics experienced subtle pressure not to publish or go public on issues that may raise the ire of government or potential research partners or lead to reputational damage The capacity for academics to 'profess' with wider social, political and economic issues such as climate change as policy activists and advocates for their specialism and for higher education more broadly as a civic responsibility to community and society and not just their university was considered by many in this study under threat. Academics refute the view that executive management represents 'the university' (Shore and Taitz 2012).

Winter Has Arrived: Covid-19, the Great Disruptor

By 2019 in Australia, previous advocates of neoliberal policies (OECD, industry leaders, economists) had recognized neoliberalism's failure due to increased social and economic inequality, a looming recession, wage stagnation and the need for structural reform (e.g. tax). 'Australia has the resources and the institutional framework to do well but it will require supreme political leadership to change gear permanently' (Tim, DVC, Utech). Then from late 2019 into February 2020, Australia, the canary in the 'coalmine' of climate change, experienced catastrophic bush fires and floods. Covid-19 followed, the unprecedented disruptor due to its speed, scale and impact across Australia and globally. Covid-19 immediately exposed the vulnerability of Australian universities with 35 per cent of international students from China (Marshman and Larkins 2020) when in March 2020, businesses with, and international borders to, China, were closed. The Prime Minister told international students unable to afford staying, 'to go home', leaving 90,000 foreign graduates 'stuck in Australia' without support (Tran and Tan 2020).

Having badly mismanaged the fire crisis, the neoliberal federal government under duress followed most economists' recommendations and initiated radical 'Keynesian' economic interventions. JobKeeper paid employers to keep employees of over a year connected to their workplaces. JobSeeker provided a Covid supplement to an already below poverty-line unemployment payment. Significantly, casual workers, those in the arts and universities, were not covered by JobKeeper, with the government changing the criteria three times to exclude universities because, the Treasurer stated, 'they had to draw the line somewhere'. Commentators considered this epitomized the Coalition government's ongoing antipathy to HE rather than good policy, ignoring the sector's contribution to the national and regional economies and as the third largest export industry. Momentarily, these 'big state' interventions promised a renewal of a social democratic imaginary of post-war reconstruction by doing the previously impossible (e.g. address climate change). Within months the federal neoliberal storyline re-emerged, putting the economy before a healthy society, only to be blocked by state governments (responsible for health) who closed state borders and prioritized health.

Embedded systemic failures and divides were immediately made transparent. Covid-19 highlighted economic and social inequalities resulting from neoliberal policies of outsourcing, privatizing and underfunding health, aged care, child care, welfare and education. The dangers of the gig economy were obvious as casual workers in hospitality, retail, security, cleaning and aged care, the majority living in the most ethnically diverse lower socio-economic suburbs were travelling between multiple workplaces transmitting the virus. They were the most affected financially and health wise as they were without sick leave. It was also a 'pink pandemic' and recession (Donald 2020). As in the university sector, the feminized and casualized education, health and 'caring' occupations upon which both responses and recovery relied were the frontline workers (Ribiero 2020). Women were more vulnerable, largely responsible for schooling at home, and were most susceptible to domestic violence in lockdown. While some men now 'enjoyed' more flexible work arrangements, single-parent families, primarily female headed, experienced greater pressure, among them sessional academics. Various 'blue recovery' schemes in 2020 focused on bolstering male-dominated construction industries and apprenticeships, the Coalition's electoral base, followed by a 'boys' budget' in October with tokenistic funds for women and no support for the arts or universities.

The pandemic foregrounded multiple leadership narratives. Globally, political leadership with Covid-19 was in disorder due to dysfunctional and divisive narcissistic politics of Johnson in the UK post-Brexit and Trump fuelling populism and inciting dangerous political and racial divisions in the United States. As Ahmed (2004: 19) states: 'It is the emotional reading of hate that works to bind the imagined white subject and nation together.' The rise of authoritarianism in Turkey, China, Iran, Myanmar and Russia has seen academics and journalists imprisoned if not worse in a hegemonic project of 'hypermasculine authoritarianism' stifling dissent (Wood 2016).

In Australia in 2019, an unexpected election result meant Scott Morrison from marketing, tourism, former Treasurer and Immigration Minister became Prime Minister of the Coalition federal government. A Pentecostalist, Morrison garnered support from a small cadre of religious and socially conservative politicians in the Liberal party, backed by the Murdoch media and right-wing radio 'shock jocks'. Morrison, forever pragmatic, having been condemned for failing to lead during the catastrophic bushfires and floods, reluctantly accepted health expertise when managing Covid-19, formed a National Cabinet of the state Premiers but excluded the federal Labor opposition leader. A new national body in charge of economic recovery was populated by big business and mining lobbyists. By contrast, state premiers put health (their responsibility) before the economy, closed state borders and introduced lockdowns 2020–1, accruing significant political capital. Unity frayed in 2021 with the NSW Liberal premier badly mis-managing the Omicron variant due to late and soft lockdowns, leading to its rapid spread to Victoria. Oncron has spread rapidly and caused more deaths because of the delayed federal acquisition of both vaccines and Rapid Antigen Tests.

By contrast, Indigenous leadership practices based on cultural knowledge of country and both-way learning through dialogue with all stakeholders worked through the Coalition of Peak Organizations (White 2010). *Black Lives Matter* was a major global disruptor in May 2020, reverberating in Australia, which continues to struggle over Indigenous reconciliation. Thousands of Indigenous and non-Indigenous people (masked) peacefully marched on June 8 in recognition of 432 *Australian Aboriginal Black Deaths in Custody*, frustrated and angry about the Coalition government's outright rejection of the Uluru Statement in 2017, the product of ten years of consensus building across over 500 Aboriginal communities to inform the Makarrata project – the Yolngu word for the process of truth-telling, resolution and justice. An additional process was set in train, despite the fact that community actions arising from Indigenous storytelling and activism indicate a widespread readiness to rewrite the Constitution to recognize Indigenous sovereignty and potentially form a republic. Indigenous leadership avoided Covid-19 cases in remote Aboriginal communities due to good communication and community-based health management until Omicron went viral in 2022. Yet community-based strategies were not called upon to implement the national vaccination rollout in 2021 or provision of RATs in 2022.

The dominant 'success' story of leadership has been the reassertion of intellectual/scientific capital with scientists informing government about how to 'flatten the curve', 'recover' the economy and manage lockdowns and vaccination rollouts. Academics disseminated research on the virus internationally, putting public good ahead of national and institutional loyalties, highlighting the importance of international research collaboration and practices of ethical collegiality central to developing a vaccine. Bio-tech research institutes (e.g. Doherty Institute) constantly provided government with modelling. The Australian Council of Learned Academies developed Rapid Research Information Forums to offer advice to the National Cabinet. Epidemiologists, virologists and science journalists have become media celebrities. The ABC, despite ongoing funding cuts, has been the primary source of facts and advice about the fires, floods and the pandemic.

The pandemic indicated the strength of democratic institutions in Australia, of a universal health system, the willingness of most Australian citizens to temporarily and voluntarily lose some individual freedoms for the public good with lockdowns and mandated masks in workplaces, and a (temporary) alliance between the state and federal governments, unions and business to protect health then jobs. By 2022, the Morrison government's popularity had waned because of overt failures in federal responsibilities for aged care health, quarantine and the late purchase and delivery of vaccines and RATS, ironically lengthening the time to open up the economy. Federal political inertia since 2013 continues with internal party conflict over climate change, same-sex marriage, abortion, religious freedoms and Indigenous reconciliation. The government's credibility has been punctuated by multiple scandals signalling what economists, retired judges and bureaucrats consider indicates a blatant lack of accountability and poor governance as the public service has been deskilled and politicized with billions spent on consultancy firms doing core policy and implementation work (Daley 2021: 3, Thodey 2019).

Morrison's ethical and moral leadership has been questioned due to his gross mishandling of gender politics when multiple incidents of gender-based violence were exposed by women in Parliament House, including an alleged rape, sexual harassment and inappropriate behaviour leading to an inquiry by the Human Rights Commissioner (Jenkins 2020). This highlighted a toxic misogynist culture, particularly in the Liberal party with 25 per cent women compared to Labor Party's 48 per cent. An online petition (Chantal Contos) naming a rape and porn culture was signed by thousands of girls with stories of how they had been abused by boys from elite private schools. Morrison was condemned for not addressing thousands of women who marched to Parliament House, for establishing internal investigations only of gender issues, for refusing to sack a male Minister under investigation for alleged rape, and for appointing anti-feminist women as Ministers responsible for women's security and well-being, adding to his failure to take responsibility, always blaming others and failing to act with integrity.

The leadership practices that gained trust and were most persuasive in this context were those where decision-making was based on evidence and fairness, where actions showed integrity, respect, care, empathy and focused on the public good and not partisan or self-interest, and where individuals took responsibility and acted ethically.

Cast Adrift: The Covid Restructuring of Australian Higher Education

The rules of the game of global higher education have radically changed. In Australia, universities were cast adrift with the federal government excluding universities and their 140,000 recorded workforce from JobKeeper, and international students from JobSeeker, which would have assisted casual staff and post-graduate student employees. International border closure left 18 per cent of international students outside Australia in March 2020 (Ziguras and Tran 2020). Those remaining without the social protections of citizens relied on university, philanthropic and community care. In contrast, student visa holders in NZ, Canada and the UK were included in unemployment programmes and government-supported universities as key employers and generators of income (Tran and Tan 2020).

Australian universities were in crisis in 2021, with at least seven of them facing financial collapse (Marshman and Larkins 2020), in part because of the reliance on international students from China, but also due to lack of preparedness and contingency funds and reliance on financial markets (Guthrie 2021b). Having invested in buildings for an enriched on-campus experience enhanced by online learning, the pandemic required a rapid move to a fully online learning environment in weeks, advantaging those universities with well-integrated blended learning and multimodal teaching practices. Many academics had to rapidly learn online pedagogical methods using digital tools on video conference platforms with little instruction in the software or technological skills. At the same time, Australian scientists were actively involved in developing a vaccine, but Australia lacked the commercial infrastructure to produce Astra-Zeneca on scale until 2021. The pandemic highlighted the mismatch between university research in the bio-sciences and industry concentration in mining and agriculture (AI 2016).

The federal government shifted blame onto the VCs' reliance on international students rather than lack of funding that encouraged that dependence. In 2021, many international students studied online but their return has been secondary to that of Australian citizens, with 12,000 returning in early 2022. Furthermore, the PM's message to 'go home' to international students potentially meant long-term reputational damage. In contrast, universities in the United Kingdom, the United States and Canada have been actively recruiting since 2020 despite the virus raging. Increasing tensions with China have encouraged discriminatory acts of racism against Chinese/Asian students with Asian-Australian academics receiving hate messages (Tran and Bui 2021). Regional geopolitics has rapidly shifted with anti-Chinese rhetoric on top of escalating trade wars and weaponization of international education. China delivered a list of fourteen complaints against the Australian government while telling students not to select Australian universities. China has been increasingly assertive militaristically, economically and diplomatically with the Belt and Road project and the exertion of soft power through expatriate pressure on Chinese-Australian press (Raby 2020); Chinese national students complaining about what is taught; surveillance of Chinese international students; through Confucius Institutes (Yang 2010); and state-based hacking of government, companies and universities (e.g. ANU in 2019). In response, Australian legislation on foreign intervention has increased federal monitoring of research collaborations. Australia has been awkwardly positioned between a more assertive United States of Biden as a defence ally in the Indo-Pacific region and China, our largest trading partner and primary source of international students.

The Coalition government left the VCs to restructure the sector. Most VCs took this opportunity to reconsider their university's future, size and shape because it was going to be a remarkably different landscape, with losses of $3–4.6 billion by 2023. The immediate response of executives was to downsize; economize across all areas; halt project expenditures and capital investment; remove 'redundant' positions (e.g. travel administrators); temporarily re-negotiate EBAs and salary reductions; and encourage staff leave taking. More consultative university executives provided a package of possibilities for staff to vote on, including voluntary redundancies and salary reductions. A few adopted a corporate hard line without consultation until required by the Fair Work Commission (Guthrie 2021b).

A less transparent strategy across the sector was not to renew contracts or recruit casual staff, a process difficult to quantify because of high levels of casualization and lack of data (NTEU 2018a). The NTEU stated to the 2021 Select Committee Senate Inquiry into Job Security in Universities: 'Universities have largely concealed the true nature of their workforce composition through vague reporting, and usage of outdated Full Time Equivalent measures'. The Casualized, Unemployed, and Precarious University Workers group legal cases led to at least three universities taken to court in 2021 for wage theft (Fenton and Kane 2021). By September 2021, there were 40,000 known job losses (20 per cent of permanent and full-time positions), with women experiencing disproportionate job cuts, and in the 2021 rounds many professors or whole sections were made redundant. This hollowing out of the public university sector will have long-term damage with regard to quality, research productivity, workforce renewal and will affect urban and regional recovery because international students are potential workers and skilled migrants.

The narrowing of a policy trajectory favouring STEMM continues. In 2020, the Coalition government changed the funding rules with the *Job Ready Graduate Act 2020* which disallowed further cost subsidization from student fees of research, compensating with a one-off payment of $1b for research. Job Ready doubled the cost of humanities and business degrees and halved that for the 'vocational' degrees in greatest demand (nursing, education, science), ignoring data that a Bachelor of Arts had the same if not better employment outcomes than science degrees (QILT 2019). Claiming to boost enrolments in STEMM, it disguised the overall effect of reduced funding per head to universities, leading to expensive courses (e.g. environmental sciences) being reduced, and increasing student numbers (e.g. education) with less funding (Gleeson et al. 2020), thus making vocational courses into 'teaching factories' due to over-enrolment. In 2022, with Australian international borders beginning to open and small cohorts of international students arriving following a second round of restructuring, consolidation or closure of courses and the disposal of institutional assets continues in 2021. HASS areas have been hard hit with Latrobe University 'cutting arts and education courses', with Federation University cutting one-third of HASS academics, Swinburne University cutting languages, the University of Melbourne streamlining STEMM undergraduate subjects and the University of Western Australia cutting sociology and anthropology (Ross 2021). Despite this, an NSW Auditor General's report in 2021 indicated many universities could have recovered without sacking staff and the Go8 remain financially solid (Guthrie 2021a, Littleton and Stanford 2021). In 2022, the Australian Research Council has been restructured to include 'industry' representatives in its governance and on all panels and ARC funds have been redeployed towards applied research, putting HASS research further in jeopardy.

Policy analysts suggest the Covid restructuring effect will be a more differentiated sector of leaner, more flexible and focused institutions – teaching-only colleges and research-intensive universities – with tighter requirements for being a university thereby institutionalizing the structural differentiation emerging over decades (e.g. Howard 2021, EY 2020). Such differentiation has long-term equity implications for women with HASS fields being numerically feminized and for regional provision because universities are 'bastions of the sociocultural profiles of cities, regions and states' (Geschwind 2019: 17). Furthermore, the downsizing of HASS ignores how the arts have been critical to social cohesion and mental health during lockdown and how the expertise in group psychology and communicative practices used by health officers, scientists and some politicians were critical to the success of lockdowns and mass vaccination (Jayasuriya and McCarthy 2021).

This is a moment of cultural reckoning about the role of universities in Australian society due to the politicization of research and crisis in trust because of how university executives have managed both before and during the pandemic. In Australia, eleven of the thirty-nine VCs are exiting in 2022. The resignation in 2020 of the University of Adelaide VC, appointed despite multiple incidents of inappropriate sexual relations, raises serious questions about the cultural norms and criteria against which university executives are selected, when only public naming and shaming that impacts on institutional reputation has an effect (Maley 2020). While Australian Chancellors are looking to standardize salary caps for VCs, academics consider 'intellectual leadership has been given away' by senior academic administrators, allowing edu-capitalism to step in' (Trenewan 2017: 256).

Anticipatory Thinking and Critical Leadership Practice

Social conservatives condemn social justice as political correctness, bleeding hearts and inhibiting freedom of speech. Many academic managers view social justice as a 'luxury' countering efficiency and effectiveness. Ironically, the word 'critical' itself is suspect within the corporate logic organizing universities. Yet being critical is not just being oppositional but is core academic and leadership work constituting the academic (and leadership) habitus. (Danvers 2016). Academic managers are surprised that practices of criticality are expected of them as informing their practice, and that they 'need to be able to deal with critique' (Middlehurst and Kennie 2019: 95). Alvesson and Spicer (2012: 375) suggest otherwise.

> Close-up studies of leadership-saturated situations often point out the fragilities, ambiguities and insecurities around leadership discourses . . . managers often struggle to adopt the identity of 'leader' in their day-to-day activities, which are usually full of administrative tasks. Often subordinates raise objections to the manager's ideas, suggestions and instructions, partly based on their detailed knowledge about work and practical circumstances.

Kezar and Posselt (2020: 5) refer to this rejection of criticality as the 'administrators' neoliberal psychic prison' which privileges the market-contractualism and a mindset focusing on efficiency, cost/revenue generation and technology rather than people.

When challenging corporate goals and values, scholars are accused of either utopian (unrealistic) thinking or dystopian despair (Bosetti and Heffernan 2021). Levitas (2000: 199) distinguishes between utopian thinking as 'compensation, escapism or fantasy' and 'anticipatory thinking' that 'focuses on social change and a better world'. In seeking to re-claim the emancipatory purpose of social transformation, Levitas (2000: 199) argues:

> Transformative utopianism requires us not just the project of desire, although it does require us to think seriously and creatively about the conditions for a sustainable and equitable future. This is the 'what' of utopia. It also requires an analysis of the present. How, and by whom, is the transformation to be made? What are the points of intervention into the present system which permit radical transformation? Who are the agents of change?

This study identifies the conditions for a sustainable and equitable future in which universities can be socially and politically responsible, environmentally sustainable (Sterling et al. 2013), as well as be inclusive and safe places of teaching and learning. To do so, academic managers first need to re-focus on maintaining the integrity of the public mission of universities by judging according to what we could or should do 'against the yardstick of an imagined good society' (Levitas 2000: 199). It means, as Brian Schmidt, VC of ANU, stated: 'you make decisions that are right [for students and staff]', citing instituting First Nations Studies as a moral and political undertaking for the university. Furthermore, there needs to be recognition that the strength of a university is that most professors interviewed considered they are not just obligated to their university but also to their disciplinary communities and the public good, committed to educating critical professionals as responsible citizens caring for others in a democratic society or relational contractualism. Such professional ethics need to be valued rather than academic values being realigned to university strategic plans (Stein 2021:16). Tierney and Almeida (2017: 106) contend that

> the responsibility, then, of the academic, is not fitting into the agenda that has been defined in a globalized world but instead focusing on creating a society without injustice. The challenge is not to provide the skills for those who are powerless in a zero-sum game so that the structural relations of power remain the same. Rather, our collective responsibility to one another and to our students is to create the conditions for a reconfigured democratic public sphere that enables voice and a diversity of public stances formed by a renewed sense of obligation to one another and the responsibility of the state for changing those structural conditions that privilege some and disable others

Relational contractualism requires critical leadership which privileges the role of a responsible university in a democracy by proactively retaining its distinctive role to educate a critically thinking and active citizenry who will seek to make a difference and being a critic of and conscience of and for society and the state.

Feminist, post-colonial, Indigenous and environmental leadership literatures speak of purposeful and proactive rather than transactional and reactive leadership (Williams et al. 2017) in which intellectual leadership comprises 'a range of mental, emotional and relational capacities that a scholar employs to build trust as the basis for wider communication and engagement' (Oleksiyenko 2019: 408). Furthermore, intellectual, affective and relational conditions to undertake critical inquiry, ethical and rigorous research requires academic freedom and relationships based on respect, recognition and reciprocity of others' (different) values, positions and feelings. While criticality takes on different meanings in different fields of research, and also different cultural contexts over time (Parker and Thomas 2011: 420), the practice of critical thinking, Andrews (2015: 50) argues, is 'when one is driven by (a) a spirit of inquiry and scepticism, (b) be able to take criticism of one's colleagues and other academics' work as part of the fabric of intellectual exchange and (c) is self-critical', based on ethics and self-reflection. Criticality is also a point of agreement upon which to re-engage with collegial relationships which are the social glue of the university or neo-collegiality (Bacon 2014).

Critical leadership practice is one that is based on equity-driven budgets, shared governance and a mindset of criticality (Jameson 2019, Tillman and Scheurich 2013). A critical leadership habitus shows a disposition to listen and question at all levels individual, team or institution about the external environment and its implications for mission and purpose; mechanisms for external and internal intelligence; an open and full engagement with the diversity of staff, students and partners, recognizing this is an operational and cultural strength; a culture that welcomes challenges to the status quo from any quarter; management structures that are non-hierarchical and which serve to foster and grow new ideas and innovative practice (Middlehurst and Kennie 2019: 95).

Nancy Fraser (2013) offers three principles of social justice that can inform leadership practice: redistributive justice based on sharing more equitably economic and material resources and services; recognitive justice which is about recognition of difference and respect for different subjectivities, experiences and knowledges; and representational justice based on including all stakeholder voices in decision-making. Finally, participatory parity requires individuals or groups having the organizational and individual capacity to influence decisions on matters that impact on them (Blackmore 2016).

Distributive Justice

Executives have the capacity to redistribute resources equitably in ways that create conditions of possibility for the next generation of academics and build leadership capacity. The first condition is to provide security and safety in all learning environment and workplaces for students and staff rather than investing in buildings, financial markets, marketing or expensive management consultants. A safe, secure and inclusive environment means restoring the psychological contract with staff by reducing casualization; paying appropriate wages for intellectual labour; recognizing that universities survive only because of structural overtime; workloads that recognize the actual hours it requires to get the job done; make work–life balance a reality rather than a conflict; provide childcare on campus; and radically reduce the administrative load on academics. Improving working conditions reduces stress, improves health and well-being and imparts a sense of trust in leadership.

Second, recognize that professional autonomy can be more cost efficient as it reduces costly time-wasting administration, and is more likely to foster collaboration, restoring the psychological contract premised on reciprocity because most academics are motivated to do their best, enacting the moral economy of industrial bargaining. Socio-material resources can be mobilized through different ways of organizing that draws on knowledge of practices that work best for academics because technologies tend to extract human labour more often than support it. Rather than digital technology being part of the 'wider struggle over the nature and role of the university-the allocation of resources, design of curricula, and working conditions of university employees' (Selwyn 2014: 121), technologies can be better used to facilitate academic work and be more user-friendly, 'designed to enable rather than constrain with greater academic involvement in the design process' (Neary and Saunder 2011: 333).

Third, executive managers and research leaders are constrained by policy and a range of external factors largely out of their control and the resources available to them, but they have the autonomy to shape institutional practice which encourages rather than undermines cooperation to achieve the aims of multiple stakeholders. University executives should buffer academics from multiple external pressures and obligations by not uncritically articulating external logics into ways of organizing by valuing and protecting the integrity of the university's public mission in terms of defining what counts. ERA provides a case study of producing counterproductive practices as an audit culture with its focus on the performative and what can be measured, and not the substance, which encourages fabrication, wastes time and money ticking boxes.

Furthermore, the inequitable effects of the default management tool of restructuring need to be recognized and avoided as poor management practice in terms of its equity effects. While many VCs struggle with what equity means in practice, equity can be embedded as a principle in strategic planning and mainstreamed through the budget process (Rothe et al. 2008), reviewing impact of financial management processes and decisions on academic practices and priorities rather than devolving equity to diversity managers and middle managers' KPIs after the damage is done (Bensimon and Malcolm 2012). An equity score card demands agreement among leaders about doing good; it is a participatory process and not someone else's problem; remediating practices are needed because past practices have failed; inquiry is seen as a change practice and an academic pursuit; and racial and gender inequality is considered a problem of practice (Bensimon and Malcom 2012). This requires full recognition and participation of academics and professional staff in the process and for executives to put equity as central to their ways of thinking, organizing and storying. An equity audit requires reviewing how resources are distributed across the university and addresses the conditions of work (tenure) which enable academic and professional career paths for all.

Finally, the pandemic highlights the failure of neoliberalism with an impending global environmental disaster. Covid-19 showed academics collaborating across national borders and political persuasion and global elite research universities on global issues (e.g. International Universities Climate Alliance) (O'Malley 2020). Vice Chancellors could use their access to governments and multinational networks to offer intellectual leadership on the national and global stage (e.g. World Economic Forum or Research Universities of the Asia Pacific Rim) (Trenewan 2017). This would require a reinvigorated Universities Australia that could offer a strong political voice promoting the value and role of the university in a democratic society as do professional organizations such as the Australian Association of University Professors and coalitions of student and academics in Public Universities Australia.

Recognitive Justice

This study indicates embedded epistemic injustice and institutional sexism and racism continue to exist in Australian universities. Women, Indigenous and non-Anglo-European academics experience the academic world differently than Anglo-European men. Kwong Lee Dow, one of the first Asian-Australian Deans in Australia, commented that leading universities in the United Kingdom and the United States explicitly commit 'to promoting cultural and ethnic diversity among their academic staff' and collect public data to monitor this aim whereas 'parallel Australian data is patchy and the prominence given to any similar commitment is muted' (Oishi 2017: 1). Making diversity policies meaningful means embedding equity principles throughout all planning. This requires both governments and Universities Australia to collect data on gender and cultural diversity. Furthermore, VCs should undertake 'dynamic institutionalization', which involves a constant review of policies based on reflexivity, resistance and policy reversal with regard to issues of class, gender and ethno-racial outcomes (Kezar and Dizon 2020: 28).

Recognitive justice requires critical leadership characterized by the reflexivity of individuals considering their positioning in terms of power imbalances, their implicit valuing and biases based on gender, race and class and realization as to the privilege of whiteness (Arday and Mirza 2018, Blackmore 2010). It is about using positional authority and resources to attend to the affective economy of the academy, taking public responsibility for a safe and fair workplace by recognizing and rejecting in policy and practice, gender or racially based discrimination, harassment and bullying. Without such practices, being badged as an equal opportunity employer becomes a form of symbolic violence.

Recognitive justice also means epistemic justice. Critical leadership practice means recognition of multifaceted and diverse knowledges and knowledge practices and the benefits of diverse ontologies, politics, identities and bodies within the academy (Blackmore 2020c). Enlightenment dualisms (hard/soft methods) are ingrained in university's institutional hierarchies and practices and government policies and need to be questioned. Knowledge hierarchies and normative models of research and quantification marginalize new knowledges, putting them at risk, exemplified by the chase for rankings. Rankings are 'poor indicators of what universities do and skew choices of students and of university executives about what courses continue and research priorities as they arbitrarily reward science and engineering, but overlook or penalize teaching quality, humanities research or subjects with little interest beyond Australia, such as local literature or history' (Baker 2020: 5). Epistemic biases during a restructuring can have unexpected outcomes counter to the public role of the university with HASS being most threatened regardless of what a good university should look like and do (Connell 2019).

Again, the pandemic foregrounded how HASS is central to how leaders understand risk and how to manage it better to maintain social cohesion and the significance of HASS for strong and fair democratic societies. For example, the HOPE project (hope-project.dk) is examining the interrelationship connecting Covid-19 trajectories, the governments and international organizational decisions, media and social media landscapes, to citizens' behaviour and well-being. It showed that in Denmark, a relatively equal and socially cohesive society, cultural and behavioural responses were critical to understanding how best to respond to Covid and a strong democracy. Sociology, politics, humanities, creative arts and cultural studies supported by a strong HASS infrastructure equivalent to that of health scientists and economists is therefore equally important in managing risk and for social cohesion (Ross 2021). This is the storyline that should be articulated by university leaders in defending HASS and the creative arts rather than using government policy to justify their demise.

Critical intellectual leadership is required to proactively change the Australian cultural sensibility of instrumentalism and anti-intellectualism in political and public fora. VCs have the capacity to modify/neuter/reject policies that reduce innovation to STEMM, that treats HASS as the 'handmaiden' to STEMM or pushes an economistic view of innovation premised upon 'constant growth, with scant attention paid to aspects such as social productivity (the reduction of poverty) or relations with developing countries amid globalisation' (Bruni et al. 2005, 218). A more expansive notion of social and inclusive innovation views innovation not merely as a product but as a practice where 'innovation is conceptualized as neither separate nor separable from learning, working and organizing' that have social benefits (Bruni et al. 2005: 218) due to its strong normative dimension and systemic perspective. 'Put simply, a social innovation is a socially desirable innovation. The notion of "doing good" or social justice (as opposed to profit maximisation) is a key motivating force for many engaging in social innovation' (Tierney and Lanford 2016: 3). The Australian Academy of Humanities (2021: 1) states:

> The humanities help people to talk about the issues, help understand and shift entrenched ideas, about the 'cost' of endless economic growth for example. The humanities share stories and express ideas through arts and cultural practice. The humanities also give us all a deeper understanding of the human experience of climate change in different places and times

The EU now refers to Responsible Research and Innovation-science for society and science with society where science includes all systemic knowledge. Social innovation means integrating notions of social innovation and Sustainable Development Goals throughout university mission statements, strategic plans and leadership storying, educating politicians and the public alike regarding the interconnected systems of innovation, sustainable economies, a healthy environment and a vigorous and inclusive democracy (OECD 2007, Martin 2013).

Representational Justice

Academics not in management at all levels in this study felt disenfranchised, that they lacked agency, that their expertise went unrecognized and was undervalued by executive management and that this signalled a lack of trust in them as professionals. Yet multiple studies show that the core work of leadership is about building relationships and nurturing trust. Universities should stand out as high-trust organizations in the context of increasing low trust in public institutions and decline of expertise in government (Quiggin 2021). Trust requires a social contract with the surrounding society that recognizes the public service role and responsibility of academics or relational contractualism (Yeatman 2002).

Critical leadership would therefore mean establishing clear fora for deliberative decision-making calling on the expertise of academics, creating structures that can act as a critical academic voice outside current structures, establishing processes with meaningful feedback loops, tracking the impact of reforms and evaluating how new initiatives impact on academic work. It means realizing the benefits of diversity in decision-making and inclusion of people from varied epistemic, biographical, gender and ethno-racial backgrounds on a participatory parity basis throughout all ranks and divisions of an organization and involving academic voices in the recruitment and appointment to leadership positions. Shared governance means a commitment to develop more collegial or distributive mode of leadership as a model of 'continuous ethico-political action that is related not only to the self but also to others' (Kezar and Dizon 2020: 27).

Structural initiatives are required to institute neo-collegiality which 'offers the restoration of broader, more collegial decision-making processes to create a professional, efficient and appropriately twenty-first-century management approach (Bacon 2014: 1). Participatory parity is critical in earning trust, in that academics need to know they can influence decision-making and this in turn leads to greater sense of ownership over, and therefore commitment to, major reforms: good management theory 101. More collaborative processes in terms of strategic planning, designing ways of organizing and change processes can lead to mutual recognition of the limits and possibilities for both academic managers and academics and therefore greater commitment to a shared sense of the university's mission.

Given the now global concerns over climate change, pandemics, cybersecurity, issues of social benefits and not just economic relevance are now foregrounded, a responsible university is one in which there is a shared understanding that a good university has a responsibility to its neighbourhood community and globally, in terms of knowledge production and dissemination, a social responsibility as well as a financial responsibility, for both quality and sustainability including risk management (Stirling et al. 2013, Sorensen et al. 2019: 4–5). Shared governance (as does peer review) is more likely to maintain research and teaching integrity and create a professional ethic of knowledge-making that distinguishes universities from other organizations, thus aiming for the 'reconstruction of the social imagination to advance a cultural politics of democracy that honours diverse voices rather than subscribes to notions of responsibilization' of individuals (Tierney and Almeida 2017: 105).

This is the moment that the principles of academic freedom and more activist academic professionalism should be translated into leadership for social justice by academic managers as well as academics. Bourdieu (2000) argues that academics as critical intellectuals should be mobilizing their expertise in political debates drawing on their knowledge of scientific expertise while being critically reflexive of their own positioning. 'Intellectuals must engage in a permanent critique of all the abuses of power or authority that are committed in the name of intellectual authority; or, if you prefer, they must submit themselves to the relentless critique of the use of intellectual authority as a political weapon within the intellectual field and elsewhere' (Bourdieu 2000: 41).

As feminists have argued, universities are where collective intellectualism can undertake a 'merciless logical critique aimed not only at the lexicon of the discourse (globalization, flexibility, employability, etc.) but also at its mode of reasoning' (Bourdieu 2000: 42) and create the social conditions for realist Utopias. Critical leadership would seek to preserve these aspects of the twentieth-century Humboldian public university, while rejecting its biases, binaries and exclusions, in order to regain a civic and critical edge to become a good (responsible, inclusive, safe and sustainable) university (Connell 2019). Critical leadership is a social practice of working with, rather than over, others, at the dialogic centre rather than out in front, inspiring trust and mutual respect and reciprocity of good will and gifting. Critical leadership is purposeful for social justice and accepts this moral obligation to lead beyond the university to actively undertake social, economic and political transformation, and to focus on what is hardest to change, such as social and economic inequality in the context of the looming global climate crisis.

NOTES

Acknowledgements

1 *Leadership in Entrepreneurial Universities: Cross-National Investigations of Engagement and Diversity* (J. Blackmore, Deakin University, PI with parallel projects led by Prof. S. Wright, Aarhus University, Denmark; Prof. N. Stromquist, University of Maryland, USA; Prof. J. Moreno, University of Saville, Spain; Prof. P. O'Connor, University of Limerick, Ireland) (DP110103700).

Chapter 1

1 An ARC Linkage grant partnered with IDP Australia: *Why Australian International Graduates in Accounting, Nursing and Engineering Were Not being Employed by Australian Employers* (2009–13) (Blackmore and Rahimi 2019). A CPA Australia project: *Cultural Perspectives on Graduate Employability in Accounting in India and China* (2016–18) (Blackmore et al. 2018, Tran et al. 2021).
2 The Group of Eight universities were all, other than Monash, established during the colonial era. They comprise an elite group equivalent to Ivy League universities in the United States and the Russell Group in the United Kingdom.

REFERENCES

Academy of the Humanities. Australia (2021), *The Humanities – Optional Extra, or Integral to Our Economic Future?* Available online: https://humanities.org.au/newsroom/discovering-humanities (accessed 13 September 2021).

Acker, J. (1990), 'Hierarchies, Bodies, and Jobs: A Gendered Theory of Organizations', *Gender and Society*, 15 (4): 139–58.

Acker, S. (2012), 'Chairing and Caring: Gendered Dimensions of Leadership in the Academe', *Gender and Education*, 24 (4): 411–28.

Acker, S. (2014), 'A Foot in the Revolving Door? Women Academics in Lower-middle Management', *Higher Education Research & Development*, 33 (1): 73–85.

Adkins, L. (1999), 'Community and Economy: A Retraditionalisation of Gender? *Theory, Culture & Society*, 16 (1): 119–39.

Adkins, L. (2005), 'Social Capital: The Anatomy of a Troubled Concept', *Feminist Theory*, 6 (2): 195–211.

Adkins, L. (2012), 'Out of Work or Out of Time? Rethinking Labor after the Financial Crisis', *South Atlantic Quarterly*, 111 (3): 621–41.

Adkins, L. and B. Skeggs (2004), *Feminism After Bourdieu*, Oxford: Blackwell.

Ahmed, S. (2004), *The Cultural Politics of Emotion*, Edinburgh and New York: Routledge.

Ahmed, S. (2006), *The Nonperformity of Antiracism*. Meridians: Feminisim, Race, Transnationalism, 104–26.

Ahmed, S. (2009), 'Embodying Diversity: Problems and Paradoxes for Black Feminists', *Race Ethnicity and Education*, 12 (1): 41–52.

Ahmed, S. (2012), *On Being Included: Racism and Diversity in Institutional Life*, Durham and London: Duke University Press.

AI Group Workforce Development (2016), *The Emergence of the Gig Economy*, Melbourne: Australian Industry Group. Available online: https://cdn.aigroup.com.au/Reports/2016/Gig_Economy_August_2016.pdf (accessed 1 September 2019).

Aikman, S. and L. King (2012), 'Indigenous Knowledges and Education', *Compare: A Journal of Comparative and International Education*, 42 (5): 673–81.

Allatt, P. (1993), 'Becomingn Proviledged. Theh Role of Family Processes', in *Youth and Inequality*, edited by I. Bates and G. Riseborough, Buskingham: Open University Press.

Altbach, P. (2006), 'The Dilemmas of Ranking', *International Higher Education*, 42 (January): 2–3.

Altbach, P., S. Reisberg and L. Rumbley, (eds) (2010), *Trends in Global Higher Education: Tracking an Academic Revolution*, Rotterdam: Sense Publishers.

Alvesson, M. and A. Spicer (2012), 'Critical Leadership Studies: The Case for Critical Performativity', *Human Relations*, 65 (3): 367–90.

Alvesson, M. and A. Spicer (2016), *The Stupidity Paradox: The Power and Pitfalls of Functional Stupidity at Work*, London: Profile Books.

Amsler, S. and C. Bolsmann (2012), 'University Ranking as Social Exclusion', *British Journal of Sociology of Education*, 33 (2): 283–301.

Analogue University (2019), 'Calling all Journal Editors: Bury the Metrics Pages!', *Political Geography*, 68: A3–5.

Anderson, C., T. Bunda and M. Walter (2008), 'Indigenous Higher Education: The Role of Universities in Releasing the Potential', *Australian Journal of Indigenous Education*, 37 (1): 1–8.

Andrews, R. (2015), 'Critical Thinking/Argumentation in Higher Education', in M. Davies and R. Barnett (eds), *The Palgrave Handbook of Critical Thinking in Higher Education*, 49–62, New York: Palgrave.

Angervall, P., D. Beach and J. Gustafsson (2015), 'The Unacknowledged Value of Female Academic Labour Power for Male Research Careers', *Higher Education Research and Development*, 34 (5): 815–27.

Anthias, F. (2012), 'Transnational Mobilities, Migration Research and Intersectionality', *Nordic Journal of Migration Research*, 2 (2): 102–10.

Apter, T. (2018), 'If Academics Do Not Understand Nuance, Who Will?', *Times Higher Education*, 6 September. Available online: https://www.timeshighereducation.com/opinion/if-academics-dont-acknowledge-nuance-who-will (accessed 1 July 2020).

Arday, J. and H. S. Mirza (2018), *Dismantling Race in Higher Education: Racism, Whiteness and Decolonising the Academy*, London: Palgrave MacMillan.

Asher, N. (2010), 'How Does the Postcolonial, Feminist Academic Lead? A Perspective from the US South', *International Journal of Leadership in Education*, 13 (1): 63–76.

Asmar, C. and S. Page (2009), 'Sources of Satisfaction and Stress among Indigenous Academic Teachers: Findings from a National Australian Study', *Asia Pacific Journal of Education*, 29 (3): 387–401.

Atewologun, D., R. Sealy and W. Atkinson (2016), 'Revealing Intersectional Dynamics in Organizations: Introducing "Intersectional Identity Work"', *Gender, Work and Organization*, 23 (3): 223–47.

Atkins, L. and M. Vicars (2016), 'Feminine Men and Masculine Women: In/exclusion in the Academy', *Education & Training*, 5 (3): 252–62.

Australian Association of University Professors (AAUP) (2022), *Pillars*, Available online: www.professoriate.org (accessed 12 April 2022).

Australian Research Council (2021), *Success Rate Statistics of Funding*, Available online: https://www.arc.gov.au/grants-and-funding/apply-funding/grants-dataset/trend-visualisation/ncgp-trends-success-rates (accessed 14 April 2022).

Bacchi, C. (2000), 'Policy as Discourse: What Does It Mean? Where Does It Get Us?', *Discourse*, 21 (1): 45–57.

Bacon, E. (2014), *Neo-collegiality: Restoring Academic Engagement in the Managerial University*, London: The Leadership Foundation for Higher Education.

Bailey, J., F. Macdonald and G. Whitehouse (2011), 'No Leg to Stand on: The Moral Economy of IR Changes', *Economic and Industrial Democracy*, 33 (3): 431–61.

Baker, D. and E. Kelan (2019), 'Splitting and Blaming: The Psychic Life of Neoliberal Executive Women', *Human Relations*. https://doi.org/10.1177/0018726718772010.

Baker, J. (2020), 'Global Ranking are Distorting University Decisions, Says ANU Chief', *The Age*, 11 November. Available online: https://www.theage.com.au/national/global-rankings-are-distorting-universities-decisions-says-anu-chief-20201111-p56do9.html (accessed 12 November 2020).

Baker, S. (2019), 'Male, 62, and a Scientist: Meet the Typical University Leader', *Times Higher Education*, 5 September. Available online: https://www.timeshighereducation.com/news/male-62-and-scientist-meet-typical-university-leader (accessed 1 July 2020).

Ball, S. (2007), 'Leadership of Academics in Research', *Educational Management Administration and Leadership*, 35 (4): 449–77.

Ball, S. (2012), *Global Education Inc.: The New Policy Networks and the Neoliberal Imaginary*, London: Routledge.

Bansel, P. and B. Davies (2010), 'Through Love of What Neoliberal Universities Put at Risk', in J. Blackmore, M. Brennan and L. Zipin (eds), *Re-Positioning University Governance and Academic Work*, 133–45, Rotterdam: Sense Publishers.

Barber, M., K. Donnelly and S. Rizvi (2013), *An Avalanche is Coming: Higher Education and the Revolution Ahead*, London: Institute of Public Policy Research.

Barnett, R. (2011), *Being a University*, Oxford: Routledge.

Barrett, T. (2015), 'Storying Bourdieu: Fragments Toward a Bourdieusian Approach to "Life Histories"', *International Journal of Qualitative Methods*, 14 (5): 1–10.

Barry, D. (2019), 'Time to Rethink Australia's Higher Education Governance', *Campus Morning Mail*, 28 July. Available online: https://campusmorningmail.com.au/news/time-to-rethink-australias-higher-education-governance/ (accessed 1 October 2020).

Bauman, Z. and R. Raud (2015), *Practices of Selfhood*, Oxford: Polity Press.

Baxter, J. (2021), *Sharing of Housework in Couple Families in 2020, Report 5*, Melbourne: Australian Institute of Family Studies.

Beck, U. (2013), *World Risk Society*, Oxford: Polity Press.

Beetham, H. and R. Sharpe (eds) (2007), *Rethinking Pedagogy for a Digital Age. Designing for 21st Century Learning*, London: Routledge.

Belfiore, E. (2015), '"Impact", "Value" and "Bad Economics": Making Sense of the Problem of Value in the Arts and Humanities', *Arts and Humanities in Higher Education*, 14 (1): 95–110.

Bell, S. (2010), 'Women in Science: The Persistence of Gender in Australia', *Higher Education Management and Policy*, 22 (1): 47–65.

Bell, S. (2017), 'University Engagement in a Post-truth World', *Transform: The Journal of Engaged Scholarship*, 1: 14–25.

Benschop, Y. and M. Brouns (2003), 'Crumbling Ivory Towers: Academic Organizing and its Gender Effects', *Gender, Work and Organization*, 10 (2): 194–212.

Bensimon, E. and L. Malcom, (eds) (2012), *Confronting Equity Issues on Campus: Implementing the Equity Scorecard in Theory and Practice*, California: Stylus Publishing, LLC.

Bentley, P. J., H. Coates, I. R. Dobson, L. Goedegebuure and V. Meek (2013), 'Academic Job Satisfaction from an International Comparative Perspective: Factors Associated with Satisfaction across 12 Countries', in P. J. Bentley, H. Coates, I. R. Dobson, L. Goedegebuure and V. L. Meek (eds), *Job Satisfaction around the Academic World*, 239–62, Netherlands: Springer.

Berg, M. and B. Serber (2016), *The Slow Professor, Challenging the Culture of Speed in the Academy*, Toronto: University of Toronto Press.

Besley, T., (ed) (2010), *Assessing Quality in Educational Research*, Rotterdam: Sense Publishers.

Bexley, E., R. James and S. Arkoudis (2011), *The Academic Profession in Transition*, Report, Department of Education, Employment and Workplace Relations. Available online: http://www.cshe.unimelb.edu.au/people/bexley_docs/The_Academic_Profession_in_Transition_Sept2011.pdf (accessed 21 April 2017).

Blackmore, J. (1992), 'More Power to the Powerful': Mergers, Corporate Management and Their Implications for Women in the Reshaping of Higher Education', *Australian Feminist Studies*, 15: 65–98.

Blackmore, J. (2006), 'Deconstructing Diversity Discourses in the Field of Educational Management and Leadership', Invited Article in Special Issue, M Coleman (Guest Editor)', *Educational Management, Administration and Leadership*, 34 (2): 188–99.

Blackmore, J. (2009a), 'Academic Pedagogies, Quality Logics and Performative Universities: Evaluating Teaching and What Students Want', *Studies in Higher Education*, 34 (8): 857–72.

Blackmore, J. (2009b), 'Anticipating Policy and the Logics of Practice: Australian Institutional and Academic Responses to the Globalizing "Quality Research" Agenda', *Access*, 27 (1 & 2): 97–113.

Blackmore, J. (2010a), 'Measures of Hope and Despair: Emotionality, Politics and Education', in E. Samier and M. Schmidt (eds), *Emotional Dimension of Educational Administration and Leadership*, 109–24, London: Routledge.

Blackmore, J. (2010b), '"The Other Within": Race / Gender Disruptions to the Professional Learning of White Educational Leaders', *International Journal of Leadership in Education*, 13 (1): 45–61.

Blackmore, J. (2014), '"Wasting Talent"? Gender and the Problematics of Academic Disenchantment and Disengagement with Leadership', *Higher Education Research and Development*, 33 (1): 86–99.

Blackmore, J. (2016), *Educational Leadership and Nancy Fraser*, London: Routledge.

Blackmore, J. (2019), 'Australia: Critical Leadership, Diversity and Feminism', in J. Jameson (ed), *Critical University Leadership: International Perspectives on Leadership in Higher Education: Critical Thinking for Global Challenges*, 130–50, London: Routledge.

Blackmore, J. (2020a), 'Identity, Subjectivity and Agency: Feminists' Re-conceptualising Educational Leadership Within/against/beyond the Neo-liberal Self', in R Niesche and A. Heffernan (eds), *Theorising Identity and Subjectivity in Educational Leadership and Research*, 13–24, Routledge, London.

Blackmore, J. (2020b), 'The Carelessness of Entrepreneurial Universities in a World Risk Society: A Feminist Reflection on the Impact of Covid 19 in Australia', *Higher Education Research and Development*, 39 (7): 1332–6.

Blackmore, J. (2020c), 'Governing Knowledge in the Entrepreneurial University: A Feminist Account of Structural, Cultural and Political Epistemic Injustices', *Critical Studies in Education*, 1–17, http://dx.doi.org/10.1080/17508487.2020.1858912.

Blackmore, J. (2022), 'Reflections on the Social Relations of Gender, Educational Leadership and Practice', in J. Showunmi and C. Shakeshaft (eds), *Handbook of Gender and Educational Leadership*, London: Bloomsbury.

Blackmore, J., K. Barty and P. Thomson (2006), 'Principal Selection: Homosociability, the Search for Security and the Production of Normalised Principal Identities', *Educational Management, Administration and Leadership*, 34 (3): 297–317.

Blackmore, J., M. Brennan and L. Zipin (eds) (2010), *Repositioning the University: Governance and Changing Academic Work*, Rotterdam: Sense Publishing.

Blackmore, J. and M. Rahimi (2019), 'How "Best Fit" Excludes International Graduates from Employment in Australia: A Bourdeusian Perspective', *Journal of Education and Work*, 32 (3): 1–13.

Blackmore, J. and J. Sachs (2007), *Performing and Reforming Leaders*, New York: SUNY Press.

Blackmore, J. and N. Sawers (2015), 'Executive Power and Scaled up Gender Subtexts in Australian Entrepreneurial Universities', *Gender and Education*, 27 (3): 320–37.

Blackmore, J., C. Gribble, M. Rahimi, L. Farrell, R. Arber and M. Devlin (2014), *Australian International Graduates and the Transition to Employment*, Melbourne: Deakin University CREFI.

Blackmore, J., M. Sanchez and N. Sawers, (eds) (2016), *Globalized Re/gendering of the Academy and Leadership*, London: Routledge.

Blackmore, J., L. Tran and M. Rahimi (2018), *Cultural Understandings of Graduate Employability in China and India*, Melbourne: CPA Australia/REDI.

Blaschke, S., J. Frost and F. Hattke (2014), 'Towards a Micro Foundation of Leadership, Governance, and Management in Universities', *Higher Education*, 68: 711–32.

Boden, R. and J. Rowlands (2020), 'Paying the Piper: The Governance of Vice-chancellors' Remuneration in Australian and UK Universities', *Higher Education Research and Development*, 41 (2): 254–68.

Boler, M. (1999), *Feeling Power: Emotions and Education*, London: Routledge.

Bosetti, L. and T. Heffernan (2021), 'Diminishing Hope and Utopian Thinking: Faculty Leadership under Neoliberal Regime', *Journal of Educational Administration and History*, 53 (2): 106–20.

Boston Consulting Group (2018), 'How Diverse Leadership Teams Boost Innovation', *Boston Consulting Group*, 23 January. Available online: https://www.bcg.com/en-au/publications /2018/how-diverse-leadership-teams-boost-innovation (accessed 1 July 2020).

Bothwell, E. (2018), 'Work-life Balance Survey 2018: Long Hours Take Their Toll on Academics', *Times Higher Education*, Feburary 8. Available online: https://www.timeshi ghereducation.com/features/wor k-life-balance-survey-2018-long-hours-take-their-t oll- academics.

Bourdieu, P. (1977), *Outline of a Theory of Practice*, Cambridge: Cambridge University Press.

Bourdieu, P. (1984), *Distinction: A Social Critique of the Judgement of Taste*, London: Routledge and Kegan Paul.

Bourdieu, P. (1986), 'The Forms of Capital', in J. G. Richardson (ed), *Handbook of Theory and Research for the Sociology of Education*, 241–58, New York: Greenwood Press.

Bourdieu, P. (1988a), *Homo Academicus*, Cambridge: Polity Press.

Bourdieu, P. (1989), 'Social Space and Symbolic Power', *Sociological Theory*, 7: 14–25.

Bourdieu, P. (1990), *The Logic of Practice*, Cambridge: Polity Press.

Bourdieu, P. (1993), *Sociology in Question*, R. Nice (trans), London: Sage.

Bourdieu, P. (1994), *In Other Words. Essays Towards a Reflxive Scoiology.* Cambridge: Polity.

Bourdieu, P. (1998), 'The Essence of Neo-liberalism', *Le Monde Diplomatique*, 8 December. Available online: https://mondediplo.com/1998/12/08bourdieu (accessed 3 September 2021).

Bourdieu, P. (1999), 'The Contradictions of Inheritance', in P. Bourdieu (ed), *The Weight of the World: Social Suffering in Contemporary Society*, 507–13. Stanford, CA: Stanford University.

Bourdieu, P. (2000), 'For a Scholarship with Commitment', *Profession*, 2000: 40–5.

Bourdieu, P. (2004), *Science of Science and Reflexivity*, R.Nice (trans), Cambridge:Polity.

Bourdieu, P. and L. Wacquant (1992), *An Inivitation to Reflexive Sociology*, Chicago: Chicago University Press.

Boys, J. (2015), *Building Better Universities: Strategies, Spaces, Technologies*, London: Routledge.

Bradley, D., P. Noonan, H. Nugent and B. Scales (2008), *Review of Australian Higher Education: Final Report*, Canberra: Commonwealth of Australia.

Branson, C. M., M. Marra, M. Franken and D. Penney (2018), *Leadership in Higher Education from a Transrelational Perspective*, London: Bloomsbury.

Brewer, A. and I. Walker (2011), 'Risk Management in a University Environment', *Journal of Business Continuity and Emergency Planning*, 5 (2): 161–72.

Brint, S. (2001), 'Professionals and the Knowledge Economy: Rethinking Post-industrial Society', *Current Sociology*, 49 (4): 101–32.

Bristow, A., S. Robinson and O. Ratle (2017), 'Being an Early-Career CMS Academic in the Context of Insecurity and "Excellence"': The Dialectics of Resistance and Compliance', *Organization Studies*, 38 (9): 1185–207.

Broadbent, K. and G. Strachan (2016), '"It's Difficult to Forecast Your Longer-term Career Milestone": Career Development and Insecure Employment for Research Academics in Australian Universities', *Labour and Industry: A Journal of the Social and Economic Relations of Work*, 26 (4): 251–65.

Brooks, A. and A. McKinnon, (eds) (2001), *Gender and the Restructured University*, Milton Keynes: Open University Press.

Brown, P., H. Lauder and D. Ashton (2011), *The Global Auction: The Broken Promises of Education, Jobs and Income*, Oxford: Oxford University Press.

Brown, W. (2015), *Undoing the Demos. Neoliberalism's Stealth Revolution*, New York: Zone Books.

Bruni, A., S. Gherardi and B. Poggio (2005), *Gender and Entrepreneurship: An Ethnographic Approach*, London: Routledge.

Bryman, A. (2007), 'Effective Leadership in Higher Education: A Literature Review', *Studies in Higher Education*, 32 (6): 693–710.

Bullen, J. and H. Flavell (2017), 'Measuring the "Gift": Epistemological and Ontological Differences between the Academy and Indigenous Australia', *Higher Education Research and Development*, 36 (3): 583–96.

Bunda, T., L. Zipin and M. Brennan (2012), 'Negotiating University "Equity" from Indigenous Standpoints: A Shaky Bridge', *International Journal of Inclusive Education*, 16 (9): 941–57.

Burford, J. (2017), 'What Might "bad feelings" Be Good for? Some Queer-Feminist Thoughts on Academic Activism', *Australian Universities Review*, 59 (2): 70–8.

Burke, C. (2016), *Culture, Capitals and Graduate Futures*, London: Routledge

Burke, C. T., N. Emmerich and N. Ingram (2013), 'Well-Founded Social Fictions: A Defence of the Concepts of Institutional and Familial Habitus', *British Journal of Sociology of Education*, 34 (2): 165–82.

Burkinshaw, P. and K. White (2017), 'Fixing the Women or Fixing Universities: Women in HE Leadership', *Administrative Sciences*, 7 (30): 1–14.

Burrows, R. (2012), 'Living with the H-Index? Metric Assemblages in the Contemporary Academy', *The Sociological Review*, 60 (2): 355–72.

Butler, J. (2004), *Undoing Gender*, London: Routledge.

Byford, J. (2011), *Conspiracy Theories: Critical Introduction*, London: Palgrave MacMillan.

Campbell, T. and S. Slaughter (1999), 'Faculty and Administrator's Attitudes to Potential Conflict of Interest, Commitment and Equity in University-Industry Partnerships', *Journal of Higher Education*, 70 (3): 309–51.

Carroll, B. and L. Levy (2008), 'Defaulting to Management: Leadership Defined by What It Is Not', *Organization*, 15 (1): 75–96.

Catalyst (2013), 'Why Diversity Matters (Tools)', *Catalyst*, 23 July. Available online: https://www.catalyst.org/research/why-diversity-matters/ (accessed 5 July 2018).

Cheal, D. (1988), *The Gift Economy*, London: Routledge.

Cheng, M. (2011), 'The Perceived Impact of Quality Audit on the Work of Academics', *Higher Education Research & Development*, 30 (2): 179–91.

Cherkowski, S., B. Kutsyuruba, B. Walker and M. Crawford (2021), 'Conceptualising Leadership and Emotions in Higher Education: Wellbeing as Wholeness', *Journal of Educational Administration and History*, 53 (2): 158–71.

Chesterman, C., A. Ross-Smith and M. Peters (2008), 'Not Doable Jobs! Exploring Senior Women's Attitudes to Academic Leadership Roles', *Women's Studies International Forum*, 28 (2–3): 163–80.

Chief Scientist (2016), *Australia's STEM Workforce: Science, Technology, Engineering and Mathematics*, Canberra: Office of the Chief Scientist.

Chubb, J. and R. Watermeyer (2017), 'Artifice or Integrity in the Marketization of Research Impact? Investigating the Moral Economy of (Pathways to) Impact Statements within Research Funding Proposals in the UK and Australia', *Studies in Higher Education*, 42 (12): 2360–72.

Chubb, J., R. Watermeyer and P. Wakeling (2017), 'Fear and Loathing in the Academy? The Role of Emotion in Response to an Impact Agenda in the UK and Australia', *Higher Education Research and Development*, 36 (3): 555–68.

Chung, H. (2016), 'The Paradox of Autonomy? Flexible Working is Making us Work Longer', *The Conversation*, 18 August. Available online: https://theconversation.com/flexible-working-is-making-us-work-longer-64045 (accessed 15 January 2021).

Clark, B. (2004), 'Delineating the Character of the Entrepreneurial University', *Higher Education Policy*, 17 (4): 355–70.

Clark, P., C. Chapleo and K. Suom (2019), 'Branding Higher Education: An Exploration of the Role of Internal Branding on Middle Management in a University Rebrand', *Tertiary Education and Management*, 26 (2): 131–49.

Clegg, S. (2008), 'Femininities/Masculinities and a Sense Self: Thinking Gendered Academic Identities and the Intellectual Self', *Gender and Education*, 20 (3): 209–21.

Clift, R., J. Loughran, G. Mills and C. Craig, (eds) (2015), *Inside the Role of Dean. International Perspectives of Leading in Higher Education*, London: Routledge.

Coates, H., I. R. Dobson, L. Goedegebuure and L. Meek (2009), 'Australia's Casual Approach to its Academic Teaching Workforce', *People and Place*, 17 (4): 47–54.

Coates, H., I. R. Dobson, L. Goedegebuure and L. Meek (2010), 'Across the Great Divide: What Do Australian Academics Think of University Leadership? Advice from the CAP Survey', *Journal of Higher Education Policy and Management*, 32 (4): 379–87.

Coates, S. K., Trudgett, M., and S. Page (2019), 'Indigenous Higher Education Sector: The Evolution of Recognised Indigenous Leaders within Australian Universities', *The Australian Journal of Indigenous Education*, 50 (2): 215–21.

Coleman, D. and S. Kamboureli, (eds) (2011), *Retooling the Humanities: The Culture of Research in Canadian Universities*, Edmonton: University of Alberta Press.

Colet, N. (2017), 'From Content-centred to Learning-centred Approaches: Shifting Educational Paradigm in Higher Education', *Journal of Educational Administration and History*, 49 (1): 72–86.

Colley, L. and C. White (2019), 'Neoliberal Feminism: The Neoliberal Rhetoric on Feminism by Australian Political Actors', *Gender Work and Organization*, 26 (8): 1083–99.

Collini, S. (2012), *What are Universities For?* London: Penguin Books.

Collins, A., L. Conner, K. McPherson, B. Midson and C. Wilson (2011), 'Learning to Be Leaders in Higher Education: What Helps or Hinders Women's Advancement as Leaders in Universities', *Educational Management, Administration and Leadership*, 39 (1): 44–62.

Collins, P. and S. Bilge (2016), *Intersectionality*, Oxford: Polity.

Connell, R. W. (2005), 'Advancing Gender Reform in Large-scale Organizations: A New Approach for Practitioners and Researchers', *Policy and Society*, 24 (4): 5–24.

Connell, R. W, (2006), 'Core Activity: Reflexive Intellectual Workers and Cultural Crisis', *Journal of Sociology*, 42 (1): 5–23.

Connell, R. W. (2010), 'Building the Neoliberal World: Managers as Intellectuals in a Peripheral Economy', *Critical Sociology*, 36 (6): 777–92.

Connell, R. W. (2013), 'The Neoliberal Cascade and Education: An Essay on the Market Agenda and its Consequences', *Critical Studies in Education*, 54 (2): 99–112.

Connell, R. W. (2016), 'Masculinities in Global Perspective: Hegemony, Contestation, and Changing Structures of Power', *Theory and Society*, 45 (4): 303–18.

Connell, R. W. (2017), 'Southern Theory and World Universities', *Higher Education Research & Development*, 36 (1): 4–15.

Connell, R. W. (2019), *The Good University: What Universities Actually Do and Why it's Time for Radical Change*, Melbourne: Monash University Publishing.

Considine, M. (2006), 'Theorizing the University as a Cultural System: Distinctions, Identities and Emergences', *Educational Theory*, 56 (3): 255–69.

Cook, H. (2019), 'Academics Pressured to Pass Struggling International Students', *The Age*, 23 January, 3.

Crimmins, G. (2019), 'A Structural Account of Inequality in the International Academy: Why Resistance to Sexism Remains Urgent and Necessary', in G. Crimmins (ed), *Strategies of Resisting Sexism in the Academy*, 3–16, London: Palgrave.

Crossley, M. (2021), 'Purpose and Community: At the Core of Universities', *Campus Morning Mail*, 22 April. Available online: https://campusmorningmail.com.au/news/purpose-and-community-at-the-core-of-universities/ (accessed 1 May 2021).

Currie, J. (1992), 'The Emergence of Higher Education as an Industry: The Second Tier Awards and Award Restructuring', *Australian Universities Review*, 35 (2): 17–20.

Currie, J. (2008), 'Research Assessment Exercises and Some Negative Consequences of Journal Rankings and Citation Indices', *Access*, 27 (1&2): 27–33.

Curtis, B. (2016), 'The Performance-based Research Fund, Gender and a Cultural Cringe', *Globalisation, Societies and Education*, 14 (1): 87–109.

Cutter-Mackenzie, A. and J. S. Renouf (2017), *Australian Educational Research Funding Trends Report: A National Stocktake and Review of Category 1 Funding in Education*, Canberra: Australian Council of Deans of Education.

Czarniawski, B. (2008), 'The Thin End of the Wedge. Foreign Women Professors as Double Strangers in Academia', *Gender Work and Organization*, 15 (3): 235–87.

Czarniawska, B. (2014a), 'Storytelling as a Managerial Tool and its Local Translations', in G. Drori, M. Höllerer and P. Walgenbach (eds), *Global Themes and Local Variations in Organization and Management*. New York: Routledge.

Czarniawska, B. (2014b), *A Theory of Organizing*, Cheltenham: Edward Elgar.

Czarniawska, B. and H. Hopfl, (eds) (2002), *Casting the Other: The Production and Maintenance of Inequalities in Work Organizations*, London: Routledge.

Dale, R. (2005), 'Globalization, Knowledge Economy and Comparative Education', *Comparative Education*, 41 (2): 117–49.

Daley, J. (2021), *Gridlock: Removing Barriers to Policy Reform*, Melbourne: Grattan Institute.

Daniels, J. and P. Thistlewaite (2016), *Being a Scholar in the Digital Era: Transforming Scholarly Practice for the Public Good*, Bristol: Bristol University Press.

Danvers, E. (2016), 'Criticality's Affective Entanglements: Rethinking Emotion and Critical Thinking in Higher Education', *Gender and Education*, 28 (2): 282–97.

Davis, A., M. J. van Rensburg and P. Venter (2016), 'The Impact of Managerialism on the Strategy Work of University Middle Managers', *Studies in Higher Education*, 41 (8): 1480–94.

Davis, G. (2017), *The Australian Idea of a University*, Melbourne: Melbourne University Press.

Davis, M. (2020), 'Reconcillation and the Promise of an Australian Homecoming: What Would Make an Acknowledgement of Country More Welcome', *The Monthly*, July. Available online: https://www.themonthly.com.au/issue/2020/july/1593525600/megan-davis/reconciliation-and-promise-australian-homecoming#mtr (accessed 1 November 2020).

Dawkins, A. (2019), 'Public Goods, Public Benefits, Public Interest', in T. Strike, J. Nicholls and J. Rushworth (eds), *Governing Higher Education Today: International Perspectives*, 219–38, London: Routledge.

Dawson, P. and D. Buchanan (2005), 'The Way It Really Happened: Competing Narratives in the Political Process of Technological Change', *Human Relations*, 58 (7): 845–65.

Decuypere, M. and M. Simons (2014), 'On the Composition of Academic Work in Digital Times', *European Education Research Journal*, 13 (1): 89–106.

Deem, R. and K. Brehony (2005), 'Management as Ideology: The Case of "New Managerialism" in Higher Education', *Oxford Review of Education*, 31 (2): 217–35.

Deem, R., S. Hillyard and M. Reed (2007), *Knowledge, Higher Education, and the New Managerialism: The Changing Management of UK Universities*, Oxford: Oxford University Press.

Deem, R., K. H. Mok and L. Lucas (2008), 'Transforming Higher Education in Whose Image? Exploring the Concept of the "World-Class" University in Europe and Asia', *Higher Education Policy*, 21 (1): 83–97.

Degn, L. (2015), 'Sensemaking, Sense Giving and Strategic Management in Danish Higher Education', *Higher Education*, 69 (6): 901–13.

Delanty, G. (2001), *Challenging Knowledge: The University in the Knowledge Society*, Oxford: Oxford University Press.

Delmestri, G., A. Oberg and G. S. Drori (2015), 'The Unbearable Lightness of University Branding: Cross-national Patterns', *International Studies of Management and Organization*, 45 (2): 121–36.

Deloitte Access Economics (2017), *Westpac Diversity Dividend Report*, Sydney: Deloitte Access Economics.

de Wit, H. and P. Altbach (2020), 'Internationalization in Higher Education: Global Trends and Recommendations for Its Future', *Policy Reviews in Higher Education*, 2020 (September): 1–19.

Diezmann, C. and S. Grieshaber (2009), *Understanding the Achievements and Aspirations of New Women Professors: A Report to Universities Australia*, Brisbane: Faculty of Education, QUT.

Do, V. H. T. and M. Brennan (2015), 'Complexites of Vietnamese Femininities: A Resource for Rethiking Women's University Leadership Practices', *Gender and Education*, 27 (3): 273–87.

do Mar Pereira, M. (2015), 'Struggling Within and Beyond the Performative University: Articulating Academia and Work in an "Academia Without Walls"', *Women's Studies International Forum*, 54 (January-February): 100–10.

Donald, A. (2020), 'The Disproportionate Effect of Covid-19 Pandemic on Women Has to be Addressed', *Times Higher Education*, 25 June.

Dopson, S., E. Ferlie, G. McGivern, M. Fischer, J. Ledger, S. Behens and S. Wilson (2016), *The Impact of Leadership and Leadership Development in Higher Education: A Review of the Literature and Evidence*, London: Leadership Foundation for Higher Education.

Dowsett, L. (2020), 'Global University Rankings and Strategic Planning: A Case Study of Australian Institutional Performance', *Journal of Higher Education Policy and Management*, 42 (4): 478–94.

Drori, G. (2016), 'Professional Consultancy and Global Higher Education: The Case of Branding of Academia', in A. Verger, C. Lubienski and G. Steiner-Khamsi (eds), *World Yearbook of Education 2016: The Global Education Industry*, 177–207, Milton Park: Routledge.

Dugas, D., A. Stich, L. Harris and K. Summers (2018), 'I'm Being Pulled in too Many Different Directions: Academic Identity Tensions at Regional Public Universities in Challenging Economic Times', *Studies in Higher Education*, 45 (2): 312–26.

Dunleavy, P. (2005), 'New Public Management Is Dead--Long Live Digital-Era Governance', *Journal of Public Administration Research and Theory*, 16 (3): 467–94.

Earick, M. (2018), 'We are not Social Justice Equals: The Need for White Scholars to Understand Their Whiteness', *International Journal of Qualitative Studies in Education*, 31 (8): 800–20.

Eddy, P. L., K. Ward and T. Khwaja, (eds) (2016), *Critical Approaches to Women and Gender in Higher Education*, New York: Palgrave McMillan.

Ekma, M., M. Lindgre and J. Packendorff (2017), 'Universities Need Leadership, Academics Need Management: Discursive Tensions and Voids in the Deregulation of Swedish Higher Education Legislation', *Higher Education*, 75: 299–321.

Elliott, K. (2016), 'Caring Masculiities: Theorizing an Emerging Concept', *Men and Masculinities*, 19 (3): 240–59.

Enders, J. and E. de Weert, (eds) (2015), *The Changing Face of Academic Life: Analytical and Comparative Perspectives*, Basingstoke: Palgrave Macmillan.

Enders, J. and R. Naidoo (2019), 'Audit-market Intermediaries: Doing Institutional Work in British Research-intensive Universities', *Studies in Higher Education*, 44 (7): 1290–301.

Engwall, L. (2008), 'The University: A Multinational Corporation?', in L. Engwall and D. Weaire (eds), *The University in the Market*, 9–21, London: Portland Press.

Ennals, P., T. Fortune, A. Williams and K. D'Cruz (2016), 'Shifting Occupational Identity: Doing, Being, Becoming and Belonging in the Academy, *Higher Education Research & Development*, 35 (3): 433–46.

Epseland, W. and M. Sauder (2016), *Engines of Anxiety: Academic Rankings, Reputation, and Accountability*, New York: Russel Sage Foundation.

Eriksen, T. (2006), 'Farewell to the Gift Economy', *Savage Minds*, 6 August. Available online: https://savageminds.org/2006/08/06/farewell-to-the-gift-economy/ (accessed 1 September 2021).

Evans, L. (2014), 'What is Effective Research Leadership? A Research-informed Perspective', *Higher Education Research and Development*, 33 (1): 46–58.

Evans, L. (2017), 'University Professors as Academic Leaders: Professorial Leadership Development Needs and Provision', *Educational Management, Administration & Leadership*, 45 (1): 123–40.

Evans, L. (2018), *Professors as Academic Leaders*. Bloomsbury Publishing PLC.

Evans, L. and J. Nixon, (eds) (2015), *Academic Identities in Higher Education: The Changing European Landscape*, London: Bloomsbury.

Evans, M. (2014), 'Liberal Values at a Time of Neoliberalism', *Arts and Humanities in Higher Education*, 13 (1–2): 17–23.

Evans, M. and A. Sinclair, (2016), 'Navigating the Territories of Indigenous Leadership: Exploring the Experiences and Practices of Australian Indigenous Arts Leaders', *Leadership*, 12 (4): 470–90.

Evetts, J. (2009), 'New Professionalism and New Public Management: Changes, Continuities and Consequences', *Comparative Sociology*, 8 (2): 247–66.

EY (2020), *A Peak of Higher Education: A New World for the University of the Future*, Downloaded 20 September 2021, Available online: https://www.ey.com/en_au/government-public-sector/the-peak-of-higher-education.

Feldman, M. and W. Orlikowski (2011), 'Theorizing Practice and Practicing Theory', *Organization Science*, 22 (5): 1240–53.

Felski, R. (2000), 'Being Reasonable, Telling Stories', *Feminist Theory*, 1 (2): 225–9.

Fenton, E. and L. Kane (2021), 'Casual Wage Theft in the Corporate University', *Arena Online*, 18 March. Available online: https://arena.org.au/casual-wage-theft-in-the-corporate-university/ (accessed 2 August 2021).

Fisher, V. and S. Kingsley (2014), 'Behind Closed Doors! Homosocial Desire and the Academic Boys Club', *Gender in Management: An International Journal*, 29 (1): 44–64.

Fitzgerald, T. (2014), *Women Leaders in Higher Education: Shattering the Myths*, London: Routledge.

Ford, J., N. H. Harding, S. Gilmore and S. Richardson (2017), 'Becoming a Leader: Leadership as Material Presence', *Organization Studies*, 38 (11): 1553–71.

Forsyth, H. (2014), *A History of the Modern Australian University*, Sydney: NSW Publishing.

Foster, G. and L. Stratton (2019), 'What Women Want (Their Men to Do): Housework and Satisfaction in Australian Households', *Feminist Economics*, 25 (3): 23–47.

Fox, C. W. and C. T. Paine (2019), 'Gender Differences in Peer Review Outcomes and Manuscript Impact at Six Journals of Ecology and Evolution', *Ecology and Evolution*, 9 (6): 3599–619.

Francis, L. and V. Shulz (2020), 'Barriers and Facilitators for Women Academics Seeking Promotion: Perspectives from the Inside', *Australian Universities Review*, 62 (2): 47–60.

Fraser, N. (2008), *Scales of Justice. Reimagining Political Space in a Globalizing World*, Cambridge: Polity.

Fraser, N. (2013), *Fortunes of Feminism: From State-managed Capitalism to Neoliberal Crisis*, London: Verso.

Fraser, N. and R. Jaeggi (2018), *Capitalism: A Conversation in Critical Theory*, Oxford: Polity.

Fredman, N. and J. Doughney (2012), 'Academic Dissatisfaction, Managerial Change and Neoliberalism', *Higher Education*, 64: 41–58.

French, R. (2019), Report of the *Independent Review of Freedom of Speech in Australian Higher Education Providers*, Canberra: Department of Education and Training Australia.

French, S. (2015), *Benefits and Challenges of Modula Higher Education Curriculum*, Available online: https://melbourne-cshe.unimelb.edu.au/__data/assets/pdf_file/0006/2774391/Benefits_Challenges_Modular_Higher_Ed_Curricula_SFrench_v3-green-2.pdf

Fricker, M. (2007), *Epistemic Injustice: Power and the Ethics of Knowing*, Oxford: Oxford University Press.

Fuller, K. (2021), *Feminist Perspectives on Contemporary Educational Leadership*, London: Routledge.

Fuller, K. and J. Berry (2019), *#WomenEd: A Movement for Women Leaders in Education*, Nottingham: University of Nottingham.

Fumasoli, T. (2019), 'The University and the Changing Structures and Processes of Academic Knowledge Production', *Higher Education Quarterly*, 73: 401–5.

Fumasoli, T. and B. Stensaker (2013), 'A Reflection on Historical Themes and Prospective Trends in Organizational Studies', *Higher Education Policy*, 26: 479–96.

Furedi, F. (2017), *What's Happened to the University: A Sociological Exploration of Its Infantalization*, London: Routledge.

Gentle, P. and D. Forman (2014), *Engaging Leaders: The Challenge of Inspiring Collective Commitment in Universities*, London: Routledge.

Gerrard, J, Sriprakash, A. and S. Rudolph (2021), 'Education and Racial Capitalism', *Race Ethnicity and Education*, doi:10.1080/13613324.2021.2001449.

Geschwind, L. (2019), 'Legitimizing Change in Higher Education: Exploring the Rationales Behind Major Organizational Restructuring', *Higher Education Policy*, 32: 381–95.

Gherardi, S. (2017a), 'One Turn…and Now Another One: Does the Turn to Practice and Turn to Affect Have Something in Common?', *Management Learning*, 48: 345–58.

Gherardi, S. (2017b), 'Shadow Organizing: A Metaphor to Explore Organizing as Intra-relating', *Qualitative Research in Organizations and Management: An International Journal*, 12 (1): 2–17.

Gherardi, S. and D. Nicolini (2001), 'The Sociological Foundations of Organizational Learning', in M. Dierkes, A. Berthoin-Antal, J. Child and I. Nonaka (eds), *Handbook of Organizational Learning and Knowledge*, 35–60, Oxford: Oxford University Press.

Gibbs, P., O. Ylijoki, C. Guzman-Valebzuela and R. Barnett, (eds) (2015), *Universities in the Flux of Time: An Exploration of Time and Temporailty in University Life*, London: Routledge.

Gleeson, D., I. Clark and S. Parsons (2020), '"Devastating": The Morrison Government Cuts Uni Funding for Environment Courses by Almost 30%', *The Conversation*, 13 October. Available online: https://theconversation.com/devastating-the-morrison-government-cuts-uni-funding-for-environment-courses-by-almost-30-147852 (accessed 1 February 2021).

Gordon, G. and C. Whitchurch, eds (2010), *Academic and Professional Identities in Higher Education*, New York: Routledge.

Gore, J. (2015), 'The Impossible Dream: Doing Deanship with Pessimistic Optimism', in R. Clift, J. Loughran, G. Mills and C. Craig (eds), *Inside the Role of Dean: International Perspectives of Leading in Higher Education*, 160–75, London: Routledge.

Gornall, L. and J. Salisbury (2012), 'Compulsive Working, "Hyperprofessionality" and the Unseen Pleasures of Academic Work', *Higher Education Quarterly*, 66 (2): 135–54.

Gornall, L., C. Cook, L. Daynton, J. Salisbury and B. Thomas, eds (2015), *Academic Working Lives: Experience, Practice and Change*, London: Bloomsbury.

Gray, E. M. (2013), 'Coming Out as a Lesbian, Gay or Bisexual Teacher: Negotiating Private and Professional World', *Sex Education: Sexuality, Society and Learning*, 13 (6): 702–14.

Gray, S. (2013), 'Activist Academics: What Future?', *Policy Futures in Education*, 11 (6): 700–11.

Gray, J. and Q. Beresford (2008), "A 'formidable challenge': Australia's quest for equity in Indigenous education", *Australian Journal of Education*, 52 (2): Article 8, Available at: https://research.acer.edu.au/aje/vol52/iss2/8.

Grenfell, M. and D. James (1998), 'Change in the Field—Changing the Field: Bourdieu and the Methodological Practice of Educational Research', *British Journal of Sociology of Education*, 25 (4): 507–23.

Gribble, C. and J. Blackmore (2012), 'Re-positioning Australia's International Education in Global Knowledge Economies: Implications of Shifts in Skilled Migration Policies for Universities', *Journal of Higher Education Policy and Management*, 34 (4): 341–54.

Grove, J. (2017), 'One in Three UK Universities Going Backwards on Female Professorships', *Times Higher Education*, 25 May. Available online: https://www.timeshi ghereducation.com/news/one-in-three-uk-universities-going-backwards-on-female -professorships (accessed 31 May 2017).

Grummell, B., D. Devine and K. Lynch (2009a), 'The Careless Manager: Gender, Care and New Managerialism in Higher Education', *Gender and Education*, 21 (2): 191–208.

Grummell, B., D. Devine and K. Lynch (2009b), 'Appointing Senior Managers in Education: Homosociability, Local Logics and Authenticity in the Selection Process', *Educational Management, Administration and Leadership*, 37 (3): 329–49.

Gunter, H. M., E. Grimaldi, D. Hall and R. Serpieri, (eds) (2016), *New Public Management and the Reform of Education*, London: Routledge.

Gupta, S., J. Habjan and H. Tutek, eds (2016), *Academic Labour, Unemployment and Global Higher Education: Neoliberal Policies of Funding and Management*, London: Palgrave Macmillan.

Guthrie, J. (2021a), 'Counting the Uncounted: Employees in Victorian Public Sector Universities', *Campus Morning Mail*, 20 September. Available online: https:// campusmorningmail.com.au/news/counting-the-uncounted-employees-in-victorian -public-sector-universities/ (accessed 1 October 2021).

Guthrie, J. (2021b), 'Universities Must Plan and Budget for the Public Good', *Campus Morning Mail*, 5 July. Available online: https://campusmorningmail.com.au/news/ universities-must-plan-and-budget-for-the-public-good/ (accessed 1 August 2021).

Hancock, L. (2020), 'Commercialization and Corporatization: Academic Freedom and Autonomy under Constraints in Australian Universities', in Z. Hao and P. Zabielskis (eds), *Academic Freedom Under Siege: Higher Education in East Asia, the U.S. and Australia*, 219–46, Cham: Springer.

Hancock, N. and D. Hellawell (2003), 'Academic Middle Management in Higher Education: A Game of Hide and Seek?', *Journal of Higher Education Policy and Management*, 25 (1): 5–12.

Hanlon, G. (2016), *The Dark Side of Management: Secret History of Management Theory*, London: Routledge.

Hao, J. and A. Welch (2012), 'A Tale of Sea-turtles: Job Seeking Experiences of Hai Gui (High Skilled Returnees) in China', *Higher Education Policy*, 25 (2): 243–60.

Harding, N., J. Ford and Lee, H. (2017), 'Towards a Performative Theory of Resistance: Senior Managers and Revolting Subject(ivitie)s', *Organization Studies*, 38 (9): 1209–31.

Hark, S. (2016), 'Contending Directions: Gender Studies in the Entrepreneurial University', *Women's Studies International Forum*, 54: 84–90.

Hassan, R. (2017), 'The Worldly Space: The Digital University in Network Time', *British Journal of Sociology of Education*, 38 (1): 72–82.

Hazelkorn, E. (2015), 'Making an Impact: New Directions for Arts and Humanities Research', *Arts and Humanities in Higher Education*, 14 (1): 25–44.

Hearn, A. (2015), 'The Politics of Branding in the New University of Circulation', *International Studies of Management and Organization*, 45 (2): 114–20.

Hearn, J. (2010), 'Men, Masculinities and Leadership', in L. Husu, J. Hearn, A. S. Lamsa and S. Vanhala (eds), *Leadership through the Gender Lens*, 21–37, Helsinki: Hanken School of Economics Research Report.

Heffernan, T. (2021a), 'Academic Networks and Career Trajectory: "There's No Career in Academia Without Networks"', *Higher Education Research and Development*, 40 (5): 981–94.

Heffernan, T. (2021b), 'Sexism, Racism, Prejudice, and Bias: A Literature Review and Synthesis of Research Surrounding Student Evaluations of Courses and Teaching', *Assessment and Evaluation in Higher Education*, 2021 (March): 1–11.

Hellström, T., E. Brattström and L. Jabrane (2018), 'Governing Interdisciplinary Cooperation in Centers of Excellence', *Studies in Higher Education*, 43 (10): 1763–77.

Hemmings, C. (2012), 'Affective Solidarity: Feminist Reflexivity and Political Transformation', *Feminist Theory*, 13 (2): 147–61.

Henman, P., S. Brown and S. Denis (2017), 'When Rating Systems Do Not Rate: Evaluating ERA's Performance', *Australian Universities Review*, 59 (1): 58–68.

Hetherington, D. (2015), *Per Capita Tax Survey. Public Attitudes Towards Taxation and Public Expenditure*, Available online: https://apo.org,au (accessed 21 September 2021).

Hey, V. and S. Broadford (2004), 'The Return of the Repressed?: The Gender Politics of Emergent Forms of Professionalism in Education', *Journal of Education Policy*, 19 (6): 691–713.

Hey, V. and C. Leathwood (2009), 'Passionate Attachments: Higher Education, Policy, Knowledge, Emotion and Social Justice', *Higher Education Policy*, 22 (1): 101–18.

Hil, R. (2012), *Whackademia: An Insider's Account of the Troubled University*, Sydney: UNSW Press.

Hil, R., K. Lyons and F. Thompsett (2021), *Transforming Universities in the Midst of Global Crisis. A University for the Common Good*, London: Taylor and Francis.

Hillman, N. (2016), 'The Coalition's Higher Education Reforms in England', *Oxford Review of Education*, 42 (3): 330–45.

Hogan, A., B. Lingard and S. Sellar (2015), 'Edu-businesses and Education Policy: The Case of Pearson', *Professional Voice*, 10 (2): 24–30.

Holvino, E. (2008), 'Intersections: The Simultaneity of Race, Gender and Class in Organization Studies', *Gender, Work & Organization*, 17 (3): 248–77.

Howard, J. (2020), *Challenges of Australian Research and Innovation*, Sydney: University of Technology Sydney Occasional Paper, April.

Howard, J. (2021), *Rethinking Australian Higher Education: Towards a Diversified System for the 21st Century*, Sydney: University of Technology Sydney Occasional Paper, February.

Hsieh, C. (2020), 'Internationalization of Higher Education in the Crucible: Linking National Identity and Policy in the Age of Globalization', *International Journal of Education Development*, 78 (October): 1–12.

Hughes, M. and D. Bennett (2013), 'Survival Skills: The Impact of Change and the ERA on Australian Researchers', *Higher Education Research and Development*, 32 (3): 340–54.

Huisman, J. (2011), 'The Great Brain Race: How Global Universities are Reshaping the World', *Studies in Higher Education*, 36 (1): 123–25.

Human Rights Commission (2017), *Change the Course: National Report on Sexual Assault and Sexual Harassment at Australian Universities*, Canberra: Human Rights Commission.

Hunt, V., S. Prince, S. Dixon-Fyle and L. Yee (2018), *Delivering Through Diversity*, Available online: https://www.mckinsey.com/~/media/mckinsey/business%20functions/organization/our%20insights/delivering%20through%20diversity/delivering-through-diversity_full-report.ashx.

Huppatz, K., K. Sang and J. Napier (2019), 'If You Put Pressure on Yourself to Produce Then That's Your Responsibility': Mothers' Experiences of Maternity Leave and Flexible Work in the Neoliberal University', *Gender Work and Organization*, 26 (6): 772–88.

IDP (2019), *International Student and Parent Buyer Behavior Research 2019*, IDP Australia.

Illouz, E. (1997), 'Who Will Care for the Caretaker's Daughter?: Towards a Sociology of Happiness in the Era of Reflexive Modernity', *Theory, Culture and Society*, 14 (4): 31–66.

Inge, S. (2018), 'Female Academics Told Image More Important Than Quality of Work', *Times Higher Education*, 24 January. Available online: https://www.timeshigher education.com/news/female-academics-told-image-more-important-quality-work (accessed 1 February 2019).

Innovation and Science Australia (2017), *The Australia 2030: Prosperity through Innovation*, Canberra: Australian Government.

Iqbal, I. (2013), 'Academics' Resistance to Summative Peer Review of Teaching: Questionable Rewards and the Importance of Student Evaluations', *Teaching in Higher Education*, 18 (5): 557–69.

Jameson, J. (2012), 'Leadership Values, Trust and Negative Capability: Managing the Uncertainties of Future English Higher Education', *Higher Education Quarterly*, 66 (4): 391–414.

Jameson, J. (2018), 'Critical Corridor Talk: Just Gossip or Stoic Resistance? Unrecognised Informal Higher Education Leadership', *Higher Education Quarterly*, 72 (4): 375–89.

Jameson, J., (ed) (2019), *Critical University Leadership: International Perspectives on Leadership in Higher Education*, London: Routledge.

Jarboe, N. (2017), *Women Count: Australian Universities 2016*, Available online: https://women-count.org/portfolio/womencount-australian-universities-2016/ (accessed 23 June 2020).

Jayasuriya, K. and G. McCarthy (2021), 'Australia's Politics of Research Funding: Depoliticization and the Crisis of the Regulatory State', in R. Eisfeld and M. Flinders (eds), *Political Science in the Shadow of the State*, 119–44, Switzerland: Springer Nature.

Jenkins, K. (2020), *Respect @Work: Sexual Harassment National Inquiry Report*, Canberra: Human Rights Commission

Jessop, B. (2017), 'Varieties of Academic Capitalism and Entrepreneurial Universities', *Higher Education*, 73 (February): 853–70.

Johnson, H. L. (2017), *Pipelines, Pathways and Institutional Leadership: An Update on the Status of Women in Higher Education*, Washington, DC: American Council on Education.

Jones, E., R. Coeli, R. Beelen and H. de Wit, eds (2018), *Global and Local Internationalization*, Rotterdam: Sense Publishers.

Jones, S., G. Lefoe, M. Harvey and K. Ryland (2012), 'Distributed Leadership: A Collaborative Framework for Academics, Executives and Professionals in Higher Education', *Journal of Higher Education Policy and Management*, 34 (1): 67–78.

Jongsma, M., W. Sanders and C. Weeda (2020), *Survey of the Extent and Effects of Structural Overtime at Dutch Universities*, Netherlands: WOinActie.

Jos, H. (2011), 'Transnational Academic Mobility and Gender', *Globalization, Societies and Education*, 9 (2): 183–209.

Juntrasook, A. (2014), '"You do not Have to Be the Boss to Be a Leader": Contested Meanings of Leadership in Higher Education', *Higher Education Research and Development*, 33 (1): 19–31.

Kallio, K. M., T. J. Kallio, J. Tienari and T. Hyvönen (2016), 'Ethos at Stake: Performance Management and Academic Work in Universities', *Human Relations*, 69 (3): 685–709.

Kauppi, N. (2015), 'The Academic Condition: Unstable Structures, Ambivalent Narratives, Dislocated Identities', in L. Evans and J. Nixon (eds), *Academic Identities in Higher Education: The Changing European Landscape*, 31–46, London: Bloomsbury.

Keane, E. (2011), 'Distancing to Self-Protect: The Perpetuation of Inequality in Higher Education Through Socio-Relational Dis/engagement', *British Journal of Sociology of Education*, 32 (3):449–66.

Kenny, J. (2018), 'Re-empowering Academics in a Corporate Culture: An Exploration of Workload and Performativity in a University', *Higher Education*, 75 (2): 365–80.

Kezar, A. and J. Dizon (2020), 'Renewing and Revitalizing Shared Governance: A Social Justice and Equity Framework', in A. Kezar and J. Posselt, (eds), *Higher Education Administration for Social Justice and Equity. Critical Perspectives for Leadership*, 21–42, New York: Routledge.

Kezar, A. and P. Eckel (2002), 'The Effect of Institutional Culture on Change Strategies in Higher Education: Universal Principles or Culturally Responsive Concepts?', *Journal of Higher Education*, 73 (4): 435–60.

Kezar, A. and J. Posselt, (eds) (2020), *Higher Education Administration for Social Justice and Equity. Critical Perspectives for Leadership*, New York: Routledge.

Kim, T. (2017), 'Academic Mobility, Transnational Identity Capital, and Stratification under Conditions of Academic Capitalism', *Higher Education*, 73: 981–97.

King, S; (2012), 'MOOCs Will Mean the Death of Universities? Not Likely', *The Conversation*, 28 August.

Kirkby, D. and K. Reiger, (2015), 'A Design for Learning? A Case Study of the Hidden Costs of Curriculum and Organizational Change', in M. Thornton (ed), *Through a Glass Darkly: The Social Sciences Look at the Neoliberal University*, 211–27, Canberra: ANU Press.

Kjeldal, S., J. Rindfleish and A. Sheridan (2005), 'Deal-making and Rule-breaking: Behind the Façade of Equity in Academia', *Gender and Education*, 17 (4): 431–47.

Klaus, K. and S. Steele (2020), 'An Exploratory and Descriptive Study of Destructive Leadership in U.S. Higher Education', *International Journal of Leadership in Education*, 2020 (July): 1–21.

Kligyte, G. and S. Barrie (2014), 'Collegiality: Leading Us into Fantasy –The Paradoxical Resilience of Collegiality in Academic Leadership', *Higher Education Research and Development*, 33 (1): 157–69.

Kloot, B. (2009), 'Exploring the Value of Bourdieu's Framework in the Context of Institutional Change', *Studies in Higher Education*, 34 (4): 469–81.

Knaus, C. (2019), 'Academics Condemn Harassment of Whistle-blower by Murdoch University', *The Guardian*, 15 October. Available online: https://www.theguardian.com/australia-news/2019/oct/15/academics-condemn-harassment-whistleblower-murdoch-university-schroeder-turk (accessed 1 November 2019).

Knight, J. (2012), 'Concepts, Rationales, and Interpretive Frameworks in the Internationalization of Higher Education', in D. K. Deardorff, H. de Wit, J. Heyl and T. Adams (eds), *The SAGE Handbook of International Higher Education*, 27–42, Thousand Oaks, CA: SAGE.

Knight, J. (2015), 'Moving from Soft Power to Knowledge Diplomacy', *International Higher Education*, 80 (Spring): 8–9.

Knight, J. and H. de Wit (2018), 'Internationalization of Higher Education: Where Have We Come from and Where are We Going?', in D. Proctor and L. E. Rumbley (eds), *The Future Agenda for Internationalization in Higher Education: Next Generation Perspectives into Research, Policy, and Practice*, xix–xxiv, New York: Routledge.

Kosonen, P. and M. Ikonen (2019), 'Trust Building through Discursive Leadership: A Communicative Engagement Perspective in Higher Education Management', *International Journal of Leadership in Education*, 2019 (October): 1–17.

Krejsler, J. (2007), 'Discursive Strategies that Individualize: CVs and Appraisal Interviews', *International Journal of Qualitative Studies in Education*, 20 (4): 473–90.

Kretovics, M. (2020), *Understanding Power and Leadership in Higher Education: Tools for Institutional Change*, London: Routledge.

Kupfer, A., (ed) (2012), *Globalization, Higher Education, the Labour Market and Inequality*, London: Routledge.

Lam, A. and A. de Campos (2015), '"Content to be Sad" or "Runaway Apprentice"? The Psychological Contract and Career Agency of Young Scientists in the Entrepreneurial University', *Human Relations*, 68 (5): 811–41.

Lane, B. (2012), 'Women Falling Foul of ERA', *The Australian*, 12 December, 9.

Langmann, A., A. Fahrleitner-Pammer, T. R. Pieber and I. Zollner-Schwetz (2011), 'Women Underrepresented on Editorial Boards of 60 Major Medical Journals', *Gend Med*, 8 (6): 378–87.

Lauder, H., M. Young, H. Daniels, M. Balarin and J. Low (2012), *Educating for the Knowledge Economy? Critical Perspectives*, London: Routledge.

Lawler, S. (2004), 'Rules of Engagement: Habitus, Power and Resistance', *The Sociological Review*, https://doi.org/10.1111/j.1467-954X.2005.00527.x.

Lea, D. (2011), 'The Managerial University and the Delcineo f Modern Thoght', *Educational Philosophy and Theory*, 43 (8): 816–37.

Leathwood, C. and B. Read (2013), 'Research Policy and Academic Performativity: Compliance, Contestation and Complicity', *Studies in Higher Education*, 38 (8): 1162–74.

Leberman, S., B. Eames and S. Barnett (2016), 'Unless You are Collaborating with a Big Name Successful Professor, You are Unlikely to Receive Funding', *Gender and Education*, 28 (5): 644–61.

Leišytė, L. (2016), 'New Public Management and Research Productivity–A Precarious State of Affairs of Academic Work in the Netherlands', *Studies in Higher Education*, 41 (5): 828–46.

Lempiäinen, K. (2015), 'Precariousness in Academia: Prospects for University Employment', in D. della Porta, S. Hänninen, M. Siisiäinen and T. Silvasti (eds), *The New Social Division*, 123–38, London: Palgrave Macmillan.

Leonardo, Z. (2013), 'The Color of Supremacy: Beyond the Discourse of "white privilege"', *Educational Philosophy and Theory*, 36 (2): 137–52.

Levitas, R. (2000), 'Discourses of Risk and Utopia', in B. Adams, U. Beck and J. van Loom (eds), *The Risk Society and Beyond: Critical Issues in Social Theory*, 198–210, London: SAGE Publication.

Liera, R. and Ching, C. (2019), 'Reconceptualizing "Merit" and "Fit"', in A. Kezar and J. Posselt (eds), *Higher Education Administration for Social Justice and Equity*, 111–31, London: Routledge.

Lightowler, C. and C. Knight (2013), 'Sustaining Knowledge Exchange and Research Impact in the Social Sciences and Humanities: Investing in Knowledge Broker Roles in UK Universities', *Evidence & Policy: A Journal of Research, Debate and Practice*, 9 (3): 317–34.

Lipton, B. (2017), 'Measures of Success: Cruel Optimism and the Paradox of Academic Women's Participation in Australian Higher Education', *Higher Education Research and Development*, 36 (3): 486–97.

Lipton, B. (2020), *Academic Women in Neoliberal Times*, London: Palgrave MacMillan.

Littleton, E. and J. Stanford (2021), 'An Avoidable Catastrophe: Pandemic Job Losses in Higher Education and Their Consequences', *The Australia Institute*, 15 September. Available online: https://australiainstitute.org.au/post/an-avoidable-catastrophe-pandemic-job-losses-in-higher-education/ (accessed 16 September 2021).

Litvin, D. (2002), 'The Business Case for Diversity and the "Iron Cage"', in B. Czarniaswaska and H. Hopfl (eds), *Casting the Other. The Production and Maintenance of Inequalities in Work Organizations*, 160–84, London: Routledge.

Livingstone, D., K. Mirchandani and P. Sawchuck, eds (2008), *The Future of Lifelong Learning and Work: Critical Perspectives*, Rotterdam: Sense Publishers.

Lokuwaduge, C. and A. Armstrong (2014), 'The Impact of Governance on the Performance of the Higher Education Sector in Australia', *Educational Management and Leadership*, 43 (5): 811–27.

Loomes, S., A. Owens and G. McCarthy (2019), 'Patterns of Recruitment of Academic Leaders to Australian Universities and Implications for the Future of Higher Education', *Journal of Higher Education Policy and Management*, 41 (2): 137–52.

Lopes, A. and I. A. Dewan (2014/2015), 'Precarious Pedagogies? The Impact of Casual and Zero-hour Contracts in Higher Education', *Journal of Feminist Scholarship*, 7 (8): 28–42.

Lorenz, C. (2012), 'If You're so Smart, Why Are You under Surveillance? Universities, Neoliberalism, and New Public Management', *Critical Inquiry*, 38 (3): 599–630.

Lovell, T, (2000), 'Thinking Feminism With and Against Bourdieu', *Feminist Theory*, https://doi.org/10.1177/14647000022229047.

Lucas, L. (2014), 'Academic Resistance to Quality Assurance Processes in Higher Education in the UK', *Policy and Society*, 33 (3): 215–24.

Lugg, C. A. (2017), 'Skipping Towards Seniority: One Queer Scholar's Romp through the Wilds of Academe', *International Journal of Qualitative Studies in Education*, 30 (1): 74–82.

Lumby, J. (2012), *What do We Know about Leadership in Higher Education?* The Leadership Foundation for Higher Education's Research: Review Paper, London: LFHE.

Lumby, J. (2013), 'Distributed Leadership: The Uses and Abuses of Power', *Educational Management Administration and Leadership*, 41 (5): 581–97.

Lumby, J. (2019), 'Leadership and Power in Higher Education', *Studies in Higher Education*, 44 (9): 1619–29.

Lumby, J. and N. Foskett (2011), 'Power, Risk, and Utility: Interpreting the Landscape of Culture in Educational Leadership', *Education Administration Quarterly*, 47 (3): 446–61.

Lupton, D. and G. Smith (2018), '"A Much Better Person": The Agential Capacities of Self-Tracking Practices', in *Metric Culture: Ontologies of Self-Tracking Practices*, 57–75, doi: 10.1108/978-1-78743-289-520181004

Lynch, K. (2010), 'Carelessness: The Hidden Doxa of Higher Education', *Arts and Humanities*, 9 (1): 54–67.

Lynch, K., B. Grummell and D. Devine (2012), *New Managerialism in Education. Commercialization, Carelessness and Gender Commercialization*, London: Palgrave Macmillan.

Lyons, M. and L. Ingersoll (2010), 'Regulated Autonomy or Autonomous Regulation? Collective Bargaining and Academic Workloads in Australian Universities', *Journal of Higher Education Policy and Management*, 32 (2): 137–48.

Macfarlane, B. (2007), *The Academic Citizen: The Virtue of Service in University Life*, London: Routledge.

Macfarlane, B. (2011), 'The Morphing of Academic Practice: Unbundling and the Rise of the Para-academic', *Higher Education Quarterly*, 65 (1): 59–71.

Macfarlane, B. (2012a), *Intellectual Leadership in Higher Education: Renewing the Role of the University Professor*, London: Routledge.

Macfarlane, B. (2012b), 'Whisper It Softly, Professors are Really Academic Developers Too', *International Journal for Academic Development*, 17 (2): 181–3.

Macfarlane, B. (2014), 'Challenging Leaderism', *Higher Education Research and Development*, 33 (1): 1–4.

Macfarlane, B. (2016), From Identity to Identities A Story of Fragmentation'. *Higher Education Research and Development*, 35 (5): 1083–5.

Macfarlane, B. (2017), 'The Paradox of Collaboration: A Moral Continuum', *Higher Education Research and Development*, 36 (3): 472–85.

Macfarlane, B. and Burg, D. (2019), 'Women Professors and the Academic Housework Trap', *Journal of Higher Education Policy and Management*, 41 (3): 262–74.

MacIntyre, S. (2010), *The Poor Relation. A History of the Social Sciences in Australia*, Melbourne: Melbourne University Press.

MacNell, L., A. Driscoll and A. Hunt (2015), 'What's in a Name: Exposing Gender Bias in Student Ratings of Teaching', *Innovative Higher Education*, 40 (4): 291–303.

Maley, J. (2020), 'Silenced for Too Long: Naming and Shaming Seems to be the Only Way to Stop Sexual Harassment', *Sunday Age*, 5 July, 26.

Manfredi, S. (2017), 'Increasing Gender Diversity in Senior Roles in HE: Who Is Afraid of Positive Action?', *Administrative Sciences*, 7 (19): 1–14.

Mansell, W. (2016), 'Should Pearson, a Giant Multinational, Be Influencing our Education Policy?', *The Guardian*, 17 July. Available online: https://www.theguardian.com/education/2012/jul/16/pearson-multinational-influence-education-poliy (accessed 10 June 2020).

Marginson, S. (2008), 'Global Field and Global Imagining: Bourdieu and Worldwide Higher Education', *British Journal of Sociology of Education*, 29 (3): 303–13.

Marginson, S. (2011), 'Higher Education and Public Good', *Higher Education Quarterly*, 65 (4): 411–33.

Marginson, S. and Considine, M. (2000), *The Enterprise University, Power, Governance and Reinvention in Australia*, Melbourne: Cambridge University Press.

Marini, G., W. Locke and C. Whitchurch (2019), *The Future Higher Education Workforce in Locally and Globally Engaged Higher Education Institutions: A Review of Literature on the 'Academic Workforce'*, London: Centre for Global Higher Education, UCL Institute of Education.

Marshman, I. and F. Larkins (2020), *Modelling Individual Australian Universities Resilience in Managing Overseas Student Revenue Losses from the COVID-19 Pandemic*, Melbourne: Centre for the Study of Higher Education, The University of Melbourne.

Martin, J. (2013), 'The Sustainable University: Green Goals and New Challenges for Higher Education Leaders', *Journal of Environmental Law*, 25 (1): 166–8.

Martin-Sardesai, A., H. Irvine, S. Tooley and J. Guthrie (2017), 'Organizational Change in an Australian University: Responses to a Research Assessment Exercise', *The British Accounting Review*, 49: 399–412.

Matchett, S. (2021), 'How to Help the Vast University Workforces that Managements Under-count', *Campus Morning Mail*, 14 April. Available online: https://campusmorningmail.com.au/news/how-to-help-the-vast-uni-workforce-managements-under-count/ (accessed 1 May 2021).

Maton, K. (2005), 'A Question of Autonomy: Bourdieu's Field Approach and Higher Education Policy', *Journal of Education Policy*, 20 (6): 687–704.

Mauleón, E., L. Hillán, L. Moreno, I. Gómez and M. Bordons (2013), 'Assessing Gender Balance Among Journal Authors and Editorial Board Members', *Scientometrics*, 95 (1): 87–114, doi: 10.1007/s11192-012-0824-4

May, R., D. Peetz and G. Strachan (2013), 'The Casual Academic Workforce and Labour Market Segmentation in Australia', *Labour and Industry: A Journal of the Social and Economic Relations of Work*, 23 (3): 258–75.

Maycock, E. (2017), *Gender Shrapnel in the Academic Workplace*, New York: Palgrave Macmillan.

McClure, K. (2016), 'Building the Innovative and Entrepreneurial University: An Institutional Case Study of Administrative Academic Capitalism', *Journal of Higher Education*, 87 (4): 516–43.

McLeod, J. (2005), 'Feminist Re-reading Bourdieu: Old Debates and New Questions About Gender Habitus and Gender Change', *Theory and Research in Education*, 3 (11): 11–27.

McManus, J. (2018), 'Are Men Just Better at Science than Women?', *Irish Times*, 14 November. Available online: https://www.irishtimes.com/opinion/are-men-just-better -at-science-than-women-1.3696662 (accessed 5 May 2020).

McNay, L. (2000), *Gender and Agency, Reconfiguring the Subject in Feminist and Social Theory*, Cambridge: Polity Press.

McNay, L. (2005), 'Managing Institutions in a Mass Higher Education Systems', in I. McNay (ed), *Beyond Mass Higher Education. Building on Experience*, 161–70, Milton Keynes: Open University Press.

McNay, L. (2012), *Leading Strategic Change in Higher Education - Closing the Implementation Gap*, Leadership and Governance in Higher Education – Handbook for Decision-Makers and Administrators, 2012 (4).

McRoy, I. and P. Gibbs (2016), 'Leading Change in Higher Education', *Educational Management Administration and Leadership*, 37 (5): 687–704.

McWilliam, E. and C. Hatcher (2007), 'Killing Me Softly: The 'Making Up' of the Educational Leader', *International Journal of Leadership in Education*, 10 (3): 233–46.

Mellors-Bourne, R. and J. Metcalfe (2013), *Principal Investigators and Research Leaders Survey (PIRLS): 2013 UK Aggregate Results*, London: Vitae.

Mendes, K., J. Ringrose and J. Keller (2018), '#MeToo and the Promise and Pitfalls of Challenging Rape Culture through Digital Feminist Activism', *European Journal of Women's Studies*, 25 (2): 236–46.

Mertz, N. (2009), *Breaking into the All-Male Club: Female Professors of Educational Administration*, New York: SUNY Press.

Metz, I., A. Harzing and A. Zyphur (2016), 'Of Journal Editors and Editorial Boards: Who are the Trailblazers in Increasing Editorial Board Gender Equality?', *British Journal Management*, 27: 712–26.

Meyer, L. (2012), 'Negotiating Academic Values, Professorial Responsibilities and Expectations for Accountability in Today's University', *Higher Education Quarterly*, 66 (2): 207–17.

Middlehurst, R. (2013), 'Changing Internal Governance: Are Leadership Roles and Management Structures in United Kingdom Universities Fit for the Future?', *Higher Education Quarterly*, 67 (3): 275–94.

Middlehurst, R. and T. Kennie (2019), 'South America: Colombia: A Case Study of Leadership and Transformation in the City of Medelllin', in J. Jameson (ed), *Critical*

University Leadership: International Perspectives on Leadership in Higher Education: Critical Thinking for Global Challenges, 91–102, London: Routledge.

Mills, A. (2010), 'Ten Things You Need to Know about Gender, Organizational Culture and Leadership', in L. Husu, J. Hearn, A. S. Lamsa and S. Vanhala (eds), *Leadership through the Gender Lens*, 21–37, Helsinki: Hanken School of Economics Research Report.

Minister of Education (2016), *The National International Education Strategy 2025*, Canberra: Australian Government.

Mirza, H. (2009), *Race, Gender and Educational Desire: Why Black Women Succeed and Fail*, London: Routledge.

Mitchell, K. and J. Martin (2018), 'The Gender Bias in Student Evaluations', *Political Science and Politics*, 51 (July): 648–52.

Mok, K. H. (2016), 'Massification of Higher Education, Graduate Employment and Social Mobility in the Greater China Region', *British Journal of Sociology of Education*, 37 (1): 51–71.

Molesworth, M., M. Scullion and E. Nixon, (eds) (2011), *The Marketization of Higher Education and the Student as Consumer*, London: Routledge.

Moreton-Robinson, A. (2004), 'Whiteness, Epistemology and Indigenous Representation', in A. Moreton-Robinson (ed), *Whitening Race: Essays on Political and Cultural Criticism*, 75–88, Canberra: Aboriginal Studies Press.

Moreton-Robinson, A. (2013), 'Towards an Australian Indigenous Standpoint Theory: A Methodological Tool', *Australian Feminist Studies*, 28 (78): 331–47.

Morgan, G. (2016), 'Cannibalizing the Collegium: The Plight of the Humanities and Social Sciences in the Managerial University', in S. Gupta, J. Habjan and H. Tutek (eds), *Academic Labour, Unemployment and Global Higher Education*, London: Palgrave Macmillan.

Morley, L. (2013), 'The Rules of the Game: Women and the Leaderist Turn in Higher Education', *Gender and Education*, 25 (1): 116–31.

Mumby, D., R. Thomas, I. Marti and D. Seidl (2017), 'Resistance Redux', *Organization Studies*, 38 (9): 1157–83.

Murgia, A. and B. Poggio, (eds) (2018), *Gender and Precarious Research Careers: A Comparative Analysis*, London: Routledge.

Naidoo, R. (2004), 'Fields and Institutional Strategy: Bourdieu on the Relationship between Higher Education, Inequality and Society', *British Journal of Sociology of Education*, 25 (4): 457–71.

Naidoo, R. and J. Williams (2015), 'The Neoliberal Regime in English Higher Education: Charters, Consumers and the Erosion of the Public Good', *Critical Studies in Education*, 56 (2): 208–23.

Nakata, M. (2017), 'Difficult Dialogues in the South: Questions about Practice', *The Australian Journal of Indigenous Education*, 47 (1): 1–7.

Neary, M. and G. Saunder (2011), 'Leadership and Learning Landscapes: The Struggle for the Idea of the University', *Higher Education Quarterly*, 65 (4): 333–5.

Neave, G. (2012), *The Evaluative State, Institutional Autonomy and Re-engineering Higher Education in Western Europe*, London: Palgrave.

Nelson, B. (2003), *Our Universities: Backing Australia's Future*, Canberra: Department of Education Science and Training (DEST).

Nicolini, D. (2013), *Practice Theory, Work, and Organization: An Introduction*, Oxford: Oxford University Press.

Nixon, J. (2015), *Higher Education and the Public Good*, New York: Continuum International Publishing Group.

Noonan, J. (2014), 'Thought-time, Money-time, and the Temporal Conditions of Academic Freedom', *Time and Society*, 24 (1): 109–28.

Norton, A. (2012), *Mapping Australian Higher Education*, Melbourne: Grattan Institute.

Norton, A. and I. Cherastidtham (2018), *Mapping Australian Higher Education*, Melbourne: Grattan Institute.

NTEU (2015), *State of Uni Survey 2015 Report No.2: Workloads*, National Tertiary Education Union, Available online: http://www.nteu.org.au/stateoftheuni.

NTEU (2018a), *The Prevalence of Insecure Employment at Australia's Universities*, Melbourne: National Tertiary Education Union.

NTEU (2018b), *Staff Experience of Student Evaluation of Teaching and Subjects/Units*, Melbourne: National Tertiary Education Union.

Nussbaum, M. (2010), *Not for Profit: Why Democracy Needs the Humanities*, Princeton and Oxford: Princeton University Press.

Oancea, A. (2019), 'Research Governance and the Future(s) of Research Assessment', *Palgrave Communications*, 5 (27): 1–12.

O'Brien, J. (2015), *National Tertiary Education Union: A Most Unlikely Union*, Sydney: UNSW Press.

O'Connor, P. (2015), 'Good Jobs – But Places for Women?', *Gender and Education*, 27 (3): 304–19.

OECD (2008), *Tertiary Education for the Knowledge Society*, Paris: OECD.

Oishi, N. (2017), *Workforce Diversity in Higher Education: Experiences of Asian Academics in Australian Universities*, Melbourne: Asia Institute, University of Melbourne.

Oleksiyenko, A. and N. Ruan (2019), 'Intellectual Leadership and Academic Communities: Issues for Discussion and Research', *Higher Education Quarterly*, 73 (4): 406–18.

Oleksiyenko, A. and W. Tierney (2018), 'Higher Education and Human Vulnerability: Global Failures of Corporate Design', *Tertiary Education and Management*, 24 (3): 187–92.

Olssen, M. and M. Peters (2005), 'Neoliberalism, Higher Education, and the Knowledge Economy: From the Free Market to Knowledge Capitalism', *Journal of Education Policy*, 20 (3): 313–45.

Olssen, M., J. Codd and A. O'Neill, eds (2004), *Education Policy: Globalization, Citizenship and Democracy*, Thousand Oaks: SAGE.

O'Malley, N. (2020), 'The World's Leading Universities Join the Climate Fight', *The Sydney Morning Herald*, 18 November. Available online: https://www.smh.com.au/environment/climate-change/the-world-s-leading-universities-join-the-climate-fight-20201117-p56ffw.html (accessed 20 November 2020).

Ong, I. (2007), 'Neoliberalism as a Mobile Technology', *Transactions of the Institute of British Geographers*, 32 (1): 3–8.

Opstrup, N. and S. Pihl-Thingvad (2016), 'Stressing Academia? Stress-as-offence-to-self at Danish Universities', *Journal of Higher Education Policy and Management*, 38 (1): 39–52.

Ordorika, I. and M. Lloyd (2015), 'International Rankings and the Contest for University Hegemony', *Journal of Education Policy*, 30 (3): 385–405. (p. 57).

O'Reilly, D. and M. Reed (2010), '"Leaderism": An Evolution of Managerialism in UK Public Service Reform', *Public Administration*, 88 (4): 960–78.

O'Reilly, D. and M. Reed (2011), 'The Grit in the Oyster: Professionalism, Managerialism and Leaderism as Discourses of UK Public Services Modernization', *Organization Studies*, 32 (8): 1079–101.

Ozga, J. T. and R. Deem (2000), 'Colluded Selves, New Times and Engendered Organisational Cultures: The Experiences of Feminist Women Managers in UK Higher and Further Education', *Discourse*, 21 (2): 141–54.

Palfreyman, D. and T. Tapper (2014), *Reshaping the University: The Rise of the Regulated Market in Higher Education*, Oxford: Oxford University Press.

Papadopoulos, A. (2017), 'The Mismeasure of Academic Labour', *Higher Education Research & Development*, 36 (3): 511–25.

Paradeise, C., I. Bleiklie, E. Reale and E. Ferlie, (eds) (2009), *University Governance Western European Comparative Perspectives*, Netherlands: Springer.

Parke, K. (2012), 'The Transformation of the Academic Profession: The Erosion of Tenure and the (E)state of the Professoriate', in M. Vukasovic, P. Maassen, M. Nerland, R. Pinheiro, B. Stensaker, and A. Vabo (eds), *Effects of Higher Education Reforms: Change Dynamics*, 219–38, Rotterdam: Sense.

Parker, L. (2002), 'It's Been a Pleasure Doing Business with You: An Analysis and Critique of University Change Management', *Critical Perspectives on Accounting*, 13 (5–6): 603–19.

Parker, M. (2014), 'University, Ltd: Changing a Business School', *Organization*, 21 (2): 281–92.

Parker, M. and R. Thomas (2011), 'What is a Critical Journal?', *Organization*, 18 (4): 419–27.

Pawlowska, B., S. Braun, C. Peus and D. Frey (2010), 'Academic Leadership: The Effect of Leader-follower Incongruence and Cognitive Processes on Perceptions of Leader Adversity', in B. Schyns and T. Hansbrough (eds), *When Leadership Goes Wrong: Destructive Leadership, Mistakes, and Ethical Failures*, 479–512, New York: Information Age Publishing.

Peirce, G., S. Deselle, J. Draugalis, A. Spies, T. Davies and N. Bolino (2012), 'Identifying Psychological Contract Breaches to Guide Improvements in Faculty Retirement, Retention and Development', *American Journal of Pharmaceutical Education*, 76 (6): 1–8.

Pelizzon, A. et al. (2021), '2 out of 3 Members of University Councils Have No Professional Expertise in the Sector' *The Conversation*, 20 November.

Pelletier, K. L. (2010), 'Leader Toxicity: An Empirical Investigation of Toxic Behaviour and Rhetoric', *Leadership*, 6 (4): 373–89.

Pells, R. (2018), 'Short Grant Call: "Unfair to Women and Carers"', *Time Higher Education*, 14 August, Available online: https://www.timeshighereducation.com/news/hasty-funding-calls-prejudiced-against-women-and-carers.

Perry, L. and L. Holt (2018), 'Searching for the Songlines of Aboriginal Education and Cultures within Australian Higher Education', *Australian Educational Researcher*, 45 (3): 343–62.

Peseta, T., S. Barrie and J. McLean (2017), 'Academic Life in the Measured University: Pleasures, Paradoxes and Politics', *Higher Education Research and Development*, 36 (3): 453–7.

Peters, M. (2011), *Neoliberalism and After? Education, Social Policy, and the Crisis of Western Capitalism*, New York: Peter Lang.

Petersen, E. B. (2011), 'Staying or Going? Australian Early Career Researchers' Narratives of Academic Work, Exit Options, and Coping Stratgies', *Australian Universities' Review*, 55 (2): 34–42.

Piattoeva, N. and R. Boden (2020), 'Escaping Numbers? The Ambiguities of the Governance of Education through Data', *International Studies in Sociology of Education*, 29 (1–2): 1–18.

Pillay, S., R. Kluvers, S. Abhayawansa and V. Vedran (2013), 'An Exploratory Study into Work/Family Balance within the Australian Higher Education Sector', *Higher Education Research and Development*, 32 (2): 228–43.

Pinheiro, R. (2015), 'Humboldt Meets Schumpeter? Interpreting the "Entrepreneurial Turn" in European Higher Education', in S. Slaughter and B. J. Taylor (eds), *Higher Education, Stratification, and Workforce Development: Competitive Advantage in Europe, the US, and Canada*, 291–310, Dordrecht: Springer.

Pinheiro, R. and M. Young (2017), 'The University as an Adaptive Resilient Organization: A Complex Systems Perspective', in J. Huisman and M. Tight (eds), *Theory and Method in Higher Education Research*, Vol. 3, 119–36, Bingley: Emerald Publishing Ltd.

Pitt, R. and I. Mewburn (2016), 'Academic Superheroes? A Critical Analysis of Academic Job Descriptions', *Journal of Higher Education Policy and Management*, 38 (1): 88–101.

Power, M. (1997), *The Audit Society: Rituals of Verification*, Oxford: Oxford University Press.

Priess, B. (2012), 'RMIT Academics not Happy about Having to be Happy at Work', *Sydney Morning Herald*, 27 March, 5.

Probert, B. (2014), 'The Rise of Teaching Only Academics: Belated Recognition or a Slippery Slope?', *The Conversation*, 22 January. Available online: https://theconversation .com/the-rise-of-teaching-only-academics-belated-recognition-or-a-slippery-slope -20438 (accessed 1 June 2019).

Proctor, D. and L. Rumbley (2018), *The Future Agenda for Internationalization in Higher Education; Next Generation Insights into Research, Policy, and Practice*, London: Routledge.

Pusey, M. (1991), *Economic Rationalists in Canberra: A Nation Building State Changes Its Mind*, Cambridge: Cambridge University Press.

Pusser, B. and S. Marginson (2013), 'University Rankings in Critical Perspective', *Journal of Higher Education*, 84 (4): 544–68.

Puwar, N. (2004), *Space Invaders: Race, Gender and Bodies Out of Place*, Oxford: Berg.

QILT (2019), *Graduate Outcomes Survey-Longitudinal*, Canberra: Department of Education, Skills and Employment.

Quiggin, J. (2021), 'Dismembering Government: New Public Management and Why the Commonwealth Can't Do Anything Anymore', *The Monthly*, September: 26–33.

Raby, G. (2020), *China's Grand Strategy and Australia's Future in the New Global Order*, Melbourne: Melbourne University Press.

Rafnsdóttir, G. and T. Heijstra (2013), 'Balancing Work–family Life in Academia: The Power of Time', *Gender, Work & Organization*, 20 (3): 283–96.

Ramsden, P. (1998), 'Managing the Effective University', *Higher Education Research and Development*, 17 (3): 347–70.

Randell-Moon, H., S. Saltmarsh and W. Sutherland-Smith (2013), 'The Living Dead and the Dead Living: Contagion and Complicity in Contemporary Universities', in A. Whelan, R. Walker and C. Moore (eds), *Zombies in the Academy: Living Death in Higher Education*, 53–66, Bristol: Intellect Press.

Rawolle, S. (2005), 'Cross-field Effects and Temporary Social Fields: A Case Study of the Mediatization of Recent Australian Knowledge Economy Policies', *Journal of Education Policy*, 20 (6): 705–24.

Rawolle, S. (2013), 'Emotions in Education Policy: A Social Contract Analysis of Asymmetrical Dyads of Emotion', in M. Newberry, A. Gallant and P. Riley (eds), *Emotion and School: Understanding how the Hidden Curriculum Influences*

Relationships, Leadership, Teaching, and Learning (Advances in Research on Teaching, Vol. 18), 49–60, Bingley: Emerald Group Publishing Limited.

Rawolle, S., J. Rowlands and J. Blackmore (2016), 'The Implications of Contractualism for the Responsibilization of Higher Education', *Discourse*, 38 (1): 109–22.

Read, B. and C. Leathwood (2020), 'Casualized Academic Staff and the Lecturer-student Relationship: Shame, (Im)permanence and (Il)legitimacy', *British Journal of Sociology of Education*, 41 (4): 539–54.

Reay, D. (2004), 'Gendering Bourdieu's Concept of Capitals? Emotional Capital, Women and Social Class', in L. Adkins and B. Skeggs (eds), *Feminism After Bourdieu*, 57–74, Oxford: Blackwell.

Reich, R. (1992), *The Work of Nations*, New York: Knopf.

Reissner, S., V. Pagan and C. Smith (2011), '"Our Iceberg is Melting": Story, Metaphor and the Management of Organisational Change', *Culture and Organization*, 17 (5): 417–33.

Rhoades, G. (2010), 'Envisioning Invisible Workforces. Enhancing Intellectual Capital', in G. Gordon and C. Whitchurch (eds), *Academic and Professional Identities in Higher Education*, 35–54, London: Routledge.

Rhoades, G. (2014), 'Extending Academic Capitalism by Foregrounding Academic Labor', in B. Cantwell and I. Kauppinen (eds), *Academic Capitalism in the Age of Globalization*, 113–34, Baltimore: Johns Hopkins University Press.

Ribiero, C. (2020), '"Pink-collar Recession": How the Covid-19 Crisis Could Set Back a Generation of Women', *The Guardian*, 24 May. Available online: https://www .theguardian.com/world/2020/may/24/pink-collar-recession-how-the-covid-19-crisis -is-eroding-womens-economic-power (accessed 20 June 2020).

Riley, D. (2017), 'Rigor/Us: Building Boundaries and Disciplining Diversity with Standards of Merit', *Engineering Studies*, 9 (3): 249–65.

Ringrose, J. (2018), 'Digital Feminist Pedagogy and Post-truth Misogyny', *Teaching in Higher Education*, 23 (5): 647–56.

Rizvi, F. (2004), 'Debating Globalization and Education After September 11', *Comparative Education*, 40 (2): 157–71.

Rizvi, F. (2012), 'Engaging the Asian Century', *ACCESS: Critical Perspectives on Communication, Cultural & Policy Studies*, 31 (1): 73–9.

Rizvi, F. and B. Lingard (2010), *Globalizing Education Policy*, London: Routledge.

Roberts, A. (2015), 'The Political Economy of "Transnational Business Feminism"', *International Feminist Journal of Politics*, 17 (2): 209–31.

Roberts, K. and K. Donahue (2000), 'Professing Professionalism: Bureaucratization and De-professionalization in the Academy', *Sociological Focus*, 33 (4): 365–83.

Robertson, S. (2007), 'Re-imagining and Rescripting the Future of Education: Global Knowledge Economy Discourse and the Challenge to Education Systems', *Comparative Education*, 41 (2): 151–70.

Robertson, S. and J. Komljenovic (2016), 'Unbundling the University and Making Education Markets', in A. Verger, C. Lubienski and G. Steiner-Khamsi (eds), *World Yearbook of Education 2016: The Global Education Industry*, 211–47, New York: Routledge.

Rollock, N. (2012), 'The Invisibility of Race: Intersectional Reflections on the Liminal Space of Alterity', *Race Ethnicity and Education*, 15 (1): 65–84.

Rosen, A. S. (2018), 'Correlations, Trends and Potential Biases among Publicly Accessible Web-based Student Evaluations of Teaching: A Large-scale Study of RateMyProfessors.com Data', *Assessment and Evaluation in Higher Education*, 43 (1): 31–44.

Ross, J. (2021), 'Pandemic Research 'Must Prioritize Human and Political Behaviour', *Times Higher Education*, 8 July. Available online: https://www.timeshighereducation .com/cn/news/pandemic-research-must-prioritise-human-and-political-behaviour (accessed 1 August 2021).

Rothe, A., B. Erbe, W. Frohlich, E. Klatzer, Z. Lapniewska, M. Mayrhofer, M. Neumayr, M. Pichlbauer, M. Tarasiewicz and J. Zebisch (2008), *Gender Budgeting as a Management Strategy for Gender Equity in Universities*, Munich: European Commission.

Rowlands, J. (2011), 'Academic Boards: Less Intellectual and More Academic Capital in Higher Education Governance?', *Studies in Higher Education*, 38 (9): 1274–89.

Rowlands, J. (2013), 'The Symbolic Role of Academic Boards in University Quality Assurance', *Quality in Higher Education*, 19 (2): 142–57.

Rowlands, J. (2015a), 'Present But Not Counted: The Tenuous Position of Academic Board Chairs Within Contemporary University Governance', *International Journal of Leadership in Education: Theory and Practice*, 18 (3): 63–78.

Rowlands, J. (2015b), 'Turning Collegial Governance on Its Head: Symbolic Violence, Hegemony and the Academic Board', *British Journal of Sociology of Education*, 36 (7): 1017–35.

Rowlands, J. (2017), *Academic Governance in the Contemporary University: Perspectives from Anglophone Nations*, Rotterdam: Springer.

Rowlands, J. (2019), 'The Domestic Labour of Academic Governance and the Loss of Academic Voice', *Gender and Education*, 31 (7): 793–810.

Rowlands, J. and T. Gale (2017), 'Shaping and Being Shaped: Extending the Relationship between Habitus and Practice', in J. Lynch, J. Rowlands, T. Gale and A. Skourdoumbis (eds), *Practice Theory and Education: Diffractive Readings in Professional Practice*, 91–107, Oxford: Routledge.

Rowlands, J. and T. Gale (2019), 'National Research Assessment Frameworks, Publication Output Targets and Research Practices: The Compliance-Habitus Effect', *Beijing International Review of Education*, 1 (1): 138–61.

Rowlands, J. and S. Wright (2020), 'The Role of Bibliometric Research Assessment in a Global Order of Epistemic Injustice: A Case Study of Humanities Research in Denmark', *Critical Studies in Education*, doi: 10.1080/17508487.2020.1792523

Ryan, P., G. Odhiambo and R. Wilson (2019), 'Destructive Leadership in Education: A Transdisciplinary Critical Analysis of Contemporary Literature', *International Journal of Leadership in Education*, 24 (4): 1–27.

Ryan, S. (2012), '"Academic Zombies": A Failure of Resistance or a Means of Survival?', *Australian Universities Review*, 54 (2): 3–11.

Ryan, S., J. Burgess, J. Connell and E. Groen (2013), 'Casual Academic Staff in an Australian University: Marginalized and Excluded', *Tertiary Education and Management*, 19 (2): 161–75.

Sahlin, K. and Ulla Eriksson-Zetterquist (2016), 'Collegiality in Modern Universities – The Composition of Governance Ideals and Practices', *Nordic Journal of Studies in Educational Policy*, 2016: 2–3.

Saltmarsh, S. and H. Randall-Moon (2015), 'Managing the Risky Humanity of Academic Workers: Risk and Reciprocity in University Work–life Balance Policies', *Policy Futures*, 13 (5): 662–82.

Saltmarsh, S., W. Sutherland-Smith and H. Randell-Moon (2011), '"Inspired and Assisted", or "Berated and Destroyed"? Research Leadership, Management and Performativity in Troubled Times', *Ethics and Education*, 6 (3): 293–306.

Samier, E. and T. Atkins (2009), 'The Problem of Narcissists in Positions of Power', in E. Samier and M. Schmidt (eds), *Emotional Dimension of Educational Administration and Leadership*, 212–23, London: Routledge.

Sang, K. and T. Calvard (2019), '"I'm a Migrant, but I'm the Right Sort of Migrant": Hegemonic Masculinity, Whiteness, and Intersectional Privilege and (Dis) advantage in Migratory Academic Careers', *Gender Work and Organization*, 26 (10): 1506–25.

Sang, K., A. Powell, F. Finkel and J. Richards (2015), '"Being an Academic is Not a 9–5 Job": Long Working Hours and the "Ideal Worker" in UK Academia', *Labour and Industry: A Journal of the Social and Economic Relations of Work*, 25 (3): 235–49.

Scharff, C. (2016), 'The Psychic Life of Neoliberalism: Mapping the Contours of Entrepreneurial Subjectivity', *Theory, Culture & Society*, 33 (6): 107–22.

Schlesinger, W., A. Cervera and C. Pérez-Cabañero (2017), 'Sticking with Your University: The Importance of Satisfaction, Trust, Image, and Shared Values', *Studies in Higher Education*, 42 (12): 2178–94.

Schulz, J. (2013), 'The Impact of Role Conflict, Role Ambiguity and Organizational Climate on the Job Satisfaction of Academic Staff in Research-intensive Universities in the UK', *Higher Education Research and Development*, 32 (3): 464–78.

Scott, G., S. Bell, H. Coates and L. Grebennikov (2010), 'Australian Higher Education Leaders in Times of Change: The Role of Pro Vice-Chancellor and Deputy Vice-Chancellor', *Journal of Higher Education Policy and Management*, 32 (4): 401–18.

Sellar, S. (2015), 'A Feel for Numbers: Affect, Data and Education Policy', *Critical Studies in Education*, 56 (1): 131–46.

Sellar, S. and D. Cole (2017), 'Accelerationism: A Timely Provocation for the Critical Sociology of Education', *British Journal of Sociology of Education*, 38 (1): 38–48.

Selwyn, N. (2014), *Digital Technology and the Contemporary University: Degrees of Digitalization*, London: Routledge.

Senge, P. (1990), *The Fifth Discipline: The Age and Practice of the Learning Organization*, London: Century Business.

Sewerin, T. and R. Holmberg (2017), 'Contextualizing Distributed Leadership in Higher Education', *Higher Education Research and Development*, 36 (6): 1280–94.

Shahjahan, R. (2014), 'From "No" to "Yes": Postcolonial Perspectives on Resistance to Neoliberal Higher Education', *Discourse: Studies in the Cultural Politics of Education*, 35 (2): 219–32.

Shahjahan, R., E. Sonneveldt, A. Estera and S. Bae (2020), 'Emoscapes and Commercial University Rankers: The Role of Affect in Global Higher Education Policy', *Critical Studies in Education*, 2020 (April): 1–16.

Sharma, D. and F. Tygstrup (eds), (2015), *Structures of Feeling: Affectivity and the Study of Culture*, Berlin: De Gruyter.

Shattock, M. (2017), 'University Governance in Flux: The Impact of External and Internal Pressures on the Distribution of Authority Within British Universities: A Synoptic View', *Higher Education Quarterly*, 71 (4): 384–95.

Sheik, A. and A. Aghaz (2018), 'The Challenges of the Faculty Members' Commitment: The Role of University Brand', *Higher Education Quarterly*, 73 (3): 312–27.

Shepherd, S. (2018), 'Strengthening the University Executive: The Expanding Roles and Remit of Deputy and Pro-vice-chancellors', *Higher Education Quarterly*, 72 (1): 40–50.

Shin, J. and J. Jung (2014), 'Academic Job Satisfaction and Job Stress across Countries in Changing Academic Environments', *Higher Education*, 67: 603–20.

Shore, C. and M. Taitz (2012), 'Who "Owns" the University? Institutional Autonomy and Academic Freedom in an Age of Knowledge Capitalism', *Globalization, Societies and Education*, 10 (2): 201–19.

Shore, C. and S. Wright (2000), 'Coercive Accountability: The Rise of Audit Culture in Higher Education', in M. Strathern (ed), *Audit Cultures: Anthropological Studies in Accountability, Ethics and the Academy*, 57–89, London: Routledge.

Showunmi, V. (2020), 'The Importance of Intersectionality in Higher Education and Educational Leadership Research', *Journal of Higher Education Policy and Leadership Studies*, 1 (1): 46–63.

Showunmi, V., D. Atewologun and D. Bebbington (2016), 'Ethnic, Gender and Class Intersections in British Women's Leadership Experiences', *Educational Management, Administration and Leadership*, 44 (6): 917–35.

Showunmi, V. P. Moorosi, C. Shakeshaft and I. Oplatka (eds) (2022), *The Bloomsbury Handbook of Gender and Educational Leadership and Management*, London: Bloomsbury Academic.

Sidhu, R. (2006), *Universities and Globalization: To Market, To Market*, New Jersey: Lawrence Erlbaum.

Skinner, T. C., D. Peetz, G. Strachan, G. Whitehouse, L. Bailey and K. Broadbent (2015), 'Self-reported Harassment and Bullying in Australian Universities: Explaining Differences between Regional, Metropolitan and Elite Institutions', *Journal of Higher Education Policy and Management*, 37 (5): 558–71.

Skorobohacz, C., J. Billot, S. Murray and L. Khong (2016), 'Metaphors as Expressions of Followers' Experiences with Academic Leadership', *Higher Education Research and Development*, 35 (5): 1053–67.

Slater, J., D. Perez and S. Fain (2008), *The War Against the Professions: The Impact of Politics and Economics on the Idea of the University*, Rotterdam: Sense.

Slaughter, S. and G. Rhoades (2004), *Academic Capitalism and the New Economy: Markets, State, and Higher Education*, Baltimore: The Johns Hopkins University Press.

Slaughter, S. and Taylor, B. (eds) (2015), *Higher Education, Stratification, and Workforce Development*, Dorchdrecht: Springer.

Small, H. (2013), *The Value of the Humanities*, Oxford: Oxford University Press.

Smith, D. (1990), *The Conceptual Practices of Power: A Feminist Sociology of Knowledge*, Boston: North-Eastern University Press.

Solanke, I. (2017), *Black Female Professors in the UK*, Leeds: University of Leeds.

Sorensen, M., L. Gesdchwindm, J. Kekale and R. Pinheiro, (eds), (2019), *The Responsible University: Exploring the Nordic Context and Beyond*, London: Palgrave Macmillan.

Spongberg, M. (2010), 'Feminist Publishing in a Cold Climate?: *Australian Feminist Studies* and the New ERA of Research', *Feminist Review*, 95 (1): 99–110.

Squire, D. (2017), 'The Vacuous Rhetoric of Diversity: Exploring How Institutional Responses to National Racial Incidences Effect Faculty of Color Perceptions of University Commitment to Diversity', *International Journal of Qualitative Studies in Education*, 30 (8): 728–45.

Stack, M. (2016), *Global University Rankings and the Mediatization of Higher Education*, Hampshire: Palgrave Macmillan.

Standing Committee on Education, Employment and Workplace Relations (2008), *Allegations of Academic Bias in Universities and Schools*, Canberra: Parliament House.

Stein, S. (2021), 'Beyond the Usual Debates: Creating the Conditions for Academic Freedom to Flourish', *Australian Universities Review*, 63 (1): 53–8.

Stensaker, B. (2015), 'Organizational Identity as a Concept for Understanding University Dynamics', *Higher Education*, 69 (1): 3–59.

Stensaker, B. and L. Harvey (2011), *Accountability in Higher Education: Global Perspectives on Trust and Power*, London: Routledge.

Stensaker, B., J. Vallimaa and C. Sarrico, (eds) (2012), *Managing Reform in Universities. Dynamics of Culture, Identity and Organizational Change*, London: Palgrave MacMillan.

Stephan, P. (2012), *How Economics Shapes Science*, Cambridge, MA: Harvard University Press.

Sterling, S., L. Maxey and H. Luna, (eds) (2013), *The Sustainable University: Progress and Prospects*, London: Routledge.

Stier, J. (2010), 'International Education: Trends, Ideologies and Alternative Pedagogies', *Globalization, Societies and Education*, 8 (3): 339–49.

Strachan, G., C. Troup, D. Peetz, G. Whitehouse, K. Broadbent and J. Bailey (2012), *Work and Careers in Australian Universities: Report on Employee Survey*, Brisbane: Centre for Work, Organization and Wellbeing, Griffith University.

Su, F., C. Erskine, T. Fitzgerald, M. Wood and J. Nixon, eds (2017), *Cosmopolitan Perspectives on Academic Leadership in Higher Education*, London: Bloomsbury.

Sullivan, T. A. (2014), 'Greedy Institutions, Overwork and Work-life Balance', *Sociological Inquiry*, 84 (1): 1–15.

Sumara, D. (2021), 'On the Power of Not Passing: A Queer Narrative Hermeneutics of Higher Education Leadership', *Journal of Educational Administration and History*, 53 (2): 144–57.

Symonds, M. R. E., N. J. Gemmell, T. L. Braisher, K. L. Gorringe and M. A. Elgar (2006), 'Gender Differences in Publication Output: Towards an Unbiased Metric of Research Performance', *PLOS ONE*, 1 (127): 1–5.

Szenes, E., N. Tilakaratna and K. Maton (2015), 'Knowledge Practices of Critical Thinking', in M. Davies and R. Barnett (eds), *Palgrave Handbook of Critical Thinking in Higher Education*, 573–91, London: Palgrave.

Thodey, D. (2019), 'Our Public Service, Our Future', Independent Review of the Australian Public Service, ©Commonwealth of Australia, Department of the Prime Minister and Cabinet

Thomas, L. (2002), 'Student Retention in Higher Education: The Role of Institutional Habitus', *Journal of Education Policy*, 17 (4): 423–42.

Thompson, E. and K. Langendoerfer (2016), 'Older Men's Blueprint for "Being a Man"', *Men and Masculinities*, 19 (2): 119–47.

Thornton, M. (2008), 'The Retreat from the Critical: Social Science Research in the Corporatized University', *Australian Universities Review*, 50 (1): 5–10.

Thornton, M. (2013), 'The Mirage of Merit', *Australian Feminist Studies*, 28 (6): 127–43.

Thornton, M. (ed), (2015), *Through a Glass Darkly: The Social Sciences Look at the Neoliberal University*, Canberra: ANU Press.

Thornton, P. and W. Ocasio (2008), 'Institutional Logics', in *Royston Greenwood,* Christine Oliver, Roy Suddaby and Kerstin Sahlin-Andersson (eds), *The SAGE Handbook of Organizational Institutionalism*, 90–130, Thousand Oaks, CA: SAGE.

Thunig, A. and T. Jones (2020), '"Don't Make Me Play Housen***er": Indigenous Academic Women Treated as "Black Performer" Within Higher Education', *The Australian Educational Researcher*, 48: 397–417.

Tierney, W. and D. Almeida (2017), 'Academic Responsibility: Toward a Cultural Politics of Integrity', *Discourse: Studies in the Cultural Politics of Education*, 38 (1): 97–108.

Tierney, W. and M. Lanford (2016), 'Conceptualizing Innovation in Higher Education', in Paulsen, (ed), *Higher Education: Handbook of Theory and Research*, Vol. 31, 1–41, Switzerland: Springer.

Tight, M. (2014), 'Collegiality and Managerialism: A False Dichotomy? Evidence from the Higher Education Literature', *Tertiary Education and Management*, 20 (4): 294–306.

Tillman, L. and J. Scheurich, (eds) (2013), *Handbook of Research on Educational Leadership for Equity and Diversity*, New York: Routledge.

Times Higher Education (THE) (2018), *Academic Workforce Survey*, Downloaded 12 June 2020.

Tinning, R. and K. Sirna (2011), *Education, Social Justice and the Legacy of Deakin University*, Rotterdam: Sense Publishers.

Tomlinson, B. (2010), Feminiism and Affect at the Scene of Argument. Beyond the Trope of An Angry Feminisy, Philadephia: Temple University Press.

Tran, L. T. (2016), 'Mobility as "becoming": A Bourdieuian Analysis of the Factors Shaping International Student Mobility', *British Journal of Sociology of Education*, 37 (8): 1268–89.

Tran, L. T. (2020), 'Teaching and Engaging International Students', *Journal of International Students*, 10 (3): xii–xvii.

Tran, L. T. and H. Bui (2021), 'Public Diplomacy and Social Impact of Australian Student Mobility to the Indo Pacific: Host Countries' Perspectives on Hosting New Colombo Plan Students', *Journal of Studies in International Education*, doi: 1028315320984833.

Tran, L. T. and G. Tan (2020), '90,000 Foreign Graduates are Stuck in Australia Without Financial Support: It's a Humanitarian and Economic Crisis in the Making', *The Conversation*, 23 April. Available online: https://theconversation.com/90-000-foreign -graduates-are-stuck-in-australia-without-financial-support-its-a-humanitarian-and -economic-crisis-in-the-making-136717 (accessed 5 June 2020).

Tran, L. T., M. Rahimi and G. Tan (2019), *The Impact of the Post-Study Work Visa*, Melbourne: REDI, Deakin University.

Tran, L. T., J. Blackmore and M. Rahimi (2021), '"You are Not as Localized as I Need": Employability of Chinese Returning Graduates', *Higher Education, Skills and Work-based Learning*, 11 (5): 949–65.

Trenewan, C. (2017), 'Who Will Win the Global Hunger Games? The Emerging Significance of Research Universities in International Relations', in C. Shore and S. Wright (eds), *Death of the Public University?: Uncertain Futures for Higher Education in the Knowledge Economy*, 253–74, New York: Bergham Press.

Tuhiwai, L. (1999), *Decolonizing Methodologies. Research and Indigenous Peoples*, Auckland: Zed.

Turner, G. and K. Brass (2014), *Mapping the Humanities, Arts and Social Sciences in Australia*, Canberra: Australian Academy of the Humanities.

Tzanakou, C. and R. Pearce (2019), 'Moderate Feminism Within or Against the Neoliberal University? The Example of Athena SWAN', *Gender, Work Organization*, 26: 1191–211.

Universities Australia (2013), *Australia's Universities*, Available online: http://www.univers itiesaustralia.edu.au/page/australia-s-universities/ (accessed 24 February 2013).

Universities Australia (2016), *Keep it Clever*. A Policy Statement, Canberra: Universities Australia.

Universities Australia (2017), *Indigenous Strategy 2017–2020*, Canberra: Universities Australia.

Universities Australia (2020), *International Students Inject $ 41b Annually into Australia's Economy*, Canberra: Universities Australia.

Universities Australia Executive Women (2009), *Mentoring for Senior Women Framework*, Melbourne: LH Martin Institute for Higher Education.

Veles, N. and M. A. Carter (2016), 'Imagining a Future: Changing the Landscape for Third Space Professionals in Australian Higher Education Institutions', *Journal of Higher Education Policy and Management*, 38 (5): 519–33.

Verger, A., C. Lubienski and G. Steiner-Khamsi (2016), 'The Emergence and Structuring of the Global Education Industry: Towards an Analytical Framework', in A. Verger, G. Steiner-Khamsi and C. Lubienski (eds), *World Yearbook of Education 2016: The Global Education Industry*, 3–23, New York: Routledge.

.Vicary, A. and K. Jones (2017), 'The Implications of Contractual Terms of Employment for Women and Leadership: An Autoethnographic Study in UK Higher Education', *Administrative Sciences*, 7 (20): 1–14.

Vickery, J. and T. Everbach, (eds) (2018), *Mediating Misogyny: Gender, Technology, and Harassment*, Switzerland: Palgrave Macmillan.

Vidovich, L. and J. Currie (2011), 'Governance and Trust in Higher Education', *Studies in Higher Education*, 36 (1): 43–56.

Vogel, A. and W. Kaghan (2001), 'Bureaucrats, Brokers and the Entrepreneurial University', *Organisation*, 8 (2): 358–64.

Vukasovic, M., P. Masseen, M. Nerland, R. Pinheiro, B. Stensaker and A. Vabo, (eds) (2012), *Effects of Higher Education Reforms: Change Dynamics*, Rotterdam: Sense Publishers.

Wacquant, L. (1995), 'Review Article: Why Men Desire Muscles', *Body and Society*, 1 (1): 163–79.

Wacquant, L. (2005), 'Habitus', in J. Beckert and M. Zafirovski (eds), *International Encyclopeadia of Economic Sociology*, 317–21, Oxon: Routledge.

Waitere, H. J., J. Wright, M. Tremaine, S. Brown and C. J. Pause (2011), 'Choosing Whether to Resist or Reinforce the New Managerialism: The Impact of Performance-based Research Funding on Academic Identity', *Higher Education Research & Development*, 30 (2): 205–17.

Wajcman, J. (2010), 'Feminist Theories of Technology', *Cambridge Journal of Economics*, 34 (1): 143–52.

Wajcman, J. and N. Dodd (2016), *The Sociology of Speed: Digital, Organizational, and Social Temporalities*, Oxford: Oxford University Press.

Walby, S. (2011), 'Is the Knowledge Society Gendered?', *Gender, Work and Organisation*, 18 (1): 1–29.

Walker, M. and M. McLean (2013), *Professional Education, Capabilities and the Public Good: The Role of Universities in Promoting Human Development*, London: Routledge.

Waring, M. (2007), 'HRM in HE: People Reform or Re-Forming People?', in D. Epstein, R. Boden, R. Deem, F. Rizvi, S. Wright (eds), *World Yearbook of Education 2008 -Geographies of Knowledge, Geometries of Power: Framing the Future of Higher Education*, New York: Routledge.

Waring, M. (2015), 'Human Resource Policies and the Individualization of Academic Labour', in L. Gornall, C. Cook, L. Daynton, J. Salisbury and B. Thomas (eds), *Academic Working Lives: Experience, Practice and Change*, 102–9, London: Bloomsbury.

Watermeyer, R. (2014), 'Issues in the Articulation of 'Impact': The Responses of UK Academics to 'Impact' As a New Measure of Research Assessment', *Studies in Higher Education*, 39 (2): 359–77.

Watt, I. (2015), *Review of Research Policy and Funding Arrangements: Report*, Canberra: Department of Education and Training.

Webb, J., T. Shirato and G. Danaher (2002), *Understanding Bourdieu*, Sydney: Allen and Unwin.

Welch, A. (2012), 'Academic Salaries Massification, and the Rise of an Underclass in Australia', in P. Altbach, L. Reisberg, M. Yudkevich, G. Androushchak and I. Pacheco (eds), *Paying the Professoriate: A Global Comparison of Compensation and Contracts*, 61–71, London: Routledge.

Welch, A. and Z. Zhan (2018), 'Higher Education and Global Talent Flows: Brain Drain, Overseas Chinese Intellectuals and Diasporic Knowledge Works', *Higher Education Policy*, 21 (4): 519–37.

Whitchurch, C. (2018), 'From a Diversifying Workforce to the Rise of the Itinerant Academic', *Higher Education*, 77: 679–94.

Whitchurch, C. and G. Gordon (2017), *Reconstructing Relationships in Higher Education: Challenging Agendas*, New York: Routledge.

White, K., B. Bagilhole and S. Riordan (2012), 'The Gendered Shaping of University Leadership in Australia, South Africa and the United Kingdom', *Higher Education Quarterly*, 66 (3): 293–307.

White, N. (2010), 'Indigenous Australian Women's Leadership: Stayin' Strong Against the Post-colonial Tide', *International Journal of Leadership in Education*, 13 (1): 7–25.

Williams, L., T. Bunda, N. Claxton and I. Mackinnon (2017), 'A Global De-colonial Praxis of Sustainability —Undoing Epistemic Violence between Indigenous Peoples and Those No Longer Indigenous to Place', *The Australian Journal of Indigenous Education*, 47 (1): 41–53.

Williams, R. (2015), 'Structures of Feeling', in D. Sharma and F. Tygstrup (eds), *Structures of Feeling: Affectivity and the Study of Culture*, 20–6, Berlin: De Gruyter.

Williamson, B. (2014), 'New Governing Experts in Education: Self-learning Software, Policy Labs and Transactional Pedagogies', in T. Fenwick, E. Mangez and J. Ozga (eds), *Governing Knowledge: Comparison, Knowledge-based Technologies and Expertise in the Regulation of Education - World Yearbook of Education 2014*, 218–31, London: Routledge.

Williamson, B. (2016a), 'Digital Education Governance: Data Visualization, Predictive Analytics, and 'Real-time' Policy Instruments', *Journal of Education Policy*, 31 (2): 123–41.

Williamson, B. (2016b), 'Political Computational Thinking: Policy Networks, Digital Governance and 'Learning to Code', *Critical Policy Studies*, 10 (1): 39–58.

Wilsdon, J. et al. (2015), *The Metric Tide: Report of the Independent Review of the Role of Metrics in Research Assessment and Management*, Bristol: HEFCE.

Wilson, A., D. Reay, K. Morrin and J. Abrahams (2021), 'The Still-moving Position' of the 'Working-class' Feminist Academic: Dealing with Disloyalty, Dislocation and Discomfort', *Discourse: Studies in the Cultural Politics of Education*, 42 (1): 30–44.

Winter, R. P. (2017), *Managing Academics: A Question of Perspective*, Cheltenham: Edward Elgar.

.Woelert, P. and L. Yates (2015), 'Too Little and Too Much Trust: Performance Measurement in Australian Higher Education', *Critical Studies in Education*, 56 (2): 175–89.

Wood, E. (2016), 'Hypermasculinity as a Scenario of Power', *International Feminist Journal of Politics*, 18 (3): 329–50.

.Workplace Gender Equality Agency (WGEA) (2020), *Gender Equality Scorecard*. Available online: https://www.wgea.gov.au

World Economic Forum (2021), *Global Gender Gap Report 2021*, Geneva: World Economic Forum. Available online: https://www3.weforum.org/docs/WEF_GGGR _2021.pdf (accessed 1 May 2021).

Wright, S. (2009), 'What Counts? The Skewing Effects of Research Assessment Systems', *Journal of Nordic Educational Research*, 29 (special issue): 18–33.

Wright, S. and J. W. Ørberg (2008), 'Autonomy and Control: Danish University Reform in the Context of Modern Governance', *Learning and Teaching: International Journal of Higher Education in the Social Sciences*, 1 (1): 27–57.

Wright, S. and C. Shore, (eds) (2017), *Death of the Public University?: Uncertain Futures for Higher Education in the Knowledge Economy*, New York: Bergham Press.

Yancey Martin, P. (2003), '"Said and Done" versus "Saying and Doing": Gendering Practices, Practicing Gender', *Gender and Society*, 17 (3): 342–66.

Yang, R. (2010), 'Soft Power and Higher Education: An Examination of China's Confucius Institutes', *Globalisation, Societies and Education*, 8 (2): 235–45.

Yeatman, A. (1990), *Bureaucrats, Technocrats and Femocrats*, Sydney: Allen and Unwin.

Yeatman, A. (2002), 'The New Contractualism and Individualized Personhood', *Journal of Sociology*, 38 (1): 69–73.

Yeatman, A. (2014), 'Feminism and the Technological Age', *Australian Feminist Studies*, 29 (79): 85–100.

Ylijoki, O. (2013), 'Boundary-work between Work and Life in the High-speed University', *Studies in Higher Education*, 38 (2): 242–55.

Youngs, H. (2017), 'A Critical Exploration of Collaborative and Distributed Leadership in Higher Education: Developing an Alternative Ontology through Leadership-as-practice', *Journal of Higher Education Policy and Management*, 39 (2): 140–54.

Zabrodska, K., S. Linnell, C. Laws and B. Davies (2011), 'Bullying as Intra-active Process in Neoliberal Universities', *Qualitative Inquiry*, 17 (8): 709–19.

Ziguras, C. and G. McBurnie, (eds) (2015), *Governing Cross-Border Higher Education*, London: Routledge.

Ziguras, C. and L. Tran (2020), 'The Coronavirus Outbreak is the Biggest Crisis Ever to Hit International Education', *The Conversation*, 6 February. Available online: https:// theconversation.com/the-coronavirus-outbreak-is-the-biggest-crisis-ever-to-hit -international-education-131138 (accessed 8 February 2020).

Zipin, L. and M. Brennan (2003), 'The Suppression of Ethical Dispositions through Managerial Governmentality: A Habitus Crisis in Australian Higher Education', *International Journal of Leadership in Education*, 6 (4): 351–70.

INDEX